Convictions

Convictions

24 Life Transforming Beliefs For Believers In Jesus Christ

By
Ed Kenerson

XULON PRESS

Xulon Press
2301 Lucien Way #415
Maitland, FL 32751
407.339.4217
www.xulonpress.com

© 2021 by Ed Kenerson

All rights reserved solely by the author. The author guarantees all contents are original and do not infringe upon the legal rights of any other person or work. No part of this book may be reproduced in any form without the permission of the author. The views expressed in this book are not necessarily those of the publisher.

Due to the changing nature of the Internet, if there are any web addresses, links, or URLs included in this manuscript, these may have been altered and may no longer be accessible. The views and opinions shared in this book belong solely to the author and do not necessarily reflect those of the publisher. The publisher therefore disclaims responsibility for the views or opinions expressed within the work.

Unless otherwise indicated, Scripture quotations taken from the Holy Bible, New International Version (NIV). Copyright © 1973, 1978, 1984, 2011 by Biblica, Inc.™. Used by permission. All rights reserved.

Paperback ISBN-13: 978-1-6628-2692-4

Table of Contents

INTRODUCTION
We Are What We Believe................................. vii

CONVICTION #1
I Believe In Jesus.. 1

CONVICTION #2
I Believe In Seeking God................................ 17

CONVICTION #3
I Believe In The Fear of God............................ 29

CONVICTION #4
I Believe In Humility.................................... 41

CONVICTION #5
I Believe In Reality... Not Fantasy..................... 53

CONVICTION #6
I Believe In Right Thinking............................. 67

CONVICTION #7
I Believe Feelings Need Control......................... 81

CONVICTION #8
I Believe In Consequences............................... 95

CONVICTION #9
I Believe That Mercy Restores.......................... 109

CONVICTION #10
I Believe That Grace Rebuilds........................121

CONVICTION #11
I Believe Faith Overcomes............................137

CONVICTION #12
I Believe God Heals..................................151

CONVICTION #13
I Believe In Godly Worship...........................163

CONVICTION #14
I Believe That Little Things Count 177

CONVICTION #15
I Believe In Using Time Well 191

CONVICTION #16
I Believe In God's Favor 203

CONVICTION #17
I Believe Balance Is A Virtue........................217

CONVICTION #18
I Believe In God's "Free" Sovereignty 231

CONVICTION #19
I Believe Sin Is Never Sophisticated 245

CONVICTION #20
I Believe Loss Can Be A Friend.......................257

CONVICTION #21
I Believe God's Will Outshines Everything!...........269

CONVICTION #22
I Believe In An "Unbelievable" Future! 285

CONVICTION #23
I Believe Culture Can Be Deadly......................302

CONVICTION #24
I Believe Convictions Build Consecration.............317

Introduction:
We Are What We Believe

"For as he thinks in his heart, so is he..."
Proverbs 23:7

The mind is a crazy place in which to live!
Each of us lives in his/her own mental neighborhood of thoughts, opinions and beliefs, which is normally quite enjoyable and mostly harmless on the face of things. We look around and make assumptions about what we see and how we should react to the world going on around us. But sometimes our thinking gets so skewed that we say or do things that are unwanted or even embarrassing.

The other day, I came across a website that recorded some of the crazy things people think and say immediately after an accident. Here's a few actual responses recorded by insurance companies, but try not to laugh too loudly.

- "The pedestrian had no idea which direction to run, so I ran over him."

- "The telephone pole was approaching. I was attempting to swerve out of its way when it struck my front end."

- "I had been driving for forty years when I fell asleep at the wheel and had an accident."

- "I don't know who was to blame for the accident; I wasn't looking."

- "The guy was all over the road. I had to swerve a number of times before I hit him."

- "I know I was going fast, I was trying to get the snow off my windshield so I could see where I'm going."

- "An Invisible car came out of nowhere, struck my car and vanished."

- "The other car collided with mine without giving warning of its intentions."

- "I pulled away from the side of the road, glanced at my mother-in-law, and headed over the embankment."
(from https://letterpile.com/humor/Funny-Excuses-Car-Accidents)

However, there are other times that the mind wanders according to its deepest impulses and beliefs about life, and not all of those are worthy of even discussing. That's because our minds are also warped according to the results of sin upon the human race, when Adam disobeyed God in the Garden of Eden. As the Bible explains, he set into play a tragic series of events, the first of which was separation from an intimate and holy relationship with his Creator. Wrenched from that wonderful and spiritual relationship of joy, purity and love, he became a manufacturer of evil thoughts and intensions. Not every thought, of course, became murderous, selfish and sensually stimulating, *but the human heart was permanently tainted with a strong propensity toward evil.* God may have clothed Adam and Eve to help them deal with sexual purity, but he didn't give them an emotional or mental cleansing at the time. The resulting debris since the Fall has been that sinful hearts have conjured up all kinds of evil to satisfy their mental urges and proclivities. Some may be funny like the above, but all of us are capable of compromised thinking that can harm ourselves deeply and others quite easily.

What Do You Believe?

The title of this book is, "Convictions," and I chose it to explore not just the random thinking of our minds, but the deeper, cognitive belief system we possess as Christians. A belief system is more than just focused thought. It is a deeper compilation of inner perspectives, which we have accumulated in childhood, in relationships, in school, and at church. Such beliefs can be good or bad, Scriptural or not, true or false, praiseworthy or degrading, whatever, which leads me to suggest that we should be very careful to only hold on to *godly beliefs*.

A belief system can be illustrated in one of two ways...a country pond or a sewer system. The pond model best describes a positive situation, where leaves and stray branches fall from above onto the smooth, slightly rippling surface of water from a cool fall breeze. Such organic things float around for a time, then sink to the bottom of the pond and decay. Eventually, these will deteriorate into a muddy compose, which proves quite healthy for the pond. Whatever unhealthy things exist on those leaves get filtered out and float away, leaving a rich, nutrient-loaded resource on the bottom for organisms to grow, a place for pollywogs to mature into frogs, and a resource for fish to indulge their appetites. All that is part of a good eco system for pond life, and it represents a mind that is rich in godly beliefs and discernment.

However, there's another "pond" like situation that's not so good, and it's that which country homes in Connecticut (where I grew up) had to install for their sewer systems. In rural living, there wasn't any town sewer system with connection pipes to every home, so when building our house, we had to install leeching fields and a sceptic tank. As I remember it, the sceptic tank was a large, buried, cement container about six feet in length, 4 feet in width and height, and having about 3" thick walls. It was the receptacle for human wastes (not garbage) that would be channeled into it from the plumbing system. Eventually, as the waste reached a certain height within the buried container, holes along the inside would allow it to flow into the long, buried, stone-filled trenches reaching out about 30 feet from the tank (each covered over with about 3 feet of dirt). All of it sat quite hidden underneath our front lawn, as it gradually decomposed over time.

I remember encountering a wicked smell when coming home from school one day and walking up the long driveway to our rather secluded home, which sat in the middle of the woods. The smell was horrendous, so I rushed into the house to ask mom what was going on. We tracked it down to the sceptic tank, which had overloaded the leaching fields, and its contents was seeping up to the surface of our lawn. We had to have the tank emptied and the leeching field trenches re-dug in order to ultimately fix that rather odiferous issue.

My point is that sometimes our minds are intaking far too much mental waste, which only putrefies within us just like a pile of buried, bacteria-infested sewer muck. It may not smell as bad, because it's not a physical thing. But it can ultimately bring disgust and shame to the spiritual home owner, if he or she doesn't keep the system clean, unplugged and refreshed with godly thinking flowing through it.

Understanding God's Truth Defines Our Convictions

What we genuinely understand and believe to be true is that which drives our passions and purposes through life. Such inner beliefs can *motivate* us or *discourage* us from obeying God, the law, our parents, or our own conscience. They only need a kick-start from some sort of life experience or desire, and we will act out that which the belief has spawned...good or bad.

Jesus similarly compared the Word of God to seed, which falls upon differing types of ground, some sprouting growth in various amounts and others lacking growth due to the poor soil upon which the seed falls. Similarly, the mind has the ability to understand and make assumptions about our inner and outer environment. It processes the intellectual seeds from philosophy, entertainment, education, relationships, and life in general. Each person evaluates, discerns and draws conclusions from these "thought seeds," possibly even acting upon them in some way. The point to remember, is that God tells us to be *discerning* about that which we hear and believe, for life success hangs in the balance.

> *"Leave your simple ways and you will live; walk in the way of insight."* (Prov. 9:6)

For instance, one belief in particular is key to gaining the peace we so much want in our lives. A mind that believes and trusts in God *is a mind of peace*.

> *"You keep him in perfect peace whose mind is stayed on you, because he trusts in you."* (Is. 26:3 ESV)

It is also important to know where we should go to gain such understanding that can bring peace into our spiritual lives. Again, the Bible is clear on this:

> *"The fear of the Lord is the beginning of wisdom, and knowledge of the Holy One is understanding."* (Proverbs 9:10)

So, believers gain life-changing wisdom and understanding from our relationship with God, as we approach him in reverent fear and respect for who he is. But, more specifically, wisdom and spiritual understanding come from the Word of God. A good New Testament verse on this is 2 Timothy 2:15, put so beautifully in the King James Version:

> *"Study to shew thyself approved unto God, a workman that needeth not to be ashamed, rightly dividing the word of truth."* (KJV)

God's Truth is always accurate, it doesn't mislead or lie, and it is fully able to correct and guide us in our understanding of what to believe and how to live.

> *"All Scripture is God-breathed and is useful for teaching, rebuking, correcting and training in righteousness, so that the servant of God may be thoroughly equipped for every good work."* (II Timothy 3:16)

However, it is important to recognize our responsibility in all this. Wisdom is usually found resting deeper than just residing in the shallows of a five-minute devotional in the morning. It most often is found by a *serious* investment of our time in studying the Scriptures, listening to wise counsel and ingesting sound teaching. Only "heart-thinking" will allow such truths to be the life-changing resources they are supposed to be. Are you serious in seeking out God's wisdom? Do you really want to find the answers to your questions and struggles with sin? Then you and I have an important responsibility before us:

> *"Listen to my instruction and be wise; do not disregard it. Blessed are those who listen to me, watching daily at my doors, waiting at my doorway."* (Proverbs 8:33-34)

> *"Then you will call upon me and come and pray to me, and I will hear you. You will seek me and find me, <u>when you seek me with all your heart</u>. I will be found by you, declares the LORD..."* (Jeremiah 29:12-14a)

> *"I love those who love me, and <u>those who seek me diligently find me</u>."* (Proverbs 8:17)

Notice the first part of Proverbs 9:6 above: *"Leave your simple ways..."* Scripture is saying that "simple thinking" is foolish, because it lacks wisdom, understanding and discernment. It's not saying that *only* scholars, philosophers and people of *great* knowledge can live for God. No, it's saying that simple thinking is that which doesn't deeply build upon God's Word for needed wisdom.

Such folks incur issues and unnecessary problems in life simply because they remain spiritually shallow or naive. Let's remember, then, that wisdom is not distinguished by an *abundance* of truth, but by a discerned *understanding* and application of it.

HOW TO BUILD A CONVICTION

As we've highlighted so far, every conviction begins in the mind. We take in information and make assumptions about what it all means. Convictions can be simple beliefs, or they can become deep and intensely heart-held beliefs about life. But they are always rooted in a *mental framework* of understanding some important slice of life, personal experience, or spiritual truth.

Each conviction has a *factual perspective* in which he or she places a high degree of trust. And, if a particular fact seems interesting and/or attractive to us, we store it away in our *motivational center*. At this point, *some degree* of emotion and/or desire has been attached to it, which can be called upon later to provide the fuel we may need to move our attitudes or actions in a given direction. In this sense, then, a conviction is more than a simple thought, an intellectual fact or just a harmless belief...it's something that "stirs and moves us," depending upon its origin as well as what we do with it.

As an example, let's say that we've never had an Oreo cookie before. We grab one at a church social, eat it, and think, "Humm... this Oreo cookie tastes great!" Then, perhaps later on in the day, while going past the cookie isle at the grocery store, the urge to buy a box of Oreo cookies suddenly comes upon us. That motivation was triggered by the original understanding that, "This Oreo cookie tastes good." At that point, this awareness hasn't accomplished much except remind us of a distant desire.

However, a strange thing could happen next. Perhaps we begin fantasizing about the creamy vanilla filling and the chocolate cookie that surrounds it. Perhaps the fantasy is increased by the suggestion that dipping it in milk would be a desirable thing. Regardless, a tiny porthole of pleasure has opened up in your mind, so you stop and turn back to the stack of Oreo cookies on the shelf. Next, you *decide* to reach up and grab one of those packages and put it into your shopping cart. Later on, at the house, you open the package and indulge your cravings for Oreo cookies dipped in milk, while watching an old rerun of NCIS. You easily down 14 cookies and enjoy every one of them!

The next day, you again find yourself at the grocery store shopping for supper. As you're going down the cereal aisle, somehow, why you don't know, a memory flashes across your mind about yesterday's afternoon delight, while watching NCIS again. You begin to remember the satisfying taste of those cookies and find yourself drawn to the cookie aisle again…5 aisles away…with eager excitement for another session of sugar enhanced indulgence!

Half way there you stop and ask yourself, "Wait a minute, I'm already 5 pounds overwait…do I really want to do this?" This question is wrapped around another conviction…that of having a healthy, disciplined sense of accountability, and it's calling you to *resist!* Back and forth goes your mind, caught in a battle of reason and desire. Who will win?

Well, no need to continue the story, for we'll let your imagination write the ending. But you recognize the struggle for **convictional domination** that occurs in our spirit all the time, when trying to do what is right…for health, for family, for God. That's the cycle of conviction that is always at work within us, but which we need to oversee and keep empowered by God's Spirit for God's glory (in far more tempestuous gales of temptation than just Oreo cookie cravings, right!)

You can see how what I just outlined works together within us to form convictions. Convictions are life-changing entities that impact what we do, sort of ongoing fuel explosions in the engine of our spirit. Convictions begin in the mind, acquire *desire* or some sort of motivation, which urge us toward a *decision* to act upon it, attitudinally or behaviorally.

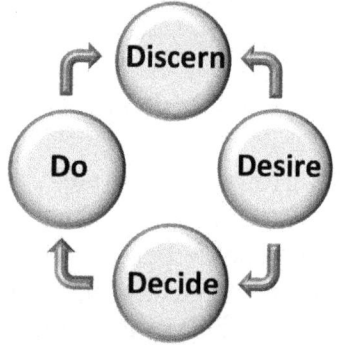

However, like anything else in our lives, God wants us to take control of ourselves and do what He wants, not what feels good… but *what is good!* So, let's turn this convictional model into a *practical sequence*, which begins with the act of discernment and continues to the complete act of obedience to do the will of God. If we master this Scripturally based sequence, we can actually **build** godly convictions, **control** ungodly ones and please the Lord in all that we do.

Truth Creates Perspective

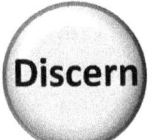

This is key, because everything important begins here. Identifying godly truth is essentially a *disciplined mental activity* in which all of us should be involved…all the time. Every inch of spiritual growth comes only as we are driven by the Word of God, which requires serious personal devotions/study, meaningful fellowship, and consistent prayer in order to infuse its truths into our minds and hearts. To discern is to *apprehend the truths of God's Word*.

Satan loves to keep us away from *God's Word*, because by doing so he takes away our understanding and awareness of God's Will. Remember the parable of the seed? Like scavenging birds, Satan comes along the hardened pathway and scoffs up the seed before it settles into the deeper soil. In addition, if he can let the seed fall upon stony and weed-infested soil, the seed won't do much more than sprout up and quickly die as well. Jesus said:

> *"But the seed falling on good soil refers to someone who hears the word and understands it. This is the one who produces a crop, yielding a hundred, sixty or thirty times what was sown."*
> (Matt. 13:23)

Look at discernment as a filter in your mind that analyzes every thought. It's like buying a filter for your kitchen faucet, which you purchase because you want to be sure all the tiny particles of dirt and/or chemicals will be removed from the drinking water. Just as impurities can cause issues in our bodies, spiritual impurities can also cause desires, decisions, attitudes, and behaviors that miss the mark of godliness.

Please keep in mind that discernment is more than factual and intellectual recognition alone. It's referring to an insightful sense of what is true and *necessary* for spiritual life and relationship with God. If God's Word is left just "hanging" in the air of sheer factual interest, it is kept from sowing itself into our heart's deepest soil...the good stuff...rich in spiritual desire and determination. Such unproductive truth is *unrooted*, cut off and incapacitated from changing us within, because it has not yet birthed conviction, just shallow thinking. If and when it spawns **some level** of spiritual *desire* and *determination,* **then** conviction will be birthed, for discernment alone (simple understanding) is not conviction. Godly discernment (deep understanding) brings motivational change from what we understand and believe to be true. Consider these "discern-less" life choices:

- We're an entertainment sponge, flittering our time away needlessly.
- We're easily bored by self-examination and spiritual thinking.
- We're soft on sin, calling adultery an "affair," or homosexuality "gay."
- We're terribly lazy and put off things of spiritual importance.
- We avoid self-disciplines of fellowship, devotions, studies, etc.
- We compromise our commitments foolishly and toy with sin.
- We fail to think consequentially, and stray from Biblical cautions.

Such attitudes can easily keep a young and immature believer, or an older and lazy one, from becoming all that God wants him or her to be. Such individuals cut off their hearts from the sharp blade of Biblical truth, and they suffer for it. Conversely, people of conviction stay connected with Christ. They're into the Word regularly and make a ***decisive effort*** to discern *its life-changing truths*. Learning to perceive God's will, to think rightly, and understand it deeply is that which the Spirit uses to change an immature person into a mighty follower of Jesus Christ.

> *"So then, just as you received Christ Jesus as Lord, continue to live your lives in him, rooted and built up in him, strengthened in the faith as you were taught, and overflowing with thankfulness."* (Col. 2:6,7)

Perspective Moves Passion

But, one thing is for sure in spiritual life and growth...*motivation is the product of the understanding that lies within it*. When one is deeply impacted by God's Truth, conviction is being created, even though it must continue to grow into intention in order to bring spiritual growth and stability. But God's Truth provides the fuel that the Holy Spirit uses to ignite *motivation* and *intention* within our soul. These are born as we allow God's Word to enroot itself into our minds at the heart level (our deepest thinking & understanding). God's Word ignites spiritual *desire* as we *discern* its truths and think as Gods thinks.

For a moment, think about a particularly important verse and what it means to you. What does it say about your relationship with God? Okay, now think about more than just that one verse. In fact, gather a slew of such truths so you can call upon them when you need strength and encouragement. As you move about in your Christian life, always seek to *enlarge, deepen and expand* your understanding and acceptance of these and many other Scriptural truths, asking yourself, "What are its implications for me and my life with Christ? What is God telling me? Why is this important to me? This type of spiritual meditation is critical for Scripture to *germinate spiritual desire*, along with its ultimate goal...*intentional change*.

> *"This Book of the Law shall not depart from your mouth, but you shall **meditate** on it day and night, so that you may be careful to do according to all that is written in it. For **then** you will make your way prosperous, and **then** you will have good success."* (Joshua 1:8).

Meditation is an interesting Word, meaning in ancient times "moaning, muttering, groaning and growling." A lion softly growls and moans as it steps guardedly through the tall, African grass, laying hidden, but intensely focused as it stalks its prey. Translators today use the word *ponder* and *meditate* for the English equivalent, but it means maintaining deep and intense focus, like a lion stealthily stalking its prey. God was telling Joshua in the above passage to focus his ***understanding*** upon God's Word, for to do so would result in a prosperous life of blessing and success. Let's ask ourselves the following question:

> *"Are you and I so deeply moved and intensely motivated by faith to search the Scriptures and apply its life changing principles?*

This is the only way to develop godly conviction(s). It's not a "MacDonald's hamburger" approach, for spirituality is rarely served up in a "fast food" manner. We've got to *diligently seek it!* (Hebrews 11:6). So, when understanding becomes a deeply held belief, it generates significant spiritual desire. That's when powerful conviction is born – for it motivates us to *want* the things of God, without which we'll drift away.

Passion Moves Purpose

We all have a part of us that's not easily defined, and it's called the ***will.*** In the Bible there are a hand full of words that are so translatable, but the most prominent ones have two meanings sort of tied together...to "wish" or to "will." One interesting verse in 1st Peter is translated somewhat differently in two versions, and gives support to what I'm saying here.

> *"The Lord is not slack concerning his promise, as some men count slackness; but is longsuffering to us-ward, not **willing** that any should perish, but that all should come to repentance."* (2 Peter 3:9 KJV)

> *""The Lord is not slow in keeping his promise, as some understand slowness. Instead, he is patient with you, not **wanting** anyone to perish, but everyone to come to repentance."* (II Peter 2:9 NIV)

People are allowed to choose spiritual death, even though God doesn't want, wish, or desire it. To say that he isn't willing, however, is inaccurate, for people do perish every day apart from knowing Christ. God wishes and wants all to respond by faith in his Son, but not everyone will believe. Simple "wishing" doesn't ultimately change anything. Shallow, marginally motivated beliefs don't change us much, for only our impassioned perspectives can empower significant spiritual commitment and determination to serve God faithfully. Ask yourself the following question:

"Does what I believe about _____
impact my attitudes, behaviors and/or
relationships for God?"

If the answer is, "Not really," then that belief is probably not a conviction, just interesting conversation. For example, a person wanting to give up cigarette smoking can't do so, if he or she sits around just *wishing* or even *somewhat* wanting it to happen. Any desire must be *strong enough* to bring about a ***decisive choice*** before bringing about eventual behavioral change on a consistent basis. Desire must grow into *purpose!*

A consecrated believer is a person of conviction, implying strong discernment, desire (varies in intensity), and *willingness to discipline one's life*. As we cultivate God's Word into our hearts, such convictional foundations will begin to "set us apart" (sanctify us) in the inner person. Then, such surrender (commitment) to the will of God will eventually change our outer person as well.

Do

Purpose Enables Practice

Remember, there are 3 things that identify genuine conviction... intellect, inclination and intention. All three must flow toward God and evidence themselves in a person's heart and life, if we are to say that one is a person of spiritual conviction. Stagnant, intellectual belief never produces spiritual conviction.

Think of it this process as building a camp fire. You're on a camp out, and it's time to cook some hot dogs and hamburgers. You get some twigs together in a pile, then throw some heavier branches on top of them. However, the wind is kicking up, so each match you light is snuffed out, for there's no lasting spark. Finally, you cover your hands around the match and lower it closer to the ground to keep that nasty wind away, then strike the match one more time. Suddenly, the spark ignites the match, so you hold it under a dry twig until a small flame appears. Your fire isn't much at this point, but it's motivated to grow bigger as you add more kindling and small branches, eventually adding some small logs.

By application, the spark of conviction always comes from *your understanding* of God's Word...a verse or spiritual truth. The small flame that occurs is an initial *burst of inclination*, and your conviction is then ignited. The more intense the flame becomes the more enflamed your inclination becomes (impassioned belief), until flowing into intention and ultimate lifestyle change (if necessary...eg. understanding a math problem won't inspire any passion; imagining and understanding what a piece of chocolate tastes like, will).

When I was a younger, my faith was enthusiastic, but immature, with clinging sins and shallow commitments. His Spirit went deeper, cutting and drilling into my inner person, helping me to understand Him with greater sincerity, motivation and intention. It was difficult and painful at times in order to yield to his purposes, but he's never deserted me or done anything without his abiding love.

God purpose was to develop a truer and deeper understanding of who he is, which produces an overflowing desire and determination to obey him without reservation. This is faith *conviction* at the heart level, where we allow the seeds of God's Word to settle deeply into our innermost person in undivided loyalty to Jesus and his will for our lives. Faith will initiate the process and form the foundation upon which other sanctifying steps are taken toward spiritual maturity. But everything must be cemented together by God's Spirit through deep seated discernment and impassioned surrender to God and his will in Christ Jesus.

When we develop that kind of spiritual mindset, we become men and women of life-changing convictions...brick by brick... until our spiritual lives are stronger and more reliable. *The deeper into our hearts and minds God's truth-seeds find themselves rooted, the more likely we can break the hold of the things that bind us.* So, if there's a key to the mystery of spiritual growth, it's this:

> Embrace God's Truth, *"...for the truth will set you free."* (Jn 8:32)

CONVICTION #1

I Believe In Jesus

"Yet to all who did receive him, to those who believed in his name, he gave the right to become children of God - children born not of natural descent, nor of human decision or a husband's will, but born of God."
John 1:12

"You're kidding," I said to the Karen, one of the other employees on this "Wilderness Learning Experience" all of us were participating in from work. We were staring at a wooden pole about six inches thick, with small metal rods sticking out from its sides every 10 inches or so all the way to the top... like a miniature telephone pole. It was about 12 feet high and had a one-foot square platform at the top, upon which you could stand...if you dared to climb to the top of the pole! Of course, that was the task!

There were about 30 of us management type people on a "fun" day off from work to learn some helpful skills about team building. My job at the time was being the corporate trainer for the company, which consisted of manufacturing grinding wheels sold throughout the country. This facility, where we were presently experiencing this wilderness learning event, was located deep in the woods about a half hour away from the rural factory where we were employed. Once we arrived, we had to put on this tethered body harness that was tied into a safety wire running above each wilderness event we had to master. There were about 7 of these difficult individual and/or group tasks at the course.

As we all approached this particular task, not everyone wanted to participate. I, of course, thought I was invincible, so I gave it a try. I hooked my tether ring tothe metal line, which tracked above me and would save me in the event of a fall.

The task was to first climb that skinny pole and somehow manage to stand up on that tiny platform...alone and swaying back and forth in the breeze. That was difficult enough, of course, but once I did that, then I had to jump out and up into the air and grab onto a red flag hanging from an extended tree branch (relying only on that tether to save me if I fell). That was the truly scary part, for it hung in the air 12 feet off the ground...*and ten feet away!* It was almost impossible, for you couldn't get any kind of a jump start up there, though you could sway the pole a bit back and forth to give yourself an edge, if you wanted (or weren't too scared to do so!).

Well, I gave it my best and leaped into thin air, as they say, hoping that whether or not I was able to grab that flag, the tether would save me. My jump came to about a foot short, but the tether held me, and I was slowly let down to the ground. It was supposedly to be a lesson in trust, for I had to trust that I wouldn't fall off the pole once I got to the top, and that the tether and the guy holding it would be able to stop me from falling to my demise. When I told my wife about it later, she almost fainted just hearing about it!

By application, just as I trusted fully in this wilderness company's expertise, so we must explicitly trust in Jesus as Savior and Lord of our lives. Part of this implies reaching out and trusting what we don't completely know or understand. But, much of what we call faith *does* involve trusting in what we *do understand* and *choose to believe.* Blind faith in anything can be a *leap* into the unknown, but usually there's *some* evidence or foundation for the trust required. Similarly, faith in Christ is also a *substantive leap*, stepping out upon the platform of *what we do understand* about life and God as revealed in the Scriptures. We certainly do not fully understand every "jot and tittle" of it, of course (that's the leap). Nevertheless, ***Gospel conviction*** *is still well-placed and well-grounded belief.*

THE WHY'S OF FAITH

Both evidence and "leaps" swirl around in the minds of believers, particularly if we're experiencing a shortfall in spiritual confidence. When facing significant indecision or stress regarding some level of trust in one's relationship with Jesus, a person is prone to vacillate in his/her spirituality, possibly succumbing to a temptation, which he or she would otherwise ignore. Lack of such spiritual confidence in the Lord isn't always recognizable and can subtly "creep" into one's life. Suggesting to someone so compromised just to "faith it through," isn't the best spiritual medicine, though still a key part of the process. However, somewhere along the way, the bridge to confidence must be recognized and rebuilt by identifying *the underlying issues* causing the collapse in the first place.

For instance, when I was in my freshman year at Christian college, I entered as a fairly confident and committed believer. I came from a good Christian home, where mom and dad knew the Lord and lived faithfully according to Biblical principles. My youth group at church was really fantastic as well, with over 70 teenagers meeting weekly for Saturday night outreach, and also through the week at school or at in-home Bible studies. I enjoyed serving on the leadership council, regularly led the worship times, and occasionally spoke at the various events.

College, however, hit me kind of hard, though others from my youth group attended the same college. Those friendships were great, but still there was the "aloneness" of being 8 hours away and stuck in the woods of upper NY state. Everything was new, and I felt unsettled, because there was no weekly youth group to attend, no youth directors to go to with your issues, and no church body for support and fellowship.

Now, it was a needed growing experience, of course, where I had to make new friends, find another church body for fellowship and begin to find more adult purposes. However, when I came face to face in the educational process with a far greater expanse of knowledge than I possessed, my fundamental beliefs became stressed. Yes, it was a fine and reputable Christian college, but inner questions raged within me...unanswered and continually attacking my spiritual confidence. It all came to a head after going to a science-fiction movie, which, looking back, was an underlying and subtle attack upon Christian beliefs, though covered over with Hollywood gloss. What was I to do?

I remember sitting down on my bunk later on at the dorm and crying out to God for the wisdom to get through all of this uncertainty. I was embarrassed by my lack of faith and frustrated by my inability to "reason it all out." Finally, in desperation, I came across the following passage in Scripture, Habakkuk 3:17-18:

"Though the fig tree should not blossom,
nor fruit be on the vines,
the produce of the olive fail
and the fields yield no food,
the flock be cut off from the fold
and there be no herd in the stalls,
yet I will rejoice in the LORD;
I will take joy in the God of my salvation."

I immediately recognized that this was God speaking to me personally, though silently. The prophet, Habakkuk, had a problem with God allowing the Chaldeans to rampage in judgment throughout Judah. He foresaw the carnage, the loss and the devastation of God's judgment, not only upon His people, but also upon the Chaldeans. Because of this, he emotionally disagreed with God, which is not a smart thing to do, right? But he eventually thought it through and realized what the Spirit was saying to him. Here's what I think he recognized.

- Judgment for sin can't be avoided, if God so wills it.

- Tough times do *not* mean that God has left us.

- Salvation is real and the most important thing to anyone.

It was the last point that really struck home to me. I can tell you that this passage settled my personal and spiritual insecurities forever.

Now, someone might say, "Well, Ed, you simply took a leap of faith, and found it reliable." No, it wasn't just the leap of faith *alone* by which God enabled me to find healing and grace, it was my ***faith perspective*** that grounded me. Just as a metal stake on top of a skyscraper is used to safely ground lightning strikes, so my faith became grounded that day in Jesus Christ. I was lifted out of doubt and found confidence in my reason for being a Christian… the ***Gospel***. I was saying to myself:

> *"Lord, no matter what happens or what nonbelievers say to erode my trust in you, I believe. I know I am a sinner. I know you exist and are holy and righteous. I know I need a Savior, and in spite of whatever I have to face in the future, I will trust in your sacrifice to save my soul. I don't care about the taunts or the unanswered questions. I'm going forward by faith in Christ."*

I really did find peace that day, and it's followed me throughout my life. There were other necessary things to add to this along the way, of course, as well as the passion and purpose to sustain this restored and renewed conviction. But God has always used this *"fundamental perspective"* to settle me down and move me more confidently forward in my Christian life.

So, faith is not *just* a leap, it's also a secure ***foundation***, a powerful and spiritually sound way of thinking. Let me review with you several principles I found that day that might help you face life with greater conviction and confidence.

FIRST, GOD IS REAL

"Ed, that's so basic...come on."

Yes...but one of the things all of us have learned in life is that more often it's the basics that people stumble over, rather than the complicated. There's a funny scene in a golf movie I've seen on television about a struggling golfer...a good one...who all of a sudden loses his touch. He doesn't know why, but he's always "shanking" it...meaning, he swings and makes contact with the ball too close to the club shaft instead of the club center. So, he puts on this crazy contraption with strings, hanging objects and mirrors in hopes, I guess, of gaining some sort of balance in his swing. It doesn't work, of course, because his real issue was just in his mind, a nervous "over-thinking" of his swing. A swing is a simple and uncomplicated thing, which enables anyone to strike the ball correctly. When he realizes this silly mistake, he corrects his focus, and the "shanks" go away.

Faith is fundamentally an *uncomplicated trust* in the person of God and in his Son, Jesus Christ. In life, however, believers are sometimes faced with unexplainable issues and questions, exaggerated by non-believers or skeptical media types, usually with no other purpose than to discredit God so they can indulge their immoral lifestyles. Belief in God, however, is just as sound as any other decision in life, because, as finite beings, faith of some sort is at the bottom of every thought and premise. For instance, we believe in electricity, though we can't really see it, except in a lightning storm. We believe in moral rights and wrongs, though many differ as to which is which. We believe in a universe of stable, recognizable, and useable natural laws, which are able to be harnessed by mankind to preserve and control life. We know garbage will spoil, cement will harden and gravity makes us fall. We believe that people who do wrong should be punished. We believe that order and design are the handiwork of intelligence, not disorder and accident. We believe that murder is wrong, compassion is good and hope moves the human spirit. All of this fundamentally relies upon our trust *that it is all true*. Why is it not just as sound to believe in our Creator God?

People who disbelieve in the existence of God, are left with nothing but a meaningless blob of empty thoughts and purposeless murmurings. The theorems of Einstein would be no more reliable than the jokes of late-night comedians. To predicate our existence as "an accident suspended between accidents," as one Pastor says, stretches one's intellectual capacity to the point of collapse! Everything in life has design and purpose written into its existence. So, it's also just as reasonable, and far more logical, to assume that the complicated design of the universe is *not* an accident, but has been intellectually driven and created.

Have you ever just sat down and looked at the immensity of the universe and the intricacies of its interworking laws? People may differ on how God began all this and put it into existence, but his handiwork is simply amazing. For instance, God's Sovereign Design is so evident in his placement of the Earth within the universe. Chance could not think up such a perfect system with which to protect life on our planet. Consider:

- Earth is at the precise distance from the sun for avoiding immediate incineration and being turned into a frozen, lifeless rock in space.

- Earth has a perfect "tilt," assuring seasons and harvesting for us all.

- Earth's water-based system is uniquely built into the fabric of our physical functionality such that life couldn't exist without it.

- Earth's protective atmosphere protects us like no other known planet from outer harmful ultraviolet light and the destructive rays from space.

- Earth's photosynthesis process is at the core of its energy producing structure and sustains all life with harmonious functionality.

- Earth's gravitational system keeps people and things from flying into space, and it holds the planets, solar systems and galaxies in perfect physical relationship and order. *

Still, all of us have talked with a few sceptics who try to deny the existence of God and hold to the inherently illogical position that a mindless, evolutionary, purposeless and haphazard series of spontaneous events spit out the intricate layout of our universe. But such random things do not create, they dissipate and destroy rather than build or benefit (e.g. the laws of entropy and thermodynamics). Only a Creator can mold and shape physical existence with persevering properties and inter-dependent design. As the Bible says, there was and had to be a beginning to it all (Genesis 1), and God's guiding hand connected everything in it with precision and harmony.

> "The *observable* universe contains 100 Billion galaxies, and each galaxy contains 100 Billion stars. Overall, the *observable* universe contains 10 thousand million million million stars (10^{22} stars)."

> "...in order for something to exist without being the result of a prior cause, that something must be eternal (i.e., something that did not come into being, but has always existed). As such, the universe could not emerge out of nothing, but it can exist as an effect of an uncaused eternal First Cause - which is precisely what God is."
(Hank Hanegraaff, president of the Christian Research Institute. Taken From God's Creative Handiwork, Dr. Richard Montagna, lecture given at WNY Church Retreat, 1-19-2018)

> "Before the mountains were born or you brought forth the earth and the world, from everlasting to everlasting, you are God." (Ps 90:2)

Let's also not forget about the intricate design of the cell and all its interworking parts, including the inner brain of it all...our DNA. Our brain itself is capable of tremendous amounts of activity in order to coordinate everything on a conscious and unconscious level - with perfect efficiency.

A supercomputer has matched our brains' performance for one second only, *with the help of 83,000 processors!* Medical science has created machines that duplicate the processes of certain organs within our body (e.g. the liver and the heart). However, each machine still has one critical part that it relies on for its functionality...*it must be plugged in!* The Master Designer of the Universe built into his creation powerful operational resources like electricity, magnetism, light, nuclear energy, etc., without which we'd be sunk! All of this again points to the handiwork of our wonderful Creator God, who designed a place for us with intricate purpose and harmony. Unfortunately, mankind ignored God's Truth and wisdom.

SECOND, SIN IS REAL

> *"...since the creation of the world God's invisible qualities—his eternal power and divine nature—have been clearly seen, being understood from what has been made, so that people are without excuse. For although they knew God, they neither glorified him as God nor gave thanks to him, but their thinking became futile and their foolish hearts were darkened. Although they claimed to be wise, they became fools and exchanged the glory of the immortal God for images made to look like a mortal human being and birds and animals and reptiles. Therefore, God gave them over in the **sinful desires of their hearts** to sexual impurity for the degrading of their bodies with one another. They exchanged the truth about God for a lie, and worshiped and served created things rather than the Creator—who is forever praised. Amen."* (Romans 1:20-25)

To deny sin, is to deny righteousness and goodness, for how would you know either without the existence of both? Frankly speaking, to even believe in moral absolutes of any nature demands that we believe in a moral Giver, who has built into life such absolutes. If there are no moral absolutes, then life is of necessity just a chaotic cloud in which we find ourselves hopelessly lost. Morality, rights and wrongs, ethics, law and order (not the tv program!), guilt and punishment, sin and evil, justice and mercy, good and bad...all of this would be pointless.

In reality, however, all of this graphically points to the existence of a Creator just as much as God's physical handiwork does.

Again, if such moral concepts are seen as nothing more than precepts without *eternal* perspective, then we are still swimming in the same chaotic soup. And, in that moral soup, all of mankind's "high thoughts" would only be evolutionary and random particles bouncing of one another for eons, which have randomly amassed into subjective, unproven, unreliable and ungrounded bits of interesting intellectual fluff.

> *"I'm against sin. I'll kick it as long as I've got a foot, and I'll fight it as long as I've got a fist. I'll butt it as long as I've got a head. I'll bite it as long as I've got a tooth. And when I'm old and fistless and footless and toothless, I'll gum it till I go home to Glory and it goes home to perdition!"*
>
> **BillySunday**
>
> https://www.whatchristianswanttoknow.com/25-christian-quotes-about-sin/#ixzz56pOmPfuQ

Wow...how's that for a sense of life purpose! But, to the contrary, God's moral nature has been stamped upon the very souls of his creatures, regardless of whether or not they comply with obedience to his will.

By the way, Satan's primary strategy is to deny all this and bend our minds into thinking that sin doesn't exist and/or that it's not a major concern for us. So, keep in mind that we are also dealing with spiritual powers that try to influence our thinking and to ignore that which is spiritually obvious, as revealed in God's Word.

> *"For our struggle is not against flesh and blood, but against the rulers, against the authorities, against the powers of this dark world and against the spiritual forces of evil in the heavenly realms."* Eph 6:12

Paul goes on to say that we must put on God's armor when going to do battle with such enemies. All of the armor he mentions is <u>mental</u> in nature…Truth, Righteousness, Gospel, Faith, Salvation, God's Word, etc. *It requires an ongoing understanding and committed focus upon the fundamentals of spiritual conviction.* Yes, the battlefield is mostly our thought life, and there are plenty of mental mines that explode upon our consciousness from the enemy. Satan ultimately seeks to commandeer our minds *so that he can steal our hearts,* for he knows that denying sin (or going soft on it) will unleash uncontrolled fleshly passions and wreak havoc in our Christian lives. Once Satan's host reaches into our <u>hearts</u> (evil passions and desires) with consistency, we're doomed by habit to fall and fail. Instead, yield your thought life to the Spirit…*protect your <u>heart</u>!*

Thirdly, Jesus Is Real

The outrageousness of Jesus, including that he calls himself the Jewish Messiah, shows that he should normally not even be given "the time of day," as one would say. In other words, no rational, stable, or psychologically sound individual would ever claim the following - to be God and the Son of God, to be sinless, to forgive the sin of others, to have lived outside of time, and to be the only source of eternal life and peace with God. He said he would rise from the dead after three days but would come back one day to take on the kings of the world in a final battle, which would bring the whole world to its knees in worship. All this would be followed by the establishment of his kingdom without end, ruled by himself and his heavenly Father, as well as the final judgement seat for all of mankind, over which he would preside as judge.

Who would possibly teach such things about himself with a straight face? Who would have looked at him and believed it to be true, and he to be God? All religions describe the spiritual searches of men seeking to please a God they do not know, but Christ claimed to actually be that God, the one who personally reached down to us in a visible and incarnate way. How utterly ridiculous...unless...*unless true!*

The exciting thing about this is that God the Father *authenticated* both the man and the message of Messiah Jesus. First, the Gospel message that was delivered by the Lord was *authenticated* by the prophets who foretold it. A multitude of prophecies were fulfilled by Christ, including the time and place of his birth hundreds of years before Jesus walked this earth.

> The likelihood of just 8 prophesies being fulfilled in this way has been calculated to be 1 in 100,000,000,000,000,000. For 1 person fulfilling 48 prophecies: 1 chance in 10 to the 157th power! http://www1.cbn.com/biblestudy/biblical-prophecies-fulfilled-by-jesus

Of course, our confidence doesn't rest in mathematical equations, but such statistical support does lift our faith a bit. *No other person in history* has such credentials of historical significance and miraculous attestation attached to his teaching and person.

Second, God authenticated his Son by miracles and his resurrection from the dead. Historians have recorded both his existence, his teaching popularity and his miraculous manifestations, thus verifying the Biblical record. He lived in poverty, had just a small band of followers, and gained no political status. Jews hated him, many of his followers left him, Rome condemned him and society nailed him to a wooden cross. Yet, his teaching garners the praise of all who hear of it and continues to change the lives of those who trust in him as Savior and Lord.

No, Jesus is no master magician who fooled everyone with slight-of-hand and planned chicanery for money or position. He was a man...*but, he was also God.* Even from an outsider's viewpoint, there's just no other credible choice to make. His life shows it, his miracles attest to it, his teaching legitimizes it, and his resurrection solidifies it. He is Almighty God, the Lord of Life!

Salvation Is Real

When all the above is considered in light of the transformational power inherent in the lives of those of us who have taken Christ at his Word, one can have the fullest of confidence in the ***Gospel Truth.*** God lives, sin is real, Christ's blood atones for our sin, and forgiveness is found by trusting Jesus as personal Savior and Lord. You and I should have the utmost confidence in our faith, for our *conviction* regarding Christ as Savior and God is as reliable as it gets!

I would be remiss not sharpen all this to a point. Everything we've been discussing here is true, reliable and trustworthy. However, since we're talking about spiritual convictions, let's remember that action is required beyond just intellectual understanding. To simply agree and understand that all of the above is true won't get you or I into heaven. People understand many things about life and God, but if those things are having no impact in your life, they are nothing more than simple intellectual interests. However, our belief in Jesus Christ as Savior and Lord **must be life changing** in order to reveal its genuineness, otherwise it is also nothing more than mental facts. James 2:17-19 says the following:

> *"In the same way, faith by itself, if it is not accompanied by action, is dead. But someone will say, "You have faith; I have deeds. Show me your faith without deeds, and I will show you my faith by my deeds. You believe that there is one God. Good! Even the demons believe that—and shudder."*

Intelligence is a good thing, and God has given it to us to make decisions that control and drive our lives into areas that are safe and productive. Spiritually speaking, God expects us to make a faith commitment to him, telling him that we not only believe in his Son, Jesus, as **Savior,** but that we also passionately and intentionally commit our lives to him as **Lord.** In other words, decision involves desire, determination and obedience, a step beyond simple understanding, as you can see. A true Christian has faith as his primary conviction, therefore...:

> He or she *worships* God by believing in Christ and in his will.
>
> He or she *wants* God and his will, and passionately seeks it.
>
> He or she *wills* to obey God, choosing his will over all other options.
>
> He or she *walks with* God and obeys his will in attitude and action.

When a person initially receives God's Gospel Truth, he or she has genuinely been converted and, therefore, has received God's Spirit within his or her soul. From there on, such genuine conviction will prompt the believer to move forward each day in order to follow through in that initial conviction, thereby growing in impassioned commitment to God and his will. Attitudes will change and behaviors will become more Christ-like, even though behavioral *perfection* will not come until heaven. There will be times of peace and serenity, and there will be times of struggle and confusion, but genuine conviction drives commitment to its ultimate end, which is salvation. That salvation is assured because of God's indwelling Holy Spirit, for it is his continuing empowerment within our hearts that saves us to the end. So, confidence in what we believe is good, but only if our conviction is genuine and life changing! C.H. Spurgeon says it this way:

"I would recommend you either believe God up to the hilt, or else not to believe at all. Believe this book of God, every letter of it, or else reject it. There is no logical standing place between the two. Be satisfied with nothing less than a faith that swims in the deeps of divine revelation; a faith that paddles about the edge of the water is poor faith at best. It is little better than a dry-land faith and is not good for much." - C. H. Spurgeon (https://www.sermonsearch.com/sermon-illustrations/2187/believe-or-reject/)

CONVICTION #2

I Believe In Seeking God

"Draw near to God and He will draw near to you."
James 4:8

We've all known individuals that start out well, but don't finish strong, right? My first Youth Director, Al Baines, told me about his mentor, who was a powerful, driving force in his initial Christian life. As a young person, Al was greatly impacted by this man's leadership in the church youth program, helping it develop into a massive outreach for Christ to the Bridgeport, Connecticut community. However, in his mentor's later years, he waned in his convictions about his call and ministry to the youth, and to the church at large. Al didn't know what caused this slow dissipation, but he recognized that the man had lost the serious drive he had most of his life for sharing the Gospel. Perhaps age had an effect, perhaps he had unanswered questions and discouragements that slowed him down…we'll never know. But it saddened Al greatly, though it didn't slow *him* down spiritually.

We've discussed above how the Christian life is built upon our convictions…faith being the first and foremost conviction of all. But, any conviction can "lose steam" over the long haul, unless it is refreshed. Consider the old locomotives that drove those original trains across our growing national landscape, particularly out West. They pulled a huge car stuffed with plenty of logs behind it in order to keep that engine fired up. When the wood was gone, so was the power to pull all those passenger cars along the tracks.

Believers have just such a power source in their relationship with Jesus Christ. To access God's power in our lives, the Bible says we should *"seek him."* Seeking means to reach out and/or search **with strong desire and personal intent**. Can this be rightly said of your relationship with Christ? Let's explore this together.

I Will Seek God's Propitiation

"Simon Peter answered him, "Lord, to whom shall we go? You have the words of eternal life." (John 6:68)

Because of the fall, man was plunged into a world of self-effort and self-reliance. Adam separated himself from intimacy with God, because that's what sin does...it pushes God away and seeks its own satisfaction and rule. But there remained in mankind the spark of spiritual life in the form of conscience.

Honestly folks, both believers and non-believers recognize the existence of sin in human affairs and relationships. Think about the school shooting in Florida, where a disturbed young man with an automatic weapon entered a school and killed so many kids, apparently just to appease his wounded ego and sense of social rejection. Think about corrupt political agendas of rogue nations such as North Korea, whose leaders are homicidally bent upon bringing nuclear destruction to the West for the sake of their own Marxists agenda? Don't forget Islamic terror, a religious political system of "conversion by conquest," which has over the years since its inception brought death by murder to over 200M people... all in the name of a self-proclaimed prophet named Mohammed. Also, think about the countless folks that steal, commit adultery, covet, hate, curse, lie, murder and live perverted lifestyles? Consider also the ungodly and carnal pleasures contrary to the will of God in which *you and I* indulge ourselves from time to time, though we know believers should not do so.

However, as believers, we have chosen to believe in Christ and seek the propitiation of God. The need for propitiation is a driving motivation for believers that keeps them on the right track. It's not that we should again seek to have our sins forgiven at the cross, for that was accomplished at one time, the time we were saved by asking Jesus to forgive us and come into our lives as Savior and Lord. However, I realize that sin is still in my life, along with Satan's presence, who constantly attacks all of us. Though I believe in eternal security, this situation still bothers me and scares me. Oh, I know we're not supposed to worry about it, but we're human, right? So, I sometimes say to myself:

> *"I hope that I'm not mistaken about the doctrine of eternal security. I mean, I understand it and believe in it, but I don't want to play with sin at all...attitudinally or behaviorally...for it would mean that I could turn away from the atonement Christ offered and saved me. So, I'm staying spiritually serious and responsible, confessing sin as it rears its ugly head in my life, and always recommitting myself in faith to my Savior."*

Now, I don't have anxiety attacks over this, or am I constantly chasing my tail in a doctrinal conundrum, nervously trying to resolve a theological issue that can't ultimately be proven, one way or the other. Yes, I scripturally favor the security side, but I know that some Christian leaders disagree. THAT'S when I remind myself of the cross and rejoice in the propitiation Christ provided for me!

The joy and peace that comes from focusing upon God's merciful grace should always drive us to our knees, calling us back from answerless worries and wayward behaviors. God's propitiation...his atoning and reconciling grace...is never something to put in jeopardy, whether it's possible or not to do so. Let it continually be the spiritual resource it should always be in your life as well.

I Will Seek God's Presence

Understanding God's Word and developing consequential thinking are both powerless unless they move the heart. As mentioned before, true *spiritual* convictions exceed simple beliefs and move us to **want** God and his Will ***more than anything*** else in this entire world. Jesus said:

> *"Whoever loves father or mother <u>more than me</u> is not worthy of me, and whoever loves son or daughter more than me is not worthy of me. And whoever does not take his cross and follow me is not worthy of me. Whoever finds his life will lose it, and whoever loses his life for my sake will find it."* (Matthew 10:37-39)

Don't' forget, however, that false and sinfully spawned convictions move us to want ***our will*** more than ***God's will***. Such convictions can be very powerful and need a spiritual plan of attack to disable and overcome them for Christ.

So, how much do we want God in our lives, even as believers? More than our accomplishments and pride? More than what we desire and/or lust after? More than our relationships and entertainments? Most of our struggles as believers come because we are like immature little children, tenaciously clinging to our impassioned toys. *Men and women of deep conviction, however, are willing to give up such things and put them in proper priority.* They don't *just* believe in Jesus, they intensely desire and pursue his presence every day!

Consider the woman who washed Jesus' feet with expensive ointment. She was chided by some for her lack of consideration for the poor, because she was "wasting" it on the Lord Jesus. But Jesus rightly corrected them, saying that his presence was enough to justify such worship. She wanted Jesus more than her expensive perfume or the wanton promiscuity of her former life. Jesus commented on her spiritual passion and worship:

> *"He that has been forgiven little, loves little.*
> *He that has been forgiven much, loves much."*

Her immoral lifestyle powerfully drove her to seek Jesus' forgiveness, for she understood, perhaps for the first time, how devastating are the consequences of sinful living. She had much to be forgiven, *so she had much to offer in worship.* We should be so passionately moved by the Spirit of God in our lives!

We, too, should show our want for Jesus, by spending time talking with him in prayer and spending personal time in worship for all he has done and is doing for us. This is the relational element to seeking God, which demands that we prioritize our lives with a dedicated eye on how much time we spend with him. It's a measure of how much we truly love him.

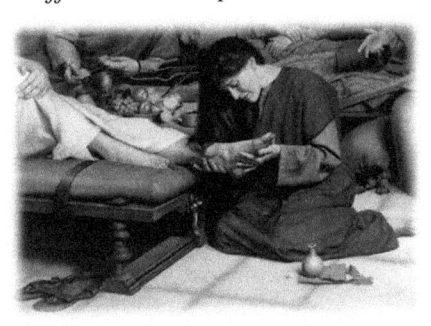

I Will Seek God's Precepts and Principles

However, this process is a very practical thing, created by God, and it's still been affected by the state of sin. Our convictions, therefore, are not always right and, even if right, they can lose their drive within us at times. In fact, we get into trouble when we fail to consistently feed our convictional engine with the logs of God's Truth. This precious resource is primarily found in the pages of the Word of God. It is the Spirit's responsibility to minister the Father's Truth into our hearts...that's the power source we desperately need and must depend upon for keeping the engine of conviction alive and productive. Listen to the Apostle John:

> *"Sanctify them by the Truth; your **word is truth**."* (John 17:17)

> *"But I tell you the truth; It is for your good that I am going away. Unless I go away, the Counselor will not come to you, but if I go, I will send him to you. When he comes, **he will convict** the world of guilt in regard to sin, and righteousness and judgment."* (John 16:7-8)

> *"...when he, the Spirit of truth comes, he will guide you into all truth. He will not speak on his own; he will speak only what he hears, and he will tell you what is yet to come. He will bring glory to me by **taking from what is mine and making it known to you**."* (John 16:12-14)

> *"**The Spirit gives life;** the flesh counts for nothing. **The words I have spoken to you are spirit and they are life.**"* (John 6:63-64)

Recently, I came down with a bronchial infection and went to the doctor. After having a deepening chest cough that sounded as if my insides were being scraped with a shovel, I went to the doctor. Unfortunately, I met with a Physician's Assistant, who was fresh out of medical school. She was fully prepped in the perspective that anti-biotics shouldn't be abused and given out by doctors to patients until it is clear that the infection is not viral (where anti-biotics *can't* help), but bacterial (where antibiotics *can* effectively work). I agreed in part, but told her that I knew my body and its reactions quite well over the years, and that this was clearly bacterial in nature. It had been over a week and things were still going painfully south. I knew that this was just my yearly battle with this type of thing, once it starts going around in the schools and at the workplace.

She still resisted, however, saying she wanted to wait another 4 or 5 days to make sure that it wasn't just a viral thing. So, I firmly informed her that she needed to talk with my primary doctor, and he would okay it...which he did. In a few days, the antibiotics had totally reversed the infection, and I was on the road to complete recovery.

Apart from the antibiotic controversy, all of us know that having the right medicine inside is a necessity for healing to occur. By application, we also need the powerful perspective of God's Word within us in order to fight off infectious and sinful impulses that attach themselves to our minds and hearts. The Word is empowered by the Spirit of God, and is powerfully invasive and deeply penetrating, enough so to bring healing and strength to our inner person. It enlightens our thinking, fuels our spiritual desire, generates renewed determination and transforms attitudes and behaviors well beyond what we can do alone. Develop and deepen your spiritual convictions by nurturing them in the Spirit and in the counsel of God's Word.

> *"For the word of God is living and active, sharper than any two-edged sword, piercing to the division of soul and of spirit, of joints and of marrow, and discerning the thoughts and intentions of the heart."* (Hebrews 4:12)

I Will Seek God's Provision

Ever heard of King Asa? He was an Old Testament king in Judah, the southern kingdom, which was composed of two tribes, itself and Benjamin. God's people were split into two kingdoms after the rule of Solomon, but the northern kingdom turned out to live in complete spiritual rebellion. Judah had some good and godly kings, however, one of which was Asa. The two nations, Israel and Judah, were like two squabbling brothers, fighting each other for power, land and prestige throughout their existence.

Though Asa was a godly king overall, I Kings 15:9-24 tells us that he made a significant mistake at the end of his days by going to the foreign king of Aram in order to secure his help against Israel. He made a treaty with him and paid him to bring his army against Baasha, king of Israel, who was seriously encroaching upon Judah's land. His strategy worked. However, God was not pleased and sent the prophet, Hanani, to inform Asa of his anger over that decision. God's reasoning was that he failed to trust in the Lord and seek his provision throughout all this, as he had in earlier years. As a result, Asa was severely judged for his failure to seek *God's* pleasure and protection. (II Chronicles 16:7-14)

The necessity and perspective of knowing and seeking God should be a rock-solid conviction for all of us, upon which all other spiritual convictions rest. One of the key purposes for doing this is to find his **blessing** and **provision** for our lives.

> *"The thief comes only to steal and kill and destroy. I came that they may have life and have it abundantly."* (John 10:10)

Asa knew of the abundant blessing of Jehovah God, for he had sought him regularly throughout his life. He saw how God delivered Judah from her enemies and richly provided for her, when they were living in a way that was righteous and godly. In his earlier days he was known for doing the right things before God, because he listened to God's prophets and acted upon their words to purge Judah from all idols and to restore proper temple worship in Jerusalem. People even came from the northern kingdom to worship in Jerusalem, because of the good things they heard about him. He even removed his wicked grandmother, Maacah, from her position as Queen, then entered into a national covenant:

> *"They entered into a covenant to seek the LORD, the God of their fathers, with all their heart and soul. All who would not seek the LORD, the God of Israel, were to be put to death, whether small of great, man or woman. They took an*

> *oath to the LORD with loud acclamation, with shouting and with trumpets and horns. All Judah rejoiced about the oath because they had sworn it wholeheartedly. They sought God eagerly and he was found by them. So the LORD gave them rest on every side."* (II Chron. 15:1-9)

Notice that God's blessing follows obedience, and it's no different for you and I today as believers in Christ. God expects us to seek his blessing upon all our efforts in providing for our families, for rearing our children, for marital growth, for our professional accomplishments, and for our ministry involvement. There should be no ultimate reliance or allegiance to anyone or anything but to our Lord Jesus.

This doesn't mean we have *no* partnerships with various people, corporations, relationships, people in authority, etc., along the way, for that would require us to leave the world and live a hermit's life in a cave somewhere in the mountains. But it does mean that our *final platform of trust* should be in Jesus, not in our own resources or of those around us. People of spiritual conviction ***seek*** and trust God to lead and provide for them.

> *"Don't love money; be satisfied with what you have. For God has said, "I will never fail you. I will never abandon you. So we can confidently say, "The Lord is my helper; I will not fear; what can man do to me?"* (Heb. 13:5, 6)

I Will Seek God's Purposes

I've never been much of a hunter, though as a kid I hunted grouse and turkeys with a bow on our land in Connecticut. I got fairly good at it, but the task of stripping off all those feathers and skinning the bird for supper, didn't really excite me. That's probably why I lost interest in hunting when entering high school.

But, when I did hunt those larger birds, I'd sneak up to them in the woods in order to get a better shot with the bow. It was easier in the snow, particularly if it was that light and fluffy stuff, for crunching through the rain-hardened, crusty snow would often just give you away. But I remember stepping quietly through the snow and slowly inching toward a bird, while trying to stay hidden long enough to creep to within 30 feet so I could get off a well-targeting arrow. To do that I had to cautiously follow its footsteps underneath and around low hanging spruce trees. It was really a lot of fun for me, but not for the bird, of course, which ended up on our dinner table that night!

I say the above because "spiritual hunters" are always seeking God's purposes. They keep praying and looking for spiritual signs, indications and leadings from God each and every day. And, as they prayerfully seek the will of God, they too, just like Asa, will be "...found by him." Being found by him suggests having our prayers answered and our provisions supplied abundantly.

I was a speaker recently at our church winter retreat, the topic of which involved, "We're going on a God hunt!" Well, we don't really hunt for God, particularly as believers, but we do seek his presence for guidance and purpose in life. Of course, we do have minds, and God wants us to think and make wise choices, not waiting for unmistakable lightning bolts of wisdom from the clouds. Asa made a good choice, based upon tactical warfare, but his fault was failing to seek God *first* and secure his approval. In that sense, he made an unwise choice.

Conversely, godly desires and intentional choices bring great blessing! There's personal joy and peace in knowing that God is in control, and that on any given day he may give you someone to help, someone to teach, something to accomplish, or someone to lead to Christ as Savior and Lord. Such a life is full of meaning and purpose, that which is the reward of godly faith and conviction.

When Elijah challenged king Ahab, Jezebel and their Baal serving prophets, he rebuked the people watching the event for not following God. He told them to stop vacillating between two choices, which means that they had two opposing desires fighting for dominance within them. Frankly, there really is no choice for the one whose faith conviction is set upon Jesus Christ. If he or she would have been there watching Elijah calling down the fire of God and burning up the altar, the choice would have been simple...

believe in Christ, and want nothing with greater desire and drive than God and his will in life. Can you say that together with me right now with the same unwavering desire and determination?

"I have sought your face with all my heart."
(Ps. 119:58)

CONVICTION #3

I Believe In The Fear of God

*"The fear of the LORD is a fountain of life,
turning a person from the snares of death."*
Proverbs 14:27

It was about 11pm at night and completely dark. I was travelling down route 9 from Torrington, Connecticut, where I had just had a business meeting with a group of folks for training purposes. It had been a productive and enjoyable night, but I was tired and anxious to get home. It was about a 45 minute trip on a fairly lonely highway that night, but the weather was good. About half way there and traveling through the hilly, wooded area of western Connecticut, I read the sign saying that I needed to stay left and switch to another highway, which I did with a relaxed yawn. About a mile down the 65mph highway, I noticed a car coming toward me on the opposite side of the road that seemed to be coming too close to my lane. It startled me at first, but the car reached me and then sped past me on my left. Again, it didn't bother me until a mile later when I saw that the signs on the road had their backs to me. *I was on a double lane highway traveling in the passing lane at 65mph...but going the wrong way!* I jumped up, focused myself and pulled over before another approaching car reached me. I just sat there for a minute or two, trying to figure out how it happened and why I survived a head-on collision. Finally, I turned around and made my way back onto the proper side toward home. When I walked through the door after arriving home, my wife said I was "as white as a ghost." I then explained to her what had happened, and she realized that the fear of what *"could have happened"* had simply gripped me all the way home.

A car accident can bring a lot of grief, even loss of life, and most people are scared enough about the possibility of having one that they are careful to avoid it. Why is it that people, believers or non-believers, are not far more interested in avoiding eternal loss, pain and/or grief? Jesus said the following:

> *"Do not be afraid of those who kill the body but cannot kill the soul. Rather, be afraid of the One who can destroy both soul and body in hell."*
> (Mathew 10:28)

I have a pastor friend who frequently says from the pulpit, "I don't like talking about it, but it's in the Bible. Hell is real." He was honest enough to say that he doesn't completely know why such a hideous and awful reality exists, but that God says it does, so it's time to listen up and be sure to avoid it.

So many folks are casually yawning their way through life, doing their own thing without much concern about sin or judgment, yet all the while they are ignoring the road signs (perhaps a generational weakness of most "millennials"). On that lonely highway at night, *I should have been watching more closely* and reading the signs properly in order to have stayed on the right road. Somehow, probably from being overly tired, I simply missed a sign and went the wrong way... toward potential disaster! Praise

God that he intervened for my safety and praise Him as well that I'm on the correct road toward heaven through Jesus Christ.

Okay, it's easy to talk about the non-believer, who needs to respond to the Gospel, if he or she is to find eternal life. But I want to focus this chapter *on the believer,* for all of us need to be concerned about having a proper and balanced "fear of God." It's not just Old Testament stuff or only about the non-Christian. Every believer needs a healthy and deep sense of spiritual fear before Almighty God, if he or she wants to walk in consistent obedience. Let's talk about that.

First of all, Christians who fear God have faith in God's __PERSON__.

If one doesn't believe in God and in his Son, why should he or she possess any degree of fear toward him. For them, he just doesn't exist, or at best, such folks just don't have any concern about searching for Him. In a way, they are like Satan and his demons.

> *"You believe that there is one God. Good! Even the demons believe that, and shudder."* (James 2:19)

In other words, even the demons have a built-in sense of fear (though, not reverence), when thinking about God. Again, it's not godly fear, for *their* belief in God *doesn't move them toward obedience.* In that sense, their "faith" is really illegitimate, for it ignores God's awesome power, his righteous expectations and his coming wrath to those who reject his will.

Biblical faith is ***obedient*** faith. Genuine Biblical faith shouldn't cause one to shudder in the corner of his house, because he or she is overcome with the fear of being struck by lightning on account of God's anger toward personal sin. Biblical fear of God centers in deep and reverent respect for the person of God. It realizes who God is and, therefore, recognizes that only a fool would disobey him and bring upon himself God's judgment, for he holds the key to earthly blessing and eternal life. Spiritual fear motivates, while unhealthy fear of God incapacitates.

Free Choice Bring Consequences.
Consequences Demand Accountability.
Accountability Brings Reward or Punishment.
Reward or Punishment Motivates the Godly.

Secondly, Christians who fear God embrace God's <u>POWER</u>.

They are deeply aware of the *awesome power* of God's omnipotent being. He created us and the universe, displaying his immeasurable capabilities and eternal nature in such a way that we are simply awestruck and over-whelmed by the power of his person. Let me give two examples of how God seeks to engender this fear within us.

First, there is Moses, who was chosen to deliver God's commandments to the Israelites. The people were to gather and hear what God had to say, but God prepared their hearts to receive his words by thunderous displays of his power.

> *"On the morning of the third day there was thunder and lightning, with a thick cloud over the mountain, and a very loud trumpet blast. Everyone in the camp trembled. Then, Moses led the people out of the camp to meet with God, and they stood at the foot of the mountain. Mount Sinai was covered with smoke, because the* LORD *descended on it in fire. The smoke billowed up from it like smoke from a furnace, and the whole mountain trembled violently. As the sound of the trumpet grew louder and louder, Moses spoke and the voice of God answered him.* And God spoke all these words:" (Ex. 19:16-19)

Then, God spoke the 10 commandments to the people. It must have been an awesome experience, which would have far surpassed the artistic capabilities of a Disney or a Spielberg, even with all their digital capabilities at hand. But what was God's intended purpose in all this?

> *"When the people saw the thunder and lightning and heard the trumpet and saw the mountain in smoke, they trembled with fear. They stayed at a distance and said to Moses, "Speak to us yourself and we will listen. But do not have God speak to us or we will die." Moses said to the people, "Do not be afraid. God has come to test you, so that the fear of God will be with you to keep you from sinning."* (Ex. 20:18-20)

The powerful display of God's powerful nature was to inspire a sense of godly fear in the hearts and minds of the Israelites so that they would obey his laws and spiritual principles for living. Here's another example...the prophet Elijah.

In I Kings 19, we again find Elijah on mount Horeb just inside a large, dark cave on the top of the mountain, after a long recuperation in the desert. He had recently and dramatically defeated wicked King Ahab's false prophets in a duel on mount Carmel. It had been a great victory, but soon after it, Jezebel, Ahab's wife, who didn't feel so enthralled with it, ordered Elijah's death. Somehow, Elijah was temporarily overwhelmed by a sudden onslaught of fear and ran off to hide, even to die. But God found him and nurtured him back to health, sending him over to mount Horeb for a conversation with Him about faith.

> *And the word of the LORD came to him: "What are you doing here, Elijah?" He replied, "I have been very zealous for the LORD God Almighty. The Israelites have rejected your covenant, torn down your altars, and put your prophets to death with the sword. I am the only one left, and now they are trying to kill me too." "The LORD said, "Go out and stand on the mountain in the presence of the LORD, for the LORD is about to pass by." Then a great and powerful wind tore the mountains apart and shattered the rocks before the LORD, but the LORD was not in the*

> *wind. After the wind there was an earthquake, but the* LORD *was not in the earthquake. After the earthquake came a fire, but the* LORD *was not in the fire. And after the fire came a gentle whisper. When Elijah heard it, he pulled his cloak over his face and went out and stood at the mouth of the cave. Then a voice said to him, "What are you doing here, Elijah?"* (I Kings 19:10-13)

Though it was the gentle whisper that brought Elijah out of the cave to talk with Jehovah, it was still the miraculous display of power that God used intentionally. As a prophet, Elijah wasn't in fear of God killing him, but I think the "fireworks display" was an announcement to Elijah that God had some *really serious issues to discuss*, and Elijah's retreat was the main topic of discussion. There was some accountability issues and irresponsible behavior on the table that needed resolution. Elijah needed *both* the whisper of God's love <u>and</u> a powerful wake up call for him to be reminded with whom he was dealing...*Almighty* God. Once God had his ear, Elijah listened and followed God's direction from then on, even sequestering Elisha as his attendant and ultimate successor.

In review, fearing God demands that we both believe in him as well as exalt his all-powerful nature. Such faith is not distant or passive but reaches out in wonder to the majesty and miraculous power of God's person. We are awestruck, almost mesmerized by the dimensions of his existence, his unlimited capabilities and his wondrous creative handiwork.

Thirdly, Christians who fear God acknowledge God's **PRECEPTS**.

Though they are awestruck by the awesome power of his divine nature, believers are also aware of his *authoritative position*. They understand that living in relationship with our almighty and eternal Creator has *spiritual responsibilities*, for we are *morally accountable to him*. God exists, he is all powerful, AND he ordains that his commandments are to be followed as behavioral absolutes and life-changing principles. He is inherently pure, holy, and without sin, and he holds us responsible to model this in our relationship with him. This humbles us, sharpening our sense of responsibility to obey as well as heightening our sense of failure, when we disobey him.

> *"The Son is the radiance of God's glory and the exact representation of his being, sustaining all things by his powerful word. After he had provided purification for sins, he sat down at the right hand of the Majesty in heaven."* (Heb. 1:3)

Not all things in our lives may be moral issues, of course, for God has told us a lot of *practical* things in Scripture to do or not do as well. Following such wise principles makes good sense, but straying from them doesn't necessarily bring down judgment upon a believer (what a situation that would be, right!).

The book of Proverbs, for instance, is loaded with such life principles, which if followed, just make good sense and bring positive life results. Here's a few:

> *"The simple believe anything,*
> *but the prudent give thought to their steps."* (14:15)
> *"All hard work brings a profit,*
> *but mere talk leads only to poverty."* (14:23)
> *"A gentle answer turns away wrath,*
> *but a harsh word stirs up anger."* (15:1)
> *"A person finds joy in giving an apt reply—*
> *and how good is a timely word!"* (15:23)

However, life itself will teach even a foolish believer such things, if he or she doesn't model such truths in their lives. God usually doesn't have to step in and discipline such an unwise believer (though he can, if he so chooses, of course). But, regarding typical moral precepts (ie. for instance, the 10 commandments, the "sermon on the mount," and other precept-type passages, etc.), it's important to discipline oneself strongly in order to avoid moral sin, guilt, and unwise distancing oneself from spiritual intimacy with Christ.

I suppose all failure can to some degree be moral failure, if one relates it to breaking a precept or principle of God. But *moral* sins usually refer to the more sensual and fleshy type things, as well as harmful attitudes or behaviors, such as hate, prejudice, pride, jealousy, covetousness, stealing, murder, lying, etc. Genuine fear of God acknowledges and accepts that such things are evil and completely contrary to will and Word of God. It produces a profound sense of either confidence before God, when one is faithful, or loss of confidence, when one has been unfaithful to the righteous character and expectations of God.

Lastly, Christians who fear God respect God's PUNATIVE ANGER.

Respect has to do with both an inner and outer response. I respect electricity, if I'm repairing an electrical socket in the wall, for I understand that it can kill me, if I'm complacent with its power. The builders of the Titanic compromised on the metal quality of that ship, not fully respecting the crushing power of an iceberg in the cold North Atlantic. Also, the Japanese army destroyed a significant part of the U.S. naval fleet, which casually sat in Pearl Harbor on December 7th, 1941. But they didn't rightfully respect the retaliating potential of the United States, until August 6th, 1945, when nuclear devastation rained down on Hiroshima, ultimately killing over 100,000 people (Manhattan Engineer District figures).

Yes, all of us need to respect God's anger against evil and sinful behavior. It's not enough for one to *just agree* with God on this, either. One must also *put that perspective into practice*, thus showing the genuineness of our fear for God's

"Sin hardens the heart, cools commitment, collapses compassion, ruptures relationships, cracks confidence, deadens spiritual desire, and incapacitates insight."

justifiable wrath toward anyone who breaks his laws…believer or non-believer.

The Bible tells us that God both hates sin and can that he can sovereignly chastise us for continued participation in it. Fearing God demands that we humbly *respect, reverence and respond to God's will,* precisely because we *deeply fear* (understand, recognize, recoil from) the consequences of a compromised lifestyle.

The saying in the margin describes the all-too-common experience of brothers and sisters in Christ, who have faltered significantly. I wrote that years ago as I contemplated the lives of folks I know, as well as my own life failures. The positiveness of popular television evangelists is encouraging, but the reality of spiritual living is that we are accountable to God. Chuck Swiindoll says:

> *"…we live in a day of pitifully shallow concepts of God. Some of today's contemporary Christian music leaves the impression that God is our buddy – a great pal to have in a pinch. A film star has said of God, "He's the great Big Daddy upstairs."…That is not the biblical view of God. That is man's feeble attempt to make God relevant."* (Moses, Charles Swindoll, WORD PUBLISHING, Nashville, 1999, pp. 269-270)

Sin angers God, and, although he always deals with us compassionately, he will at times let us experience pain, loss or disfunction, when we continue to be engaged in it. Chastisement is not pleasant, but often necessary for any of us.

> *"Endure hardship as discipline; God is treating you as his children. For what children are not disciplined by their father? If you are not disciplined—and everyone undergoes discipline— then you are not legitimate, not true sons and daughters at all. Moreover, we have all had human fathers who disciplined us and daughters at all. Moreover, we have all had human fathers*

> *who disciplined us and we respected them for it. How much more should we submit to the Father of spirits and live! They disciplined us for a little while as they thought best; but God disciplines us for our good, in order that we may share in his holiness. No discipline seems pleasant at the time, but painful. Later on, however, it produces a harvest of righteousness and peace for those who have been trained by it. Therefore, strengthen your feeble arms and weak knees. "Make level paths for your feet," so that the lame may not be disabled*, but rather healed." (Heb. 12:7-13)

"An old legend tells of a merchant in Bagdad who one day sent his servant to the market. Before very long the servant came back, white and trembling, and in great agitation said to his master: "Down in the market place I was jostled by a woman in the crowd, and when I turned around, I saw that it was Death that jostled me. She looked at me and made a threatening gesture. Master, please lend me your horse, for I must hasten away to avoid her. I will ride to Samaria and there I will hide, and Death will not find me." So, the merchant lent him his horse and the servant galloped away in great haste.

Later the merchant went down to the market place and saw Death standing in the crowd. He went over to her and asked, "Why did you frighten my servant this morning? Why did you make such a threatening gesture?"

"That was not a threatening gesture," Death said. "It was only a start of surprise. I was astonished to see him in Bagdad, for I have an appointment with him tonight in Samaria." (from Peter Marshall, "John Doe, Disciple: Sermons for the Young in Spirit," ed. Catherine Marshall, New York: McGraw-Hill, 1963), 219-20).

Believers do not have an appointment with *spiritual death*, for they have been delivered from that in Christ, and instead look forward to heaven and eternal life. However, they could still have an appointment with *physical death* as a punishment, if they enter a season of continuing disobedience.

> "...let a person examine himself, then, and so eat of the bread and drink of the cup. For anyone who eats and drinks without discerning the body eats and drinks judgment on himself. That is why many of you are weak and ill, and some have died. But if we judged ourselves truly, we would not be judged. But when we are judged by the Lord, we are disciplined so that we may not be condemned along with the world." (I Cor. 11:28-32).

More likely, perhaps, is that such an appointment could be a purposeful season of suffering, sickness, or loss in this present life, if God decides to just wake them up and correct their disobedient and/or compromising lifestyle. Either way, genuine faith in God should never become complacent or forgetful. A person of spiritual conviction hates sin, just as the Father hates sin.

Keep in mind also, that Christ is our Savior now, but one day he will also be the judge of both believers and non-believers. Non-believers will then be forced to respect his wrath for eternity, while believers will be judged for how they have lived, and it will affect their rewards in heaven. Please remember, even though God's love is real, his wrath over sin is just as real.

So...what's your pleasure?

CONVICTION #4

I Believe In Humility

◦━━◆━━◦

*"My sacrifice, O God, is a broken spirit;
a broken and contrite heart
you, God, will not despise."*
Psalm 51:17

When I was a teenager, I attended a church that had a fantastic youth program. We had Saturday night outreach events each week, Bible Studies throughout the week and caring youth workers, who spent huge amounts of personal time with the teenagers in order to disciple them.

One of the event things we did was to play some of the town softball league teams as an outreach to the community. Playing at that level meant finding some real good teenage players, which we were able to do and had great times beating the older guys! All of us thought we were pretty good, of course, and liked to stroke our own egos by recalling all the great plays we made.

Well, one summer we attended a Christian camp that was nestled in the foothills of the Adirondack mountains. We had over 75 teenagers there and rented out the entire camp for a week, bringing in our own speakers and running our own activities. Most of the guys on our team were at the camp that week, and the Camp Director, Phil, over-heard our bragging. In front of everyone, he challenged our team to a game against the camp staff, since we thought we were so good...and we took the bait. What we didn't know was that he was a former softball pitching pro and was formerly known as one of the best "windmill" pitchers on the entire east coast!

That afternoon we all gathered at the softball field, ready to squelch this "old" guy, who dared to challenge our reputation. At first, he shocked us by saying that he only needed 3 other players.

We looked a bit befuddled. "What do you mean?" we asked.

"I only need a catcher, a shortstop, a first baseman and a single outfielder. And, I'll be pitching, of course," Phil replied.

We chuckled inwardly, assuming the game would be over in no time...and it would have been. But not the way we would have figured the outcome!

When Phil strode to the mound and warmed up, we all practically barfed up our breakfast! If you blinked when he released the ball, it would be in the catcher's mitt. WHAM...WHAM...WHAM! That's three swings, fella, so you're out! The spin he put on the ball made it jump two feet from four different directions over the plate. He'd send it up and over from the lower right or left, as well as down and in from the upper right or left. All of us teenagers faced him for the first four innings out of a 5-inning game with knees shaking so much it sounded like a drum corps practice! Man...was he incredible!

Contrition

Now, I told myself that I would not be so *ostentatiously* defeated in the presence of my friends. But I also knew I had *no chance* of hitting that ball with any predictability whatsoever. However, I noticed that Phil rarely missed the strike zone...dead center. So, I decided to just casually swing the bat in the center of the strike zone, hoping the ball would hit my bat instead of me trying to hit the ball.

I set up, looked at the mound and Phil released his usual bullet. I casually but firmly dropped the bat into the strike zone and... *"boom!"* The speed of the ball hitting the bat sent the ball flying over his one fielder's head far enough for me to make it around the bases. I couldn't believe it...that one score won us the game. Of course, it was sheer luck on my part...but...well, I don't remember telling that to anyone!

Humility lessons abounded that day on the mound and in the field. My team was overconfident, myself included. A critical component of spiritual maturity in Christ is remaining in proper authoritative position before God. Look at Paul's clear direction for the church:

> *"But I want you to realize that the **head** of every man is Christ, and the head of the woman is man, and the head of Christ is God." (I Cor. 11:3)*

Now, we're not dealing with marital or church relationships at this point, just the relationships between individual believers and God. But, the term "head" is a military-based term, implying submission to authoritative rank. And, when it comes to you and me, we are not spiritual generals or sergeants or anything else... just simple recruits. We may have differing levels of responsibility both in marriage and in the church, as well as different degrees of giftedness in areas of ministry. However, *all of us* must keep in mind *at all times* that we are not the purpose givers or the power source of spirituality. We should be fully compliant and humbled before the Lord Jesus, who loved us enough to save us from a hopeless situation of spiritual depravity and guilt. We need an ongoing *conviction of contrition!*

I had an individual in my men's group at church years ago that had an ego problem, which was clearly evident to all who knew him. He wasn't blatant or verbally conceited, but all of us easily sensed the self-posturing that came across as he said things in the study. He's not alone in this weakness, by the way, for all of us have seasons in our lives when we pontificate a bit, looking for praise because of what we know or do. It's often subtle, but it can easily creep inside our soul, causing us to frustrate God's Spirit and his loving purpose for our lives.

The interesting thing about it was that he was a man I would definitely go to for spiritual advice. On the one hand, he was extremely knowledgeable, but on the other, he seemed driven to present everything with subtle arrogance, which repelled people from associating with him. At one point, even the Elders of the church had to address the issue. What a shame, frankly, because of what a powerful resource he could have been, if only he would have humbled himself. To this day, I would still consider him a friend and a resource. But I am saddened that this thorny situation still somewhat remains in his walk with Christ.

So, lesson one is to be sure that our spiritual posture evidences the inner *conviction of contrition.* God will not share glory with anyone. He looks with distain at the prideful displays like that of the Pharisees praying on the street corners in long colorful robes, trying to garner spiritual points for themselves before God. Jesus said about them, "They have their reward." What a sad statement about misplaced priorities, where one works so hard to "be somebody" in the eyes of others, but misses out on what God really wants to give them now and in eternity.

> *"Those that cling to worthless idols*
> *forfeit the grace that could be theirs."* (Jonah 2:8)

Compassion

Second, Phil and his staff were just plain good. They weren't interested in showing off, but content to have a tie score in the end to help us learn a lesson about having too much pride or self-confidence. They were willing to lose in order to show their love for us.

In this regard, there's a Scriptural doctrine called *depravity*, which teaches that we are all so separated and sinful before God, that we can never "pull ourselves up by our bootstraps" and earn... on our own...the favor of God. In fact, Adam's sin was passed on to us, and each of us bears that mark of corruption upon our spirits, which keeps us from fully seeking God and his goodness. Our world remains scarred by unbelievable hate, prejudice, spiritism, fighting, sexual debauchery, and other horrible sins.

However, Scripture also teaches that there remains in mankind an *image* of God's love and holiness, stamped as it were upon our consciences. Because of this, not everyone is as evil in attitude or practice *as they could be*. There is a degree of goodness and capability out there – a sort of pre-fall "leftover" - which is seen in the general way people give to others, show compassion, have righteous laws, reward goodness and punish evil.

In addition, God allows a measure of grace for mankind manifested in many ways so that he will not completely be given over to Satanic evil (perhaps this is also the "restrainer" that Paul refers to in I Thessalonians, which will one day be removed before the appearing of the Anti-Christ). However, too much over-confidence in self and one's moral strength is definitely wrong. But, remember, so is beating to death the "dead horse" of depravity to the point of not recognizing God's love for us. He may punish and hate sin, but he loves us in spite of it.

I have a former pastor friend who was a wonderful preacher and counselor. He did a great job in communicating with the church by sending out a weekly updated prayer list for members. In a church of 600 people, it was a very helpful thing to do for folks to keep up with names and issues. However, when he started doing this, he ended the list with the following salutation: "

Just A Hopeless Worm, _____" (followed by his name). Now, there's no right or wrong here. But I believe that our humility before God doesn't mean we are worms in his sight, nor should we feel we are just a worm in our relationship with Him. He continues to recognize great value in us, and he loved us enough to send his Son to die in place of us in order to provide a way to spend eternity with him. That's not the case of a worm.

I understand that my friend liked using that theological idea found in older theological writings. Writers used to compare our sinfulness in regard to God by using what is referred to as *worm theology*, which states that God, in his majesty, sovereignty and holiness, stands far above anything we can ever hope to be apart from his intervention in Christ. So, yes, we are damaged goods due to sin, and in those areas, we *are* no more than a lowly worm *by comparison*, which is true. But, that's as far as the comparison should go, for we are not <u>worms</u> in terms of God's love for us and our value to him. We are a special people of great <u>worth</u> to God.

> *"But you are a chosen people, a **royal priesthood**, a holy nation, God's special possession, that you may declare the praises of him who called you out of darkness into his wonderful light."*
> (I Peter 2:9)

I've gone into this detail *not* to pick on a former Pastor, but to suggest that we should have a balance in the way we relate to the Lord. The truth is, God certainly doesn't need us to do his work. However, the other side is equally inadequate and unscriptural. A person who thinks that he or she is "just a useless worm" before God in *every* way, is not going to present themselves as a member of a **royal priesthood**, but as an inadequate, useless and worthless piece of humanity…perhaps even a divine mistake. That's not going to bring many sinners to repentance or encourage many believers to step out and confidently share the love of God. Yes, sin has devastated God's handiwork in our world, deformed our bodies with disease and death, and corrupted our spirits with selfishness and guilt. On the other hand, God's gift of life in the first place, his gracious forgiveness in Christ and his ongoing desire to intimately know and use us...all this teaches us to have a *conviction of compassion*...for we are deeply loved by God. Though unworthy of his grace, we are much more than just worms, folks. Worm thinking and such semi-spiritual put downs will not assign you a better standing with God or with others.

> *"...God demonstrates his own love for us in this: While we were still sinners, Christ died for us."*
> (Romans 5:8)

As we share the Gospel with the folks in our workplace and in our daily travels, as well as from the pulpit, we should let people know that they are special in God's sight...sinners, yes, but loved and sought after by a loving and merciful God. For sure, they cannot dip into the well of grace without first seeking God's forgiveness at the cross of Christ, for they (or us) are not in any sense worthy of it *on their own*. Why? *Because God's compassion cannot simply erase God's justice*; he must of necessity deal with our sinfulness. But, because God values this fallen and fractured race so greatly, he wants all to come into his spiritual family. They must come in repentant faith and humbly remain so in the body of Christ. But they are asked to follow a Savior who loves them beyond anything they can imagine.

> *"I pray that out of his glorious riches he may strengthen you with power through his Spirit in your inner being, so that Christ may dwell in your hearts through faith. And I pray that you, being rooted and established in love, may have power, together with all the Lord's holy people, to grasp how wide and long and high and deep is the love of Christ, and to know this love that surpasses knowledge—that you may be filled to the measure of all the fullness of God."*
> (Eph. 3:16-19)

Confidence

Third, I was completely humbled, when I initially saw my team hopelessly strike out. I also had no capability of hitting a home run that day, I simply submitted myself to a plan that had more luck in it than skill... and it happened to work.

There were no "self-praises" after the game, for the victory was sheer luck, from a human point of view. Similarly, humility before the Lord is the only way to face the issues and challenges of your life. Again, it doesn't mean we are bankrupt of any ability to act intelligently. But it does mean that *we do not ultimately trust in anything else...* in our own strength, our own ingenuity, or in anything or any other person. It's the *conviction of confidence...* in God and *only* in God.

Here's another example of this. Have you ever been in a car accident? Hopefully not, but if so, you can probably remember the helplessness you felt in the midst of it. Well, one day I was on the way home from delivering a training session in Rochester, New York, about an hour's drive from away. It was late afternoon in January, and it began to snow, not too heavily, but enough to put a glaze on the surface of the highway. So, one tries to stay in the tracks of the car in front of you, which provides some measure of stability on slippery roads.

At this particular time, there were no other cars around at all, except for the tractor trailer I was approaching up ahead of me. He was going about five miles per/hour slower than I, so I pulled out to pass him on the left. Again, there was no traffic and the highway, though it was somewhat slick, but it was certainly safe to pass someone.

About the time I started to pass him, the driver swerved his back end into my lane...intentionally, not wanting anyone to pass him (a trucker friend of mine says that's not as unusual as it may sound). I pumped my ABS brakes to slow down enough to miss his careening back end, and did so, but at the same time my vehicle went into an uncontrollable spin (never pump ABS brakes in such a situation, just apply a firm peddle, and they will keep this from happening). Unfortunately, I continued to spin several times at 60 mph on the slick pavement, bounced off the road, and slid down the metal guard railing to the left. I bounced back onto the highway for another spin and finally swerved back to the center guard rail for another 30 feet of scraping and screeching before coming to a stop. I looked around and saw that both my front and back windshields were smashed, mostly missing, with pieces of broken glass resting everywhere inside. The leftover salad I had finished before I left was now all over the back seat of the car. As I got out of the car, I saw that both sides were completely dented inward, bumpers hanging, and...well, it was quite a mess. I was thankfully free from any cuts, bumps or scratches, even getting back into the car and driving it off the median and along the side of the highway to the toll booth up ahead, about a mile away. How that car could even move is a mystery, but it did noisily crawl along.

I remember during the whole event, which probably only lasted 8 seconds, that I was whispering, "Lord save me...Lord save me!" Now, I tried to maneuver the car and get out of the incessant spinning, but apart from some minor efforts on my part, I do believe that I had little to do with my survival that day. The truck could have actually hit me and sent my car flipping over and over into who knows what...but it didn't. There could have been a boulder, a pilon or a tree in the median, instead of a guard rail...but there wasn't. There could have been other cars in front or in back of me that could have posed some disastrous results... but there weren't. Essentially, I was on a ride that I was unable to change in any way and could only trust in God's providential protection over my life.

That feeling of helplessness has always stuck with me as I face life responsibilities and difficulties, and I've learned two things from it. First, we should always do what we call "our due diligence." While in the midst of that crazy accident, I still needed to think about how to steer, work the brakes and guide my careening car correctly. By application, life's circumstances still require us to use wisdom, to think through our choices and make wise decisions. Nevertheless, in actuality, we are all at the mercy of God *in every situation*, undergirding us and overseeing our life down to the last detail at every point. Humility should, therefore, be a sincere and abundant part of our everyday responsibilities, for going it alone without faith and trust in Christ is not a good situation in which to be found.

Second, while doing my due diligence, I must still *find my ultimate confidence in God*... and only God...to uphold me, as well as to fulfill my plans according to his will. In that car, I didn't stop praying for God to bring me to safety. Humility, then, doesn't eliminate us from our own responsibility and effort, for God didn't give us a mind to ignore. We have freedom of choice, but only within the kind boundaries of God's providential love for us in Christ Jesus.

> *"Trust in the LORD with all thine heart; and lean not unto thine own understanding. In all thy ways acknowledge him, and he shall direct thy paths."* (Prov. 3:5,6)

Compliance

Well, at the end of the game, which we won by a lucky homerun, the Camp Director and his three-man team acted like the mature believers they were. There was no complaining, even though they knew that they were the better team. There were no excuses, trying to say that Phil was just "off his game." No, each one of them congratulated us and thanked us for taking them on. They modeled humility well. One of the most important things I learned from this event was that ultimately, it is the will of God that I must always seek and for which I should be truly thankful.

In the end of the game of life, we will face God, not in judgment for sin, but for how well we've played the game. How foolish to argue with our spiritual coach that he messed up and shouldn't have done this or allowed such and such to happen. God knows what he's about and choose circumstances and events in our lives to accomplish his purposes, not ours. Yes, we do have personal choices and situations that demand discernment and wisdom in order to do the right thing. But whatever happens or doesn't happen is not something for which we should blame God, because God's nature is perfect and beyond blame in all things. I would call this a *conviction of compliance*, where we humble ourselves before the will of God in acceptance and praise, regardless of our thinking or judgment.

In summary, there is a unique blend of responsibilities as we apply spiritual principles to our daily lives. First, we must place our confidence, trust, hope and reliance upon Jesus Christ our Lord to do what we cannot do. Second, we must do our best to do what is required of us, while continuously praying for his oversight, mercy and grace over it all.

CONVICTION #5

I Believe In Reality... Not Fantasy

⚜

"Finally, brothers and sisters, whatever is true, whatever is noble, whatever is right, whatever is pure, whatever is lovely, whatever is admirable - if anything is excellent or praiseworthy - think about such things."
Philippians 4:8

When I was a boy, fantasy television for kids was mostly filled by Lone Ranger westerns, Superman and Jungle Jim adventures, and Saturday morning cartoons such as Bugs Bunny, Daffy Duck and Road Runner episodes. On weekday afternoons I never missed my favorite show…the Mickey Mouse Club, with its award winning and engaging serials like "Spin & Marty" and "The Hardy Boys." Night time shows included, "Wagon Train," "The Rifleman," and "My Three Sons." Soon after those came "The Brady Bunch," The "Six Million Dollar Man," and "Little House on the Prairie."

But, when Star Wars came along, a whole new avenue of imagination swept the country. From its digital beginnings grew a seemingly unlimited capability of transferring all kinds of creative situations onto a visual tapestry of believable plots and characters, formerly limited by one's own imagination. Soon aliens, vampires, werewolves, Martians, and robotic creatures were given new life. Spielberg and others even dwarfed Walt Disney's imaginative story lines, cinematic technologies and theatrical presentations.

Most of these shows were great entertainment, until moral swamps began to emerge, sucking the industry down into liberal agendas, immoral quicksand and off-color humor. Hollywood has blurred Biblical values, made fathers into buffoons, transformed women into John Rambos, and morphed kids into independent citizens, who can imprison their parents, if they try to control their kids' behaviors too much. I am not suggesting that *all* entries on the electronic stage are evil in either intent or presentation, but certainly many, perhaps most, are *not* acceptable for spiritually healthy viewing. Such things have become cultural carnivores!

What I can say, however, is that all of the above…good or bad…are *fantasies*. They are imaginatively created, technologically enhanced scripts originating from the minds of human beings, those either given to Biblical values or those not so given. The programs, movies, stage shows, videos, video games, etc., are, therefore, either vehicles for transmitting what is true or what is false. Superman, Captain Kirk, Luke Skywalker, Indiana Jones, the Goonies gang, Ripley, Leroy Jethro Gibbs, Captain America, John McClain or Optimus Prime are just imaginative visions espousing beliefs or moral values intentionally manufactured by Hollywood elitists. These folks rarely care about supporting conservative cultural values and often have a clearly antagonistic bent on undermining them. When you put these two social chemicals together… technologically enhanced fantasies along with liberalized, anti-Christian agendas…you often get a spiritual explosion of evil intention that can rock the faith of the immature believer. It has also transformed the world's greatest Christian-grounded culture into a dis-functional soup of diversified moral values spilling over and spoiling its once godly driven social character. And, guess what…it's all fantasy, just imagination gone amuck! Let's talk for a moment about some of these cultural fantasies that the non-believing world is caught up in and how to recognize them.

First...

There are no monsters, aliens, Klingons, yeti's, ghosts or even Ghost Busters...for Pete's sake!

I know that Hollywood producers don't want you to know about it, but that's how they make their money...by creating or spreading myths that stir folks up and make them come and see their entertaining products. One show that I watched for a few of weeks was about a group of scientists going into the Canadian Rockies, trying to catch a bigfoot on camera. After two weeks of falling cameras just at the wrong time and tripped wires that sent camera men running...they always *just missed* bigfoot. Yes, it's obvious that bigfoot doesn't exist except in the money driven minds of Hollywood producers.

Now, mind you, if a large creature *is* found that resembles a bigfoot, one thing is for sure, it's either a hilarious, hairy homo-sapien, or it's an elusive, ape-like animal of some sort. Why? Because the Biblical message doesn't allow for "missing links" formed from purposeless atoms haphazardly bombarding into each other over millions of years, then spontaneously developing into intermediary kinds of pre-human orangutans. If so, they would then have had to gradually develop - apart from purposeful design and through random selection - into spirit possessing, image-of-God bearing, logically thinking, morally driven and self-conscious creatures. Now...*that's science fiction!*

Second...

Satan is not a red-horned goat with a pointed tail. However, there <u>is</u> a real and intelligent spirit world all around us, motivated by evil and awaiting God's judgment at the second coming of Jesus Christ

The world tends to take some truth and blow it up into something that's false. When approaching the spirit world, it either denounces it all, or it makes movies about crazed characters like Freddie Kruger in "Nightmare On Elmwood Street."

However, there *is* a spirit world that the Bible clearly references, and it can be a bit scary or intimidating to naïve believers. As far as we are told, it is composed of spiritual beings, once heaven dwelling angels, who turned away in rebellion from God. Satan, a self-posturing being from among them, is alive and well, and he rules over this evil bunch, while roaming free through the earth and causing havoc beyond belief. Some of these creatures seemed bound to what the Bible refers to as the "pit" of hell, and Jesus sent some of them, those who harmed human beings, back to that "pit." In Paul's letter to the Ephesians, he also tells us that we are fighting a spiritual war, a fight that *"...is not against flesh and blood, but against the rulers, against the authorities, against the powers of this dark world and against the spiritual forces of evil in the heavenly realms."* (Eph. 6:12) So, many demons do occupy this world outside of that pit, and we must know how to resist them.

So, how do we deal with this unknown world? Well, it's real and populated by fallen angels, commonly called demons, and these beings do *influence* personal choices, cultural values, and belief systems. Satan and his host, however, are under the *complete authority* of God's Spirit, who sovereignly *allows or thwarts* whatever influence they exert against people and society. Although demonic powers can be oppressively influential, bringing unwanted harm and havoc at times, *they cannot <u>possess</u> genuine believers nor can they do anything apart from the will of God* in our lives...or even in society at large.

So, again, our focus should not be upon that which is evil, but upon God and his awesome power over evil…demons or otherwise! Jesus taught his disciples to pray confidently, "Deliver us from evil." And, that should be our goal as well!

Third…

Learn to recognize the fantasies of our progressive and morally bankrupt friends on the political and educational "left."

Here is the top 5 list of "leftist fantasies," which they try to sell to our kids.

Evolution   Socialism   Multi-Culturalism   Transgenderism   Homosexuality

It is not my intention to expound in great detail upon each one, but *all of these* rest upon the untenable foundation of atheism and moral pluralism (living apart from moral absolutes). Without a belief in God, moral certainty is impossible and anything becomes acceptable in lifestyle, politics, corporate ethics, whatever. The Christian response to all this is the following:

- Evolution is impossible, for life could not have spontaneously developed and then continue to develop without intentional and cohesively purposeful design. Without this, life would be nothing more than mindless chaos…an amoral soup of uncertainty leading ultimately to personal carnality and social corruption. On the contrary, **life does have recognizable, repeatable and reliable order to it,** which can only be postulated as coming from the hand of our creator God.

- Socialism is evil in the sense that it allows people to live off the productivity of others. Yet, Scripture says that man was given a task of gardening and providing for himself. Man must sow, and he should only reap from his own efforts, not live off others' efforts in a welfare-state society. "If a man will not work, he should not eat." (II Thess. 3:10)

- Multi-Culturalism is a fact of life on the one hand, for differences exist around the world in societal values, morals, laws, and opinions. However, there is a prevalent agenda being espoused today, which suggests that all beliefs, values, religions and lifestyles are inherently acceptable and morally sound, whether they differ or not. This, of course, is **philosophical nonsense and moral absurdity,** for such differences cannot coexist together... they are opposites. Common ground may exist among some cultures, but beyond this, that which is morally wrong cannot at the same time be what is morally right. Hence, the Bible says, *"Woe unto him that calls evil good and good evil."* (For a more detailed study on this, please get my book, *"How To Survive The Spiritual Jungle."*)

- Transgenderism is one of the saddest things happening to our fallen world today. Life and Scripture (and common sense) teach that God created two definitive sexes, male and female. But the world's pluralistic belief system has few moral boundaries anymore. Because of this, social elitists have been busily re-engineering historically sound and physically obvious sexual distinctives in such a way as to allow folks to choose their sexual identity, thus enabling their carnal lusts to create illegitimate avenues of sexual satisfaction. So, "crossing over" from one sex to the other, particularly with the advantage of surgical manipulation, is suddenly fashionable and acceptable. However, God created them "male and female," so again, no other choice for the believer is acceptable other than that which is defined at birth. Manipulating it by choice, surgery, drugs, behavioral conditioning and/or psychological counseling is as spurious as deciding to be a horse (either sex, of course, to be politically correct!).

- Homosexuality is another "abomination" to God, because it causes men and women to sin against their own bodies (which heterosexual sin does as well), and which the Apostle Paul says is a grave evil.

> *"Run from sexual sin! No other sin so clearly affects the body as this one does. For sexual immorality is a sin against your own body."*
> (I Cor. 6:18)

I take this to mean that sexual sin rejects God's creative purposes in designing our bodies for sexual satisfaction within the singular scope of male and female relationships and marital fidelity. Perversion, prostitution or any other sophisticated twist man wishes to place upon sexuality, is simply a carnal enablement of fallen flesh.

Fourth...

There are also religious fantasies and cultic influences that dominate people and society at large.

Regardless of their claims to revelation, all of the religious and cultic entities in the world can be broken down to the same basic, anti-Christian doctrinal similarities. Christ's teaching stands out so uniquely from all these false religions, showing that Biblical Truth is truly distinctive and trustworthy. Here's a short list of seven doctrinal disasters most of them espouse:

- **Man is mostly good...**
  <u>Their teaching</u>: "Listen, nobody's perfect, but for the most part mankind is able to pull himself out of spiritual degradation. The earth is full of well-meaning and good people. Give all men the chance of a good education and a good home life, and they will end up okay, morally speaking."

  <u>The Bible</u>: *"...righteousness from God comes through faith in Jesus Christ to all who believe. There is no distinction, for all have sinned and fall short of the glory of God."* (Romans 3:22-23)

- **God is mostly love...**

    Their teaching: "We all fail, of course, but God understands all that. His mercy exceeds his desire to punish folks for their shortcomings and mistakes. We're not Hitlers, you know, for crying out loud. God forgives!

    The Bible: God is equally just as he is compassionate. He cannot overlook sin without also offending his sense of justice - apart from Christ.

    "For the wages of sin is death, but the gift of God is eternal life in Christ Jesus our Lord." (Romans 6:23)

- **Jesus is mostly man...**

    Their teaching: "Jesus was a wonderful prophet, a good man, outspoken and inspiring. But he was divine only in the sense of being inspirational. He had some of the truth, but he wasn't perfect."

    The Bible: "'I and the Father are one." Again, his Jewish opponents picked up stones to stone him..." (John 10:30-31)

    "In the beginning was the Word, and the Word was with God, and the Word was God." (John 1:1) [By picking up stones to kill Jesus, they were testifying that Jesus was indeed saying that he was claiming to be God, thus committing blasphemy...punishable by death].

- **Sin is mostly acceptable...**

    Their teaching: "God mostly overlooks sin, because we're all good people just trying to do and be the best in everything. Yes, some are worst sinners than others, but... hey, no one is perfect. God understands that."

    The Bible: God does not and cannot simply overlook sin and guilt. It is never acceptable, hence the need for Christ's atoning sacrifice.

    "...it is appointed for man to die once, and after that comes judgment..." (Heb. 9:27)

"Therefore, just as sin entered the world through one man, and death through sin, and in this way death came to all people, because all sinned." (Romans 5:12)

- **Salvation is mostly earned...**

    <u>Their teaching</u>: "Faith is good, but it alone isn't enough to save your soul. God will judge every man to see if that man lived a good enough life to enter heaven. Integrity is what counts in the end."

    <u>The Bible</u>: That's right...integrity counts with God. But no man has it in the quality or quantity that God's nature demands it.

    "For it is by grace you have been saved, through faith--and this is not from yourselves, it is the gift of God—not by works so that no one can boast." (Eph. 2:8, 9)

- **Morality is mostly cultural...**

    <u>Their teaching</u>: "Hey, people see things differently, particularly in cultural settings. Similarly, religious morals and social values will differ."

    <u>The Bible</u>: Two inherently different moral absolutes cannot exist together. Opinions, beliefs, and personal values may at times differ, but never do absolute truths and/or moral values. Knowing the difference is key and why God gave us his Word.

    "See to it that no one takes you captive through hollow and deceptive philosophy, which depends on human tradition and the elemental spiritual forces of this world rather than on Christ." (Col. 3:8)

- **Eternal life is mostly assumed...**
  Their teaching: "Most people aren't going to hell, for most people are good people. Most of us...if not all...are going to end up in heaven."

  The Bible: No one is good "enough." The depravity of mankind is only held in check by God's Spirit, both personally and in society. Everyone may not be as bad as they could be, but they are as bad as they choose to be, and all men and women are held accountable for those choices.

  "Whoever has the Son has life; whoever does not have the Son of God does not have life." (I John 4:12)

  Jesus answered, "I am the way and the truth and the life. No one comes to the Father except through me." (John 14:6)

Fifth...

Believers are not without their spiritual fantasies, either. Here's a list of several popular but erroneous mis-truths about God and Christian living.

Fantasy #1: God Blesses Faithful Believers With Prosperity

Correction: Biblical prosperity is not to be equated with wealth, but with God's blessing and favor. Although the OT does speak often about favor for the godly, *this in no way implies monetary riches for all.* Generally, the word for prosperity in the O.T. is "towb," which means "beautiful, best, better, bountiful, cheerful... favor." It can have a "numerical" context at times, but it *doesn't*

categorically imply riches or financial wealth, only favorable and abundant goodness from the hand of God. Riches and wealth (measured in the OT by ownership of land) comes from the Hebrew word "chul," which implies strength, armies, efficiency, and wealth. So, there is *no absolute implication* in Scripture that faith and godliness assure anyone of money in the bank or huge 401K's (whatever) in today's economic situation. Jesus spoke of providing us with an "abundant" life, but such favor and blessing is not to be understood as financial riches alone.

God's favor, goodness and blessing are abundant and pleasurable, but distributed in various ways to those who are godly believers in Christ. For some, financial wealth might be his will, but not for all. For others, favor and/or blessing could be having special ministry enablement or family concerns taken care of, or daily needs met through the intervention of caring people at church.

Fantasy #2: Everything Always Works Out For The Best

Correction: No, but God *is* working *in* everything *for* good (Romans 8:29). Things that are not good...war, disease, sin, etc. – still exist. Believers will sometimes experience failure, disease, pain, loss, etc., which are not necessarily "best" for them (humanly speaking, with painless, happy endings type-stuff). Their own failure or innate selfishness may have even caused some difficulties or unwanted sinful debris to fall upon them. Nevertheless, for the believer, God is still sovereignly working to bless and sanctify us into Christlike vessels in the midst of "a good world gone bad." So, *everything* doesn't always work out for *"our best,"* but God's Will prevails in everything to accomplish what is sovereignly *the best*.

Fantasy #3: Christians With Enough Faith Will Always Be Healed

Correction: Faith is a necessary component of life in Christ, and it's an important ingredient for asking and receiving specific manifestations of God's mercy and grace. But it alone doesn't mean all diseases can be avoided or healed because one has it, regardless of its depth. Disease and difficulty can be great tools in the hands of God and used for our good.

I had a wonderful Christian lady in my adult Sunday School class for a while, until she contracted a very uncommon, post-surgery infection for a fairly minor procedure at the hospital. She slipped in weeks from minor discomfort to complete inability to talk or move her limbs because of it. The Elders of our church went and prayed for her, along with many of her friends over the years, but to no avail...God simply wasn't going to heal her.

I'm not sure what purpose God had for her in acquiring this unfortunate disease, but people did visit her from time to time to encourage her. She remained full of faith in the Lord all of her remaining years, eventually passing away years before she would "normally" have done so. Only heaven will reveal God's will in all of this, but it teaches us that the depth of one's faith is not the only medicine for healing, nor is the will of God that everyone should find healing.

Fantasy #4: God Always Protects Me, My Family and My Nation From Evil

Correction: Evil men cause seasons of great harm, which affects believers and non-believers together. Jesus said, "In the world you will have tribulation." The Bible also says that God sends rain for harvests to believers and even non-believers at times, so truly he is a compassionate God. However, the believer has entered a special, spiritual sphere of mercy and grace through faith in Christ. God wants us to trust him and seek his favor in all things, never trusting in our own plans (Prov. 3:5,6). He promises to provide for our needs abundantly (read about the Hebrew word "towb" above, once more). So, we can have great confidence in his love and care over us. Still, we know that Satan is allowed to travel in this world and, therefore, there is a degree of pain or difficulty inherent for everyone who breathes the breath of life. One day, we will draw deep, refreshing and pain free breaths of heaven's air along with all who have been given the gift of eternal life in Christ Jesus...what a day that will be!

"He will wipe every tear from their eyes. There will be no more death' or mourning or crying or pain, for the old order of things has passed away." (Rev. 21:4)

Fantasy #5: God Blesses A Faithful Person With Freedom From Harm

<u>Correction</u>: God never promises a life of ease and safety. The Bible does say, however, that he is aware of our needs and will provide for us according to his good will. Hardship, suffering and persecution, again, can at times be sanctifying tools in God's hands. If, however, prosperity is to be understood as complete sovereign protection and productivity in all things, then the Apostles certainly missed out, as you can see below:

> **Peter and Paul:** Both martyred in Rome about 66 AD, during the persecution under Emperor Nero. Paul was beheaded. Peter was crucified upside down at his request, since he did not feel he was worthy to die in the same manner as his Lord.
>
> **James:** The Jewish historian. Josephus, reported that James was stoned and then clubbed to death.
>
> **Matthew:** Some of the oldest reports say he was not martyred, while others say he was stabbed to death in Ethiopia.
>
> **Matthais:** Was the apostle chosen to replace Judas. Tradition says he was put to death by burning.
>
> **John:** Sent into exile and died of natural causes while there.
>
> **Andrew:** Andrew went to the "land of the maneaters," in what is now the Soviet Union. Christians there claim him as the first to bring

the gospel to their land. He also preached in Asia Minor, modern-day Turkey, and in Greece, where he is said to have been crucified

Thomas: Tradition has him preaching as far east as India, where the ancient Marthoma Christians revered him as their founder. They claim that he died there when pierced through with the spears of four soldiers

Philip: He possibly had a powerful ministry in Carthage in North Africa and then in Asia Minor, where he converted the wife of a Roman proconsul. In retaliation the proconsul had Philip arrested and cruelly put to death. [https://www.christianity.com/church/church-history/timeline/1-300/whatever-happened-to-the-twelve-apostles-11629558.html]

In a world driven by cinematic creations, digital entertainment, philosophical dreamers, educational elitists, and advertising moguls, fantasies abound for those *gullible enough to embrace them*. But, Biblical doctrine and the resurrection of Jesus Christ remain as historically sound bolts of divine lightning to anyone discerning enough to recognize reality. God's Word is trustworthy in every aspect for understanding life and eternity.

> *"For the word of God is alive and active. Sharper than any double-edged sword, it penetrates even to dividing soul and spirit, joints and marrow; it judges the thoughts and attitudes of the heart. Nothing in all creation is hidden from God's sight. Everything is uncovered and laid bare before the eyes of him to whom we must give account."* Hebrews 4:12, 13

CONVICTION #6

I Believe In Right Thinking

"For we did not follow cleverly devised stories when we told you about the coming of our Lord Jesus Christ in power, but we were eyewitnesses of his majesty. He received honor and glory from God the Father when the voice came to him from the Majestic Glory, saying, "This is my Son, whom I love; with him I am well pleased." We ourselves heard this voice that came from heaven when we were with him on the sacred mountain."
II Peter 1:16-18

In the last chapter we discussed the danger of fantasy, for it keeps us from understanding and accepting the reality of life and God. Now let's discuss other thoughts that *should be travelling back and forth within our minds*...thoughts that please God and open our lives up to his blessing.

First, "think about" what is TRUE.

I take this to mean that we are not to follow lies or untruths meant to suck us down into spiritual swamps. It's *not* saying, for instance, that going to Disneyworld is necessarily an evil activity or that seeing a movie, reading a novel, attending a play, watching television, or listening to a song is wrong, *just because it's all made up*. Jesus sometimes used stories to teach truth, but the details or characters of his illustrations weren't necessarily real. They taught spiritual truths, of course, but the stories were obviously created to get the attention of the listeners so that God's Truth would impact their lives.

If the intended content of the activity is to propagate false narratives and ungodly teaching, then it should be kept off our "fantasy entertainment" list. An older, but recently revived television show example would be "Will and Grace," a show which clearly depicts homosexual living as acceptable…that's its message, while using humor as a vehicle to do it. Such a show violates the principle "focus upon what is true," and directly undermines Christian morality.

One friend of mine suggested that humor is a dangerous thing when in the hands of the wrong person. A person (or Satan) often uses humor to soften the listener's moral sensitivities, allowing him or her to subtly enjoy a joke or movie scene that they would avoid in another setting. If one laughs at something risqué or sexually immoral enough times, it "takes the edge off" the precept or principle of behavior, thus diluting its truth and our commitment to it. It's also called "boiling the frog slowly," because a frog immersed in warm water doesn't know when the water reaches a boil…its senses are too dulled, so it simply dies.

One would also apply this principle to what we read, what we say and what we believe. Naively listening to media that often intentionally lies against what is real and true (ie. books, entertainment, news outlets, advertising, etc.) exposes ourselves to evil thinking and spiritual error. I just viewed a *"Christian"* website sponsored by a woman who said that Jesus would be called a feminist today. As I read her website, it was obvious that her understanding of the original language and intent of Scripture was warped by today's culture. One example was how she tried to downsize the concept of "headship" in Paul's letters into simple differences in "responsibility," thereby suggesting that women and men are to share equal roles regarding church ministry and family authority. Such "thinking" exhausts the imagination, when one looks correctly at the text and the context. Scripture clearly delineates a *distinctive difference* of role, where the man is to be the authoritative lead (ie. "rank" in Greek) in both church and marriage...though always gentile, loving, and supportive, of course. Jesus loved women and elevated their role as important, and Scripture certainly condemns male despotism or demagoguery in both marriage and society. But both he and the other New Testament writers were no equality-espousing feminists, that's for sure!

Another example of "truth bending" happened at my church the other day, as I was moving about the crowd in our "hospitality time" between services, sipping on a cup of coffee. One older gentleman came over and shared an interesting book he was reading (in his opinion). The author was stating that Jesus really wanted to start a revolution of sorts, but the culture and inadequacy of his disciples to spawn it made that impossible. Now...that's sheer nonsense, for any evangelical Bible school or seminary would never teach such poor history or Scriptural heresy. Jesus' mission was never to revolt against and then change society by force. His mission was to be a humble, itinerate preacher, always being sure to avoid a societal uproar. His purpose was to quietly die upon a Roman cross in order to make atonement for the sins of the world and let people be free to choose God's kingdom by faith, not by force.

Fortunately, I knew the man had tendencies to start controversies, so I simply nodded and went back for another cup of coffee. It was not the place to correct him, nor would he have been open at that point for the truth...a future discussion would be better. But, again, listening to such erroneous theology or tolerating it is dangerous, particularly to those who are less mature or are new believers.

Second, "think about" what is <u>Noble</u>.

This is an interesting principle, for noble can mean a couple of things. First, there is nobility recognized as positive attitudes and godly behaviors.

> *"Blessed is the land whose king is of noble birth and whose princes eat at a proper time-- for strength and not for drunkenness."* (Eccl. 10:17)

And, there are also noble people, those of high ideals and character:

> *"A wife of noble character is her husband's crown, but a disgraceful wife is like decay in his bones."* (Pro. 12:4)

If we make a simple connection between noble and "high," we realize that what is noble *stands above* the norm in whatever one is talking about. A noble house is one of *noted* and *remarkable* appearance, size and quality...a *cut above* the normal house. A noble horse is a model of *exceptional* quality in appearance, stamina and/or performance...a "noble steed." The Greek word used in our Philippian's passage above can also mean "honorable," which implies being *above and beyond the norm*, such that people want to give praise and honor to the thing being discussed. So, by application, we should think thoughts and hold beliefs that are honorable, because they are *worthy to be modeled and praised* by people of high ideals and character, as well as by the Lord.

An example of noble thought would be the Declaration of Independence, a *noble* document, which outlined America's reasons for seeking separation and severing itself from England's political control.

> *"When in the course of human events it becomes necessary for one people to dissolve the political bands which have connected them with another and to assume among the powers of the earth, the*

separate and equal station to which the Laws of Nature and of Nature's God entitle them, a decent respect to the opinions of mankind requires that they should declare the causes which impel them to the separation. We hold these truths to be self-evident, that all men are created equal, that they are endowed by their Creator with certain unalienable Rights, that among these are Life, Liberty and the pursuit of Happiness."

Why is it noble? Because it highlights the *Creator's purposes* in creating mankind and honors that which is innately and truly God in human government. It has gained the respect of millions of people and the admiration or many nations since its birth over 200 years ago. Please keep in mind that crazed leftist and neo-Marxists are gaining a strong foothold in our country today. Under the false dogma of "white supremacy," they are propagating and instilling reverse racism into the minds of our children and our society at large. They do not value truth, only their own aims of collapsing our nation and rebuilding it into a socialist dream. But, in fact, it's a coming nightmare of societal chaos, economic destruction and spiritual corruption.

America's ideals are good and historically sound, though at times and with some, they have at times stumbled along the way. But, we as a nation (2021) are not racist at the core for sure, and will not be persuaded by politically motivated lies and evil agendas. Godly driven people, though imperfect in practice at times, are the ones who established and built America into probably the greatest nation ever known to mankind (thank God for that!). Still, it can easily falter, as so many nations have, and fall into the human abyss of moral dissipation and political corruption. But let's not let Marxist agitators and political pawns bring this about. Instead, we must continue to hold on to the crystal clear commitments of our Founding Fathers' ideals, which are rooted in Christian precepts and principles.

Third, "think about" what is <u>Right</u>.

The word translated "right" means to be "just" in the eyes of God. Ultimately, the only things that can be right or just are things considered morally acceptable by God. Human ideals of genuine authority or worth can only be derived from God, because they come from his eternal and immutable nature.

So, six-year-old Johnny looks angrily at mom, after being corrected by her for snitching a cookie from the cookie jar after school. He had eaten half of it.

"You can't tell me what to do!" he angrily responds. Apparently, his friend tried that one on his older sister, and it worked, sending her away in tears. But mommies don't respond to such bold and authoritative words.

"If I can't, Johnny, then who can?" Johnny thought for a moment, then responded with a smirk, looking at the remaining half cookie in his greedy hand.

"Daddy...just Daddy!" Johnny smiled, thinking he just won the argument. But mommy wasn't persuaded and offered a bluff.

"Okay...let's call Daddy at work and see what he would say. By the way, I think he said that he'd give you a good licking, if you got into those cookies again, right?

Johnny paused and thought it over. "Well, Daddy's not here!

"He will be shortly," responded Mom. Again, Johnny paused thoughtfully.

"Well...ah...okay," he replied, looking down at the remaining half cookie in his hand. "Here's half of the cookie, anyway...don't bother dad about the other half!"

Poor Johnny, he said everything he could to win his case and avoid punishment, but too many things were stacked against him. Whether Dad was home or not, or whether he returned half the cookie, all that really didn't matter to mom, for the deed was done...and it was wrong and against the family's rules. Well, God has rules and principles that define right from wrong. In the above passage, the Apostle Paul is saying that we shouldn't even be thinking about, considering, or meditating upon things that are evil.

One of the most dangerous aspects of the effects of marijuana, for instance, is that it is a "gateway drug" for other hardcore drugs such as heroin or cocaine. Because the illegal cost of such drugs is within reach these days, great numbers of marijuana users have moved on to heroin, adding to the opiate crisis all of us are hearing about. But, it's no surprise for, in general, sin always seeks to dig its hooks deeper into us to increase its grip upon carnal pleasure. In the same way, any sin begins enticingly in the mind, lingering subtly in one's thought life...just before it pouches with ungodly fury upon our exposed spiritual bellies.

So, thinking "right" means avoiding such illicit fantasies, compromising attitudes, wandering imaginations, questionable considerations and roving rationalizations. It respects the danger inherent in unguarded contemplations, and avoids mental entrapments. The wisdom of Proverbs 4:25-27 should help us here:

Let your eyes look straight ahead;
fix your gaze directly before you.
Give careful thought to the paths for your
feet and be steadfast in all your ways.
Do not turn to the right or the left;
keep your foot from evil

Fourth, "think about" what is <u>Pure</u>.

I remember a painting job my friend, Dan, and I had one summer. Our mutual friend, Duane, hired us to paint the interior of his house, including the living and dining rooms, as well as the hallway leading to the bedrooms. Both of us had ample experience painting, but that day didn't turn out so well.

The trouble began when Dan opened up the 3rd can of paint around lunch time and mixed it with half a can of remaining paint. It was the same brand and color, so it should not have been a problem, so we poured it out into our paint containers, dunked our rollers into it, and began a second coat. But the paint seemed to go on differently...it was "goopy" and had some odd discolorations in it, but we continued, hoping they would simply disappear...but they didn't. I noticed that the paint was blotchy on the walls and had streaks of various shadings, so I went into the back room to check the paint can labels. I shouted from the back room, "Dan, what's going on with this paint?" Unfortunately, Dan had unknowingly bought 2 cans of water-based paint and 2 cans of oil-based paint, then mixed the two together. At this point, however, it was too late, for all the walls dried in streaks and shadows, leaving no option other than to return the next day and redo the whole thing. The final job turned out fine, but we kid ourselves continually that there's enough coats of paint in the house to withstand a category five tornado!

The truth I'm aiming for is that purity implies something that is undefiled, unpolluted, untainted and unadulterated in any way. My son works as a scientist in a company that produces special solutions for biological testing, which contain *"cell, protein and molecular biology technologies ranging from lipofectamine reagents, cloning kits, and platinum enzyme-blotting technologies, antibodies, and gene synthesis services."* Now, that's a mouthful, when describing the types of substances with which they're involved. But, all of it demands (as he told me) pristine purity in order to assure that customers will gain testing accuracy.

God's standards of spiritual life also demand absolute purity in attitude and action. It is true that this side of heaven will never see this level of purity in the lives of believers, even though positionally we have been granted it as a gift through faith by Christ's atonement. But, on the earthly and *sanctification* side of salvation, let's remember that's the goal of why we're living…to obey God with purity of thought and lifestyle.

> *"Love the Lord your God with all your heart and with all your soul and with all your strength and with all your mind…"* (Luke 10:27)

Unfortunately, the culture in which we find ourselves immersed is not very pure. Spiritual pollution abounds on every corner of life to the point where, like the Israelites of old, God asks:

"Are they ashamed of their detestable conduct? No, they have no shame at all; they do not even know how to blush..." (Jer. 6:15)

Think of media advertisements and how they don't seem to be able to sell anything without some sort of sexual stimulus. Think of television programs and content, as well as novels, plays and music videos. Is there much of anything not defiled with questionable emphases upon bloody murders, avarice, rape, graphic violence, and sensuality? How about those Hollywood gossip "rags" at the checkout counter in the grocery stores, which used to be considered unacceptable social content. But now their titillating ilk has spread onto live interview shows, where people enjoy show plot lines like, "Who's really the father of this child?" and "Her lesbian lover tells all!" One can then watch all the shouting, fighting, and hating as it's paraded upon the viewer, sitting there enjoying it all with popcorn and pop. This is not the type of purity that should find its way into the focus of mature believers in Jesus Christ. Yet, it seems so difficult at times to extract oneself from borderline contact with blended values and compromised content, doesn't it. But, it shouldn't, and according the continuing passage above in Jeremiah, the prophet gives us the challenge to make some decisive changes.

> "Believers need to avoid illicit fantasies, compromising attitudes, wandering imaginations, inquisitive considerations and roving rationalizations."

"This is what the LORD says: "Stand at the crossroads and look; ask for the ancient paths, ask where the good way is, and walk in it, and you will find rest for your souls. But you said, 'We will not walk in it.'" (Jer. 6:16)

Yes, again, purity is a principle of spiritual living, which like everything else, will to some degree, be left unattained this side of heaven. But believers can certainly do better than we are at ridding ourselves of the compromising and overly comfortable values we so tightly hang on to in this impure culture that surrounds us. Perhaps this is why the hand of God has been demonstrably absent in our evangelistic and discipleship endeavors these days. We have wandered from the "ancient paths" and stubbornly clung to cultural compromise. Let's be willing to step out and away from these clinging carnalities and subtle sensualities. God waits for those who sincerely seek God for his personal and ministerial blessing.

> *"Finally, brothers and sisters, whatever is true, whatever is noble, whatever is right, whatever is pure, whatever is lovely, whatever is admirable — if anything is excellent or praiseworthy — think about such things."* Philippians 4:8

Fifth, "think about" what is Lovely.

It's been said that beauty is in the eye of the beholder. Perhaps that's true to a degree, but what someone personally believes to be admirable could also be gross and ugly to God. So, let's define the word first. The word for "lovely" involves the following:

> "Affectionate caring for something proper and worthy of personal affection; something dearly prized and worth the effort to have and embrace." (http://biblehub.com/greek/4375.htm)

Something lovely to God, then, should be worthy of personal endearment. But, the *fantasies* of unbelievers or wandering believers are often just that... unworthy and immoral. They don't have any moral integrity to them and, therefore, never can be "personal endearing" by any stretch of the imagination. When people are driven by ungodly personal pleasures, they will justify such things and then call beautiful what God calls ugly. And, if they begin to indulge those fantasies, they create behavioral links, which entrap and chain themselves to those very fantasies. Folks, such habitual behaviors are ugly, not lovely, particularly when they imprison a person's will from living in the beauty of God's Spirit and in the majesty of his Word.

Samson was a man that was confused about this whole concept of loveliness. He definitely was called and used by God to bring judgment to the Philistines, but he had a great "personal endearment" to lust. As a Nazarite, he had been given special strength as a tool to fight the ungodly Philistines that surrounded the Israelite people. But his calling and blessing demanded that he obey his Nazarite vow, which included avoiding three things...wine, touching dead bodies and cutting of his hair. However, because of his attraction to the "loveliness" of Philistine women, he eventually fell into sin with Delilah and lost God's gift of strength. Toward the end of his life, he prayed for God to forgive him and return his strength for one last challenge. God heard his prayer, and he brought down the temple of Dagon to a heap of stone, along with the many Philistines within it. In that feat of strength and divine judgment, he was also killed in its wake.

Samson's problem was that he seemed continually compromised by his love for women. His unacceptable marriage to a Philistine woman, his dabbling in sex with prostitutes on occasion, and his ultimate affair with Delilah shows his "Achilles heel," if you will.

Yes, in spite of his poor choices, God still used him to accomplish much good for Israel and also to bring judgment upon the surrounding Philistines. But Samson was forever mistaken about what spiritual *loveliness* involves, for he was a man too often "endeared" to sexual lust and power, instead of spiritual obedience, like Joseph was, for instance. Joseph rejected the passing beauty and pleasures of sexual temptation, eventually being blessed and used by Jehovah to protect God's people and secure the lineage leading to Messiah Jesus. All of us should critically think about what is spiritual lovely, desirable and ultimately endearing to Jesus and his will for our lives...and nothing else.

Sixth, "think about" what is admirable.

Consider the 1987 photograph by the American artist and photographer Andres Serrano. It depicts a plastic crucifix submerged in a small glass tank of the artist's urine. It won the Southeastern Center for Contemporary Art's "Awards in the Visual Arts" competition, which was sponsored in part by the National Endowment for the Arts.

Such "art" exists only in the mind of those who have compromise fantasies and is certainly not praiseworthy in any sense of the word. It is unnecessarily crude in its presentation, seeking to make an artistic statement apart from a basic sense of reverence for God and those who worship him. No surprise here, for without a spiritual foundation, self-posturing artists recognize no limits to their imaginations and no restraints upon the expressions of them.

In the book of Acts, the story is recounted of Peter's encounter with a magician named Simon in Samaria. Through the preaching of Philip, Simon and many others believed Philip *"...as he preached the good news of the kingdom of God and the name of Jesus Christ, they were baptized, both men and women. Simon himself believed and was baptized. And he followed Philip everywhere, astonished by the great signs and miracles he saw."* (Act. 8:12-13)

As one who formerly delved into magic and showmanship, he was also intrigued by the miraculous manifestations of Philip and later Peter, when he came down to Samaria. Before long, he asked Peter to give him the same power.

> *"When Simon saw that the Spirit was given at the laying on of the apostles' hands, he offered them money and said, "Give me also this ability so that everyone on whom I lay my hands many receive the Holy Spirit." Peter answered: "May your money perish with you, because you thought you could buy the gift of God with money."* (Acts 8:18-20)

Simon wanted a shortcut toward spiritual maturity and a showboat access to ministry. The excellence, purity and integrity of the

Spirit's ministry in Samaria was not to be a magician's sideshow for all to see, or for him to be praised and admired, while having his financial pockets filled. God's ways are praiseworthy, man's ways are usually self-gratifying and unworthy of admiration.

I heard on the news today about a Black actor, who has uniquely "risen to prominence" by his bold acceptance and declaration of his own homosexuality (apparently, there is a shortage of *black* actors, who have "come out of the closet.") I would suggest that he is not risen to prominence as much as he has fallen into disfavor with both God and right-thinking people (black or white). Of course, my comments about him do not fit within the boundaries of their agenda.

In summary, we should focus our creative imaginations upon things that rise above schemes, dreams and fantasies alone. Then we can repeatedly garner praise from those who value true godliness, uncompromising truth and spiritual purity centered in the Word of God. Right thinking always leads to right living!

> *"The heart is deceitful above all things and beyond cure. Who can understand it? I the Lord search the heart and examine the mind to reward a man according to his conduct, according to what his deeds deserve."* (Jer. 17:9-10)

CONVICTION #7

I Believe Feelings Need Control

*"Life is not about what feels good;
it's about what is good!"*
John 1:12

It "feels good" to have sensual pleasure, to be comfortably rich, to please people, to be successful, to be praised for your accomplishments and/or spiritual gifts, to be entertained, to rest and relax...well, you get the idea. Every person has activities that "feel good," which he or she seeks to repeat and enjoy. For example, I just got back from a long bike ride, kicked up my feet and sat down to enjoy an old western video just for the fun of it...*and it felt good!*

So, what's your favorite place to eat? One of my wife's favorite and mine, too, is the Olive Garden. Great salads and fantastic pasta dishes! What's your favorite ride at Disney World? Ours is Splash Mountain, a water ride where you float in and out of a mountain crafted after Disney's movie, "Song of the South." It's got great music and special landscapes as you ride along to a final, breathe-taking plunge, 50 feet down into a river of water! You can't help but get wet, but the fun is inescapable!

However, the problem with "feel good" behaviors, is that some of them can either be directly or indirectly involving us with sort of sin, or make us unwisely susceptible to it. But God doesn't define good by what "he feels is good," but by what is *innately* good...in accordance with his nature and his revealed standards for our attitudes and actions. In fact, the Bible says that the foolish easily become addicted to pleasurable feelings:

> *"For at one time we too were foolish, disobedient, misled, enslaved to all sorts of desires and pleasures..."* (Titus 3:3)

It also says that Moses was a good man, who **refused** such wayward indulgence:

> *"...choosing rather to endure ill-treatment with the people of God than to enjoy the passing pleasures of sin..."* (Heb. 11:25)

So, though we have the capacity by God to enjoy pleasurable feelings and emotions, such things need careful oversight and should always be controlled. Let's look at this whole idea of "feel good" activities and emotions.

Sensual Feelings

Each of us has five, God-given senses to use...sight, smell, hearing, touch and taste. The first thing to remember about these senses is that they are *innately and morally good*. Why? Because they were created by God and ordained for us to enjoy. However, caution and self-discipline are spiritual attributes *also* created by God to be employed in the experience of pleasurable indulgence. Sugary desserts weren't created by God, even though the taste to enjoy them was. So, we must remember that unbalanced or uncontrolled intake of sweets can eventually kill us. Food intake is both pleasurable and enhances our "feel good" attitudes, but too much of it makes us uncomfortable and overweight, even to the point of cardiovascular disease. Relaxation after a workout or some other physical exertion feels good, but too much of it makes one lazy, unproductive and fat. Sexual pleasure is also a good thing, but having it with prostitutes is evil.

Did you know that our bodies actually have built in neurotransmitters that enhance our "feel good" sensations? We generally call them "happy hormones."

> "What are "happy hormones." Happy hormones generally refer to **endorphins, serotonin, dopamine, and oxytocin**. Endorphins block pain. An easy way to remember this is that "endorphins" is the shortened term for "endogenous (containing) morphine". They are the body's natural painkillers. When rigorous exercise depletes our muscles of glycogen (oxygen stores), endorphins allow us to push on. This is why we often feel blisters for example only after and not during the activity. Serotonin boosts our mood and makes us more agreeable and sociable. Lack of it can cause irritability and depression. Dopamine is a "pleasure" hormone and is stimulated when we strive towards a goal. It helps motivate us to take action to achieve the goal so we can experience the pleasure of the reward. Oxytocin is the "love" hormone released upon physical contact. Intercourse and childbirth release large amounts of oxytocin, but even a good old hug works. Oxytocin provides feelings of love and trust, which is why relationships boost our happiness."
>
> (http://www.joyfuldays.com/happy-hormones)

However, the fact remains that sin has corrupted many of the pleasures God has provided for us to experience. By this I mean that some of us have exaggerated, extreme or evil-based sensual "magnets" hiding in the caves of our inner person. They can greatly influence our feelings and motivations and are deadly, to be quite blunt about it. They must be categorically controlled and incapacitated or they will eventually corrupt all that is good in one's life.

Recently, while on vacation, I received news about a church friend, whom I have known for over thirty years and who died unexpectantly. He had no heart condition or disease that I knew about, so my wife and I checked out the obituary to find out some of the details (he and his family had moved away from our state over 10 years ago). What we found out shocked us and all who knew him, for he had been an abused child, who as an adult had abused children himself. Though claiming to be a believer, he had apparently struggled with pedophilia all his life, eventually committing suicide. I believe he was indeed a genuine believer that never genuinely confronted his inner demons through proper counseling, accountability groups and self-discipline. He apparently became more and more indulgent in his aberrant behaviors to the point of totally indulging the evil feelings of his damaged and sin-bent heart. What a shame, and what devastation he also brought upon the children he had abused. Folks, we must decisively distinguish between pleasurable feelings that are godly and those that are immature or ostentatiously evil.

At the end of God's creative activity, the Bible records God's reaction as saying, "God saw all that he had made, and it was very good..." (Genesis 1:31)Good, therefore, is a statement of moral worth and value, and the "author of good" created pleasurable feelings for us to enjoy guilt free...as long as we indulge them *within the parameters of his will*. Unfortunately, Adam and Eve failed in this and sought to experience pleasure outside the will of God, seeing fruit that was appealing and were enticed by Satan to indulge those desires. They sinned and missed the mark of God's expectations, thereby corrupting their relationship with God and bringing destruction upon God's "good creation." This included both physical destruction (ultimately) and spiritual death (relational separation).

Again, we can enjoy sensual feelings from pleasurable activities and interests, but only within the guidelines God has given us for them. With God's help, we must employ self-discipline as a tool for traveling down the many turbulent rivers of sensuality. Know when to stop a particular indulgence that is overflowing God's boundaries for it. Try listening to that inner, rational voice of God's Spirit, who says, "Hey, bub, you're getting too close to immaturity, over-indulgence and carnal lust. Start paddling in a different river, okay, or your runaway desires may swamp your spiritual boat!" The wisdom of Proverbs 4 below, verses 23 – 27, should be our guide. Bottom line...*don't just do what feels good, do what is good!*

> *"Above all else, guard your heart, for everything you do flows from it...Give careful thought to the paths for your feet not turn to the right or the left; keep your foot from evil."*

Relational Feelings

Relationships come with a host of feelings. Some folks are overly sensitive in this regard, and you can say something that offends them without ever believing that what you said would be offensive. Others are like a human shell and cannot easily be emotionally influenced by the way others think, speak or act.

King David had to fight a battle with misplaced feelings, when facing how to deal with his rebellious son, Absalom. His son sought to steal the throne for himself in a wicked and deceitful plot to overthrow his own father's rule. David eventually had to confront the rebellion, at the cost of many lives.

> *"Then David mustered the men who were with him and set over them commanders of thousands and commanders of hundreds."* (II Samuel 18:1)

David gathered his army and went out to put down the rebellion, giving his commanders the following orders:

> *"And the king ordered Joab and Abishai and Ittai, "Deal gently for my sake with the young man Absalom." And all the people heard when the*

king gave orders to all the commanders about Absalom." (II Samuel 18:5)

Notice the softness and love exhibited by David for his son, even though his very life was threatened by Absalom. But these were not very inspiring words for his commanders, as they went out to face Absalom in the battlefield. Nevertheless, the battle between father and son was a fierce one.

"So the army went out into the field against Israel, and the battle was fought in the forest of Ephraim. And the men of Israel were defeated there by the servants of David, and the loss there was great on that day, twenty thousand men. The battle spread over the face of all the country, and the forest devoured more people that day than the sword." (II Samuel 18:6-8)

The sad thing about the whole affair was that even though David won the battle, David's "feelings" got in the way of his kingly responsibilities and leadership. When he learned that Absalom had been killed, his response was understandable, but still misplaced from a kingly point of view.

"And the king was deeply moved and went up to the chamber over the gate and wept. And as he went, he said, "O my son Absalom, my son, my son Absalom! Would I had died instead of you, O Absalom, my son, my son!" (II Samuel 18:33)

And, later on he continued to cry out even publicly.

"It was told Joab, "Behold, the king is weeping and mourning for Absalom." So, the victory that day was turned into mourning for all the people, for the people heard that day, "The king is grieving for his son." And the people stole

into the city that day as people steal in who are ashamed when they flee in battle. The king covered his face, and the king cried with a loud voice, "O my son Absalom, O Absalom, my son, my son!" Then Joab came into the house to the king and said, "You have today covered with shame the faces of all your servants, who have this day saved your life and the lives of your sons and your daughters and the lives of your wives and your concubines, because you love those who hate you and hate those who love you. ***For you have made it clear today that commanders and servants are nothing to you, for today I know that if Absalom were alive and all of us were dead today, then you would be pleased.*** *Now therefore arise, go out and speak kindly to your servants, for I swear by the LORD, if you do not go, not a man will stay with you this night, and this will be worse for you than all the evil that has come upon you from your youth until now." Then the king arose and took his seat in the gate."* (II Samuel 19:1-8)

David could only think of his grief and the pleasures of loving his son, instead of his kingly responsibilities. No doubt, his soul was filled with the enjoyable memories of sitting in front of the castle fireplace with his son in years past, teaching him God's commands and enjoying the pleasures of life in the royal family. But such relational feelings must be carefully overseen like everything else in our lives, no matter how much we care about someone, or how much we dislike someone. We must channel our behaviors by making decisive, behavioral choices based upon what is right and wise, not what feels good.

Remember, however, that it is not always an easy thing to take control of our feelings. So, let's not judge David's reactions too quickly, for doing the right thing with our feelings is not always easy. Still, in the end, feelings should never be allowed to grasp the

steering wheel of our minds or hearts. They must always remain as back seat passengers, while God directs our travels down our relational highways. Here's a simple guideline that might help us:
Always act, but never react.
The truth here lies at the core of our heart's motivation in times of stress, disagreement or disapproval. Feelings are reactive and, therefore, may not necessarily be well-advised or appropriate in any given situation. They are often "tied" to the way we've been raised, the circumstances of our lives and the spiritual mindset that we've adopted. It's like crossing a swollen, rain-gorged stream in the woods. You're out for an energetic hike and come across this small flow of water usually about a foot deep and 4 feet wide curling lazily down from higher ground. However, it's *now* about fifteen feet across, and over three feet deep, with a very fast current driving it. You're not sure if you should cross it, but you don't want to take the long way around to where you're going, so you say to yourself, "Well, okay, I'll just be careful." So, you step in and move cautiously across. But, half way across you suddenly begin slipping under the growing pressure of rampaging water. You have a choice...give in to the powerful currents and let them drown you, or, carefully and wisely retreat to safety? A well, thought-out response will determine your relationship with this stream. *Will you let it rule your actions, or will you resist its domination and get out of the grip of its pressure.*

Relational feelings – good or bad - flow all around us...at work, at home, in church, at school, on the television, with friends, etc. Just today, two service personnel came to the house, one to fix the new dryer, the other to deliver a new couch. Both were extremely pleasant and helpful to deal with, so my feelings weren't charged with anything but acceptance. However, the other day I drove my granddaughter to her cheering practice, and she was untalkative and pouting about something. To her on this particular day, I was just a taxi, not an appreciative Grampa that cared for her enough to take some time and help her out. Yes, I had some feelings of disappointment and anger, but I did not vent them to her. I just let them fall to the ground, understanding that something was bothering her. If it went on beyond that day, I would have talked with her about having a kinder, more appreciative attitude for those who go out of their way to help her. But, for now, I simply corralled my feelings and kept an uncritical spirit about me.

There are times, however, when feelings are torrents of tremendous pressure driving us to react in negative ways. At other times, they are more subtle, quietly tempting us to make hasty, self-satisfying, and ungodly choices. Either result can be destructive, if it frustrates the flow of God's Spirit and his powerful promptings to do the right and loving thing instead. Wisdom and God's Word should be our guide in such situations, never our feelings alone. We dare not just *react* according to the way we "feel." This is why Paul urges us to *take captive **every thought** (and its feelings) and make it obedient to Christ"* (II Cor. 10:5). When Christ died on the cross for our sins, his love overshadowed his anger regarding our endless sins and selfishness behaviors. There is no better model of having a forgiving spirit and mastery over negative feelings than our Lord Jesus.

Feelings About Failure

I'm thinking about our inner impulses and/or emotions regarding moral behaviors and our relationship to God. Built into each one of us is a conscience, which we might call our *moral referee*. When we do something right and godly, our moral feelings become pleasurable, confident and content. But, when that moral referee recognizes that we have sinned against God's demands and expectations, it becomes sad or depressed, even ashamed (before God, if we're believers), even anxious. More *simple* reactions of emotion will occur, when we face *simple* transgressions. But, more complex or *debilitating* emotions result, when we become more deeply involved with intentional sin. Our moral referee can be very harsh and bitter toward our sense of worth. So, how do we control it?

First, we must accept whatever is true in what our moral referee says, but certainly reject whatever is false. This may sound easy at first, but it is always a difficult process to learn, for we are prone to either shut him out of our mind's ear or let him crush us with accusations and guilt. The truth of it all, however, lies somewhere in between these two. In Hebrews 12:4-6, the writer refers to this

> *"In your struggle against sin, you have not yet resisted to the point of shedding your blood. And have you completely forgotten this word of encouragement that addresses you as a father addresses his son? It says, 'My son, **do not make light of the Lord's discipline**, and **do not lose heart when he rebukes you**, because the Lord disciplines the one he loves, and he chastens everyone he accepts as his son.'"*

In the above verses, notice two wrong directions to take when it comes to managing guilty feelings. First, never make light of God's discipline. A believer who has a mature outlook (or "conviction") regarding what to do with failure and sin, should **own it and change**. This involves *listening* to God's Spirit and confessing the sinful activity. After David sinned with Bathsheba, he described his inner turmoil in Psalm 51, verses 1-2, saying...

> *"Have mercy on me, O God,*
> *according to your unfailing love;*
> *according to your great compassion*
> *blot out my transgressions.*
> *Wash away all my iniquity*
> *and cleanse me from my sin.*

A sincere follow-up to that would also include taking any necessary corrective and/or any disciplinary actions God seems to be suggesting to you, instead of ignoring those things. *The wise and repentant believer makes the necessary changes to the situation in order to avoid inappropriate relationships, unwise activities, or anything else which was causal and led up to the problem in the first place.* Otherwise, the future will only bring repetitive failure and more guilty feelings.

In the past, when I've been dealing with a particularly annoying sin, I've found that taking a day and fasting through breakfast and/or lunch brings a welcome time to pray, read scripture and re-consecrate myself to the Lord. Obviously, it needs to be a day when I'm home and alone, and it gives me 8 hours of mental renewal and spiritual restoration. I've found that lasting change is much more likely to follow such a focused and humbling effort. Most importantly, it keeps me from burying myself in unnecessary guilt and restores relational intimacy with the Lord. It also, I believe, can avoid further discipline from God, for *"if we judged ourselves truly, we would not be judged."* (I Cor. 11:31) The fasting itself has no efficacy, but it does help us to genuinely approach God in righteousness and confession.

The second thing to avoid is to allow our failures to lead to *unnecessary* discouragement or depression *("Do not lose heart when he rebukes you")*. Again, Satan knows that repetitive sins can get us so down on ourselves that we start avoiding devotions or withdrawing from fellowship times...not what you want, if you're trying to get beyond some annoying weakness, problem or habit. Do you remember the story of Jesus and the woman "caught in adultery?"

> *"Jesus returned to the Mount of Olives, but early the next morning he was back again at the Temple. A crowd soon gathered, and he sat down and taught them. As he was speaking, the teachers of religious law and the Pharisees brought a woman who had been caught in the act of adultery. They put her in front of the crowd.*
>
> *"Teacher," they said to Jesus, "this woman was caught in the act of adultery. The law of Moses says to stone her. What do you say?" They were trying to trap him into saying something they could use against him, but Jesus stooped down and wrote in the dust with his finger.*
>
> *They kept demanding an answer, so he stood up again and said, "All right, but let the one who*

has never sinned throw the first stone!" Then he stooped down again and wrote in the dust. When the accusers heard this, they slipped away one by one, beginning with the oldest, until only Jesus was left in the middle of the crowd with the woman.

Then Jesus stood up again and said to the woman, "Where are your accusers? Didn't even one of them condemn you?"

"No, Lord," she said.

And Jesus said, "Neither do I. Go and sin no more."

Worshipful Feelings

What are you talking about, Ed? Worship should feel good, shouldn't it? Well, worshiping God usually does evoke a sense of peace, joy, and contentment, among other things. But, worship itself has nothing to do with emotion, it really doesn't. Emotions are just personal reactions to what we believe and sense, and they vary greatly from person to person. I've known people dying in a hospital bed that one could easily see were worshiping God with all they had, yet still struggling with the agony of pain and death. *Worship is not about us and what we want to feel, it's about God and what we understand him to be.*

True worship is finding peace at the cross of Christ, finding inner joy in knowing you are saved, and that God is at work in your life for good - regardless of the circumstances. It's never the pulsating percussion of an electronically wailing worship band, swaying with emotionalized and repetitive lyrics. That most often produces only manipulated attitudes mimicked by the use of cultural cues. No, worship...pure and simple...is bowing one's heart and mind before God in whatever life environment you happen be and praising God for how great he is.

Feelings will vary in intensity and expression, of course, but worship is primarily a matter of head and heart humbled before the throne of Almighty God. It's needs no propping up with accommodating "feel good" styles or pulsating musical rhythms. It simply rejoices in the knowledge and sovereignty of God. Worship praises God for his worth and character, while avoiding the quest for just another spiritual high (which will only dissipate anyway, when the sanctuary doors close).

I pray that your faith and mine will never be propped up with gimmicks and manipulative crowd pleasers. If we need a feeling fest in which to indulge ourselves, let's do it in the privacy of our homes, instead of the church.

Certainly, feelings can be moving and worthwhile, and can accompany God's Spirit as he brings conviction to our disobedient hearts or joy to our submissive ones. But we should always enjoy feelings authentically, with propriety, and with control, while we focus upon the deep truths (convictions) behind them. Feelings, therefore, follow in the wake of events and beliefs and are greatly influenced by personal experiences, previous life choices, early family issues, relationships, and by how we may "feel" in any given moment. Thus, feelings are untrustworthy to build into our relationship with Jesus. Having a proper understanding of life, where one takes feelings into account, but never lets them become a platform for what you believe and do, is the safest way to go. (more on this later)

CONVICTION #8

I Believe In Consequences

*"When You Choose An Action,
You Choose Its Consequences"*
Graemme Marshall

The words in the little heading above describe the all-too-common experience of brothers and sisters in Christ, who have faltered significantly. I wrote that down years ago as I contemplated the lives of folks I know, as well as my own life failures. The positive thinking of the popular television evangelist from Texas is encouraging, but the reality of spiritual living is that we are accountable to God. Sin angers God, and, although he always deals with us compassionately, he will at times let us experience pain, loss and disfunction, when we continue to be engaged in it. Chastisement is not pleasant, but often necessary for all of us.

Are you a "consequential thinking" person? This is a critical thing to recognize, if you want to live an effective life for Christ. It's a kernel of truth repeated in the Bible, and it can straighten out a lot of our immaturities and sins, if we start applying the concept with spiritual depth and consistency.

Think of a mom and dad with two children, Johnny and Sally. Johnny is very compliant and obedient, but Sally is often stubborn-willed and disobedient. What do mom and dad need to do to get Sally moving on a more consistent path?

Well, a coordinated program of discipline will usually go a long way in turning such a child in the right direction. Her parents must clearly tell her what their expectations are, and then enforce loving yet firm disciplines, if she fails. She learns quickly (hopefully) that there are consequences to her choices and behaviors. Such consequences are painful reminders that it's better to please mom and dad than it is to disappoint them by doing wrong.

You and I are spiritual children, learning about God and his Will and how to please him in our attitudes and actions. A foundational conviction to almost everything in the Bible *is that God holds us accountable for our choices*. If we choose rightly, he will bless us accordingly, but if we choose wrongly, then one of two options can occur.

First, he can mercifully and graciously allow us time to learn and grow out of the immaturity and sinful propensities. Like a child, we simply come to recognize our weaknesses and learn how to make important changes until significant growth begins to take root. Eventually, some degree of persevering spiritual fruit will hopefully reveal itself.

Secondly, however, he can certainly discipline or chastise us for our mistakes and sins. However, I think he usually does that only when necessary, perhaps when we've been too repetitive in our failures and/or stubbornly fixated on some sort of sin. That's when our wise heavenly Father has to "speak much louder" to us in order to get our attention. In such cases, like any loving father, the Lord may need to use pain, sorrow or loss in order to get us back on the right track.

In either case, the Lord *can use consequences* to chasten us… the simple and "semi-sovereign" results of our own poor choices. When I say "semi-sovereign," I'm suggesting that habitual sins and foolish decisions to disobey God bring consequences…and may have little to do with God implementing a purposeful decree of judgement in our life. We just find ourselves immersed in a resulting season of shame and/or disfunction ***due primarily to our own foolishne***ss. For example, we choose a selfish course of action, and we hurt others that we never thought we would hurt. The damaging fallout happened because we didn't think things through deeply enough and refused to accept that which the Spirit and the Scriptures were warning us to avoid.

In other words, consequences bring circumstances and life events that can hurt us and those around us. Though such resulting consequences aren't necessarily sent by God (though they can be), nevertheless, they can be quite upsetting and painful to experience. Sin is a distasteful and often devastating thing to have to deal with, both personally and in the church at large.

But no matter what type of consequence occurs, it can be used by God to mature the growing believer...if he or she allows it to do so. Maturity ultimately comes when the wounded, but repentant believer comes to sincerely recognize that sin brings more fallout, debris, the damaging results than he or she wants to endure. Such a person has learned to *think consequentially* (a rooted conviction) before going habitually down the wrong path toward ultimate self-destruction.

> *"Godly sorrow brings repentance that leads to salvation and leaves no regret, but worldly sorrow brings death."* (II Cor. 7:10)

Consequential thinking is something that must be developed at the heart level within every mature believer. I'm focusing upon it now, because it is a strong understanding of life that must be accepted and practiced. Such deeper learning is usually a seasonal thing, but when we yield to it, the Holy Spirit can do remarkable things in our lives thereafter.

Consequential thinking provides fuel for all our convictions, but it only comes by learning *to want God more than anything else*, more than those same old sins and temptations we've known for too long. It is finally coming to the *realization* in a given area that it ONLY makes sense to reject sin and embrace God's will...no matter what pleasure or gain is attracting us - in spite of all. This usually involves the person saying the following at some strategic point in dealing with a particularly invasive sin:

> "Lord, I believe in You, why am I so willing to throw away all that is good and blessed in my life for a moment of continuing passion and pleasure with **inevitable, unavoidable and devastating repercussions?**"

Always see the big picture with sin...its destructive consequences for personal health, ministry, family, job, and future security in Christ Jesus. When *that* type of conviction takes root in our hearts, we're on the road to spiritual maturity!

> "We have much to say about this, but it is hard to make it clear to you because you no longer try to understand. In fact, though by this time you ought to be teachers, you need someone to teach you the elementary truths of God's word all over again. You need milk, not solid food! Anyone who lives on milk, being still an infant, is not acquainted with the teaching about righteousness. **But solid food is for the mature, who by constant use have trained themselves to distinguish good from evil."** (Heb. 5:11-14)

Let's discuss in greater detail how the consequences of life affect our conviction about sin and what it does to God, to us, to others and to our life calling. I think you'll be surprised at how destructive and disastrous sin really is.

What Sin Does To God

> *"Jesus answered and said to him, "If anyone loves Me, he will keep My word; and My Father will love him, and we will come to him and make our home with him."*
> (John 14:23)

God loves men and women, he really does, and he desires relationship with us not because he needs to, but because he wants to. That's why he created mankind in the beginning, to have intimate communication and ongoing relationship. His good pleasure is to show forth the essence of his *glorious nature*, which protects, encourages, and blesses believers with his loving favor.

> *"The LORD is not slow in keeping his promise, as some understand slowness. Instead, he is patient with you, **not** wanting anyone to perish, but everyone to come to repentance."* (II Peter 3:9)

God is also omniscient, which means that he knew that his creatures would choose to disobey him, if he gave them the freedom to choose. But, he did so anyway, which severed the relational intimacy and loving relationship he previously had with Adam and Eve. Why? Because even the fall of man allowed God to show is gloriously redemptive and merciful nature. Sin, though painful to him in a way we cannot understand, was ultimately overcome by his personal act of loving-kindness shown to the world by sending his Son, Jesus, to die.

> *"For God so loved the world that he gave his one and only Son, that whoever believes in him shall not perish but have eternal life."* (John 3:14)

Now, in Christ, that relationship has been eternally restored. It cannot be broken, because the atoning blood of Christ has forever washed our guilt away before God. Nevertheless, sin still *disappoints God* and can cause his just nature to punish or chastise the spiritual wanderer. God's wrath, however, is eternally **"propitiated"** (ie. satisfied) in Christ for those who come to him as Savior and Lord.

> *"For by one sacrifice he has made perfect forever those who are being made holy."* (Hebrews 10:14)

Though God **hates** sin, he never ceases to love sinners, even though we as believers, may still fall into sin from time to time. Again, this grieves him, of course, but it also brings glory to him when we repent, confess and return to a full and favored relationship in our daily walk.

> *"And do not grieve the Holy Spirit of God, with whom you were sealed for the day of redemption."* (Gal. 4:30)

When we confess our sin, God is pleased, because his anger is **appeased** by the blood Christ shed on the cross. Like a king's decree, our spiritual relationship with God has been sealed and stamped with the Spirit's pledge of *eternal* love and redemption. We can no longer be separated from this royal family relationship with Jesus, the Son of God.

Again, all of the above is never an excuse for one who persistently, intentionally and habitually chooses to live a lifestyle of sin. John speaks to this clearly.

> *"No one who lives in him **keeps on sinning**. No one who **continues** to sin has either seen him or known him."* (I John 2:6) ("continues" in the Greek means to habitually, consistently and intentionally sin against God and his will. Such a situation best describes a non-believer, not a believer struggling to master a grievous sin.)

What Sin Does To Us

"...your iniquities have separated you from your God; your sins have hidden his face from you, so that he will not hear." (Isaiah 59:2)

This Old Testament passage above is directed toward the rebellious and disobedience nation of Israel. It teaches a general rule that sin completely distances God from blessing his people, when they are involved with intentional, ongoing sinful behaviors.

They were a people of God in name only, for most of their hearts were unfaithful and distant from Jehovah, who had led them out of Egypt. Sin had completely corrupted their relationship with God as a people, such that he would not hear their prayers, protect them from their enemies, nor bless their crops.

For New Testament believers, the first and most obvious thing sin does to us is to **destroy our intimacy** with God, even though the relationship cannot be *completely* broken in Christ. But ongoing and intentional sin can still *encumber* our relationship with God significantly. It keeps our hearts from seeing him clearly, because our lusts, pride, jealousy and self-will pushes away God's blessing from our lives. Our hearts can become calloused and hardened, causing him to close his ears toward our prayers. Remember what God asked Cain?

> "Then the LORD said to Cain, "Why are you angry? Why is your face downcast? If you do what is right, will you not be accepted? But if you do not do what is right, sin is crouching at your door; it desires to have you, but you must rule over it." (Genesis 4:6-7)

Notice the anger and depression that infested itself in Cain, because of his jealousy over God's preference for Abel's offering. That inner battle within Cain over satisfying his sinful desires verses satisfying his godly conscience ended with Cain murdering his brother in vicious hatred.

We cannot sin without causing inner pain to ourselves, as well as those around us. Our relationships, including our marriages, can be harmed, at first subtly, then more obviously, as sin becomes more repetitive. Our work or ministry can be stripped of meaningful results and productivity, because our intimacy with Christ is not there to bear the fruits of patience, diligence and integrity. Our own minds can be permeated by unclean and damaging thought patterns, which plant little hooks of sinful memory within us that repetitively disable one's moral stability and character growth. It could be years until spiritual balance is restored.

Left unchecked, mental and emotional harm can cause both disease and physical disability, afflicting the physical body of the continually disobedient believer. . God, of course, is always ready and willing to restore the repentant believer, but, unfortunately, that repentance often comes after years of spiritual, emotional and/or physical deterioration.

In addition, **sin short-circuits our integrity**. I remember watching my father fix the wiring in an electrical socket in our newly built country home. I was on the other side of the dining room, while he was putting a new electrical plug unit into the wall. Normally, when you do this, one is wise if he turns off the power in the house first. That way, if one crosses the wires by accident, no electrical shock will occur. However, my father was in somewhat of a hurry and decided to avoid that which was the wiser course of action, so he just told himself to be careful.

> The debris of sin can be a backwash of lust-filled impulses, reoccurring fears, emotionalized responses and habitual patterns of both thinking and behavior.
>
> Climbing out of the hole of such self-dug pits is never easy and requires a total renewing of mind and heart, which by God's merciful grace, can be accomplished in his time.

The wall switch was off, and he carefully adjusted the wiring, when...bang! Across the floor he went...12 feet or more...and landed about a foot from me. Somehow, the hot and cold wires crossed, connecting the 110- volt circuit and throwing my father across the room. I jumped a mile myself, then realized what had happened. Dad was dazed, but okay, just shook up a bit. He later promised to never again skip the wiser choice of turning off the power before fooling around with a "hot" electrical box!

Electricity is dangerous, something one cannot hold on to or touch without facing some painful consequences. Sin is also something one should not touch, tolerate or hold on to, for it will "bite" back with painful tenacity somewhere in our lives. I've seen too many lives disrupted and/or destroyed by carelessly fooling around with it, even my own.

One significant issue that sin leaves in our lives is a ***loss of innocence.*** By way of example, let me share a bit about a friend of mine who suffers from PTSD (Post Traumatic Stress Disorder). He served in the military and had some sort of horrible confrontation with death in a battle zone arena that hurt him so much inside his spirit that he's never been able to fully shake the event. He has sleep problems and relational problems, among others, that keep resurfacing from time to time, bringing much grief and pain along the way.

By application, the deeper and more consistently we fall into the hands of repetitive sin the more likely it will cause inner pain and life struggles. That's because one's mind has been "branded" by sin in such a way that no longer will such a person be mentally and emotionally *free* from the knowledge or memory of it. There's something inescapable about sin's effect upon our soul, and both David and Paul address it:

> *"My iniquities have overtaken me, so that I am not able to look up."* (Psalm 40:12)

> *"To the pure all things are pure, but to those who are defiled and unbelieving nothing is pure; but even their mind and conscience are defiled"* (Titus 1:15).

On the other hand, both spiritual intimacy and integrity over time generate an *innocent relationship with God*, without memories and enticements from former times of rebellion or resistance to God's will. One's heart is clean from duplicity, and such a person can honestly say that he or she loves the Lord without invading thoughts of guilt, lust or fear. Because nothing clouds that relationship from the warmth of his love, such a person can eagerly expect God's fullest favor in life.

> *"Love the Lord your God with all your heart and with all your soul and with all your mind."* (Matt. 22:37)

One last thing that happens to us when we become repeatedly involved with sin...***we lose intention.*** Imagine with me that you're at a fall football game on this cloudy October day. You're almost at the end of your High School team's season, but this is a crucial game, which decides whether you'll catch an end run to the playoffs. A few stray snowflakes fall upon your shoulder and you shudder as a cold breeze whips across your face. It's a final kickoff to the opposing team with only 15 seconds to go...and you'll win the game and make the playoffs.

You're ahead 5 points, so only a touchdown will overtake your team. There goes the kick...the opposing team catches it and runs. Before you can even catch your breath, the runner dodges everyone on your team and crosses the goal line! You can't believe it...you're just stunned! Your team loses in these last seconds *and the finals are now out of reach*, though you've still got a final game to play.

Here's my question*: "When you get to next week's final game, with no chance to achieve the playoffs, how will you feel? Do you even want to play that game?*

Spiritually speaking, sin similarly weakens our resolve and dampens our desire to love and serve the Lord. Jesus said, *"No servant can serve two masters. Either he will hate the one and love the other, or he will be devoted to the one and despise the other. You cannot serve both God and Money."* (Luke 16:13)

Little sin areas or larger habitual sins correspondingly diminish our commitment to Christ. Yes, confession cleanses our spirits with mercy and grace, but sometimes it takes a fair amount of time for us to forgive ourselves. Better to stay away before intention to serve God deteriorates into inclination to satisfy lust, pride, fear, jealousy, anger, whatever. It can be an ongoing battle in some areas, but many who have given in to the wrong master have *struggled* to gain back lost yardage in their spiritual hearts.

What Our Sin Does To Others

"For nothing is hidden that will not be made manifest, nor is anything secret that will not be known and come to light." (Luke 8:17)

Eventually, all sin will be exposed, whether in this life or at the hand of the Lord at time of judgment. Sin, hidden or not, always has the ever-present power to hurt and harm the church, family, friends and our witness at large.

Do you remember the "TV Evangelist Scandals" of the 90's? Who knows how much harm was done to the name of Christ, because of the exposed failures of those once godly servants. But the harm went deeper than just the loss of position and integrity. Think of their families and friends who had to go through all the turmoil, distrust and defamation along with those fallen leaders. For instance, do you think that there might have been even just one unfortunate soul whose faith was scared or weakened, a family member who experienced debilitating depression, or a friend that determined never to trust a Christian again? What about the weakness of those men's preaching while living in their sin? Think about the anemic loss of power to really help those under their spiritual care. Yes, though all of us fall short of God's expectations, the greater our failure, the greater the negative results of it in the lives of those around us. As a typical teenager has no doubt recounted to his friends in the youth group at church, "Sin sucks!" Yes...it does.

> "Sin cannot pay enough dividends to justify our investment in it."

I just heard a rather *depressing* presentation of the Gospel at a funeral in a nearby evangelical church. There was no mention of the necessity of placing one's faith in Christ as Savior and Lord at all, nor was there any mention of the atoning blood of Christ shed on Calvary in order to find forgiveness and reconciliation with God. It was just a half-hearted explanation about repenting and being obedient thereafter. Now, that's true, but it's not the complete Gospel. I humbly believe that no one is going to be saved by such a message, though it might be characteristic of a eulogy at a typical non-Christian funeral, perhaps. Without a clear presentation of the cross of Christ, the Spirit of God has nothing with which to convict the heart about sin and our need of salvation by faith alone.

Is it possible that genuine churches today are so afraid of *offending* others with truth, that they are often found backing off from the truths of the Gospel? The doctrine of sin is meant to be clearly presented to unbelievers and continually reviewed in the church in order that God's Spirit can cleanse us from its presence. We must hate it no less than our Lord does. The Psalmist says, *"The sacrifices of God are a broken spirit; a broken and contrite heart, O God, you will not despise."* (Psalm 51:17)

I was asking the question at a men's Bible study the other night, "Why is it that God allows us to fail...even miserably so? Couldn't he have joined salvation with sanctification at point of faith, and then let us be examples of maturity for others? Then we could be free of some of the nasty little habits we have and hide, eliminating those seasons of doubt, or lust, or pride, etc. Hey, we'd be more productive for God, right? Why doesn't God just remove the memories, the impulses, and the debris of previous sins?

Well, the guys came up with some good reasons. One suggested that it's because God wants relationship with us anyway. Another suggested that without issues and problems on our part, we might be tempted to feel that we just don't need him any longer.

CONSEQUENCES

Whether only ripples of compromise or waves of carnality," what could have been" easily evaporates into the pain of "what is." Shattered dreams, broken relationships, dysfunctional families and squelched expectations in ministry or profession can drown a disobedient believer. Sin's consequences also flood into other lives around the sinner, causing pain and problems to innocent loved ones, friends and neighbors. The debris of his or her own indulgent choices can be utterly devastating.

However, there is another significant reason to explain why God doesn't just deliver us spontaneously from an enrooted sin or allow us to keep struggling against it, or even to be recaught in its tentacles. The reason may be that God desires to *test* our faith, our commitment, our resolve, our character, and our loyalty. Deliverance wouldn't challenge or change anyone inside (unless it's some sort of last resort on God's part for an extremely stubborn believer's situation). But, struggle, loss, pain and other consequences from persistent sin bring us face to face with our accountability to God...the prime motivation for change. Consequences provoke personal responsibility in ways that sovereign deliverance simply won't do. Most often *we've just got to hurt, if we're going to grow.* I don't think that's always the reason, but I do believe it's a common one.

Over all, our lives should gradually be moving toward the goal of Christlikeness in spiritual character. Our attitudes should be defined by love, gentleness, kindness, patience and longsuffering, and our behaviors should model persevering purity and moral obedience. Fewer spiritual "gaps" should be clinging to our lifestyle, as we learn to starve self and feed the Spirit. It's a massive undertaking, of course, to change fallen sinners into Christlike saints, but the process is guaranteed, even though it's accomplished over time and by many difficulties.

The two guys in this picture happened to be waiting along with us in the foyer of the Canadian pavilion at EPCOT in Florida's Walt Disney World. I took the picture because of how similar these two friends appeared as they were looking at their cell phones (probably trying to sign up for fast passes!). Similarly, you and I, though different in some areas, should appear to others as genuinely committed believers of Jesus Christ, having the same positive characteristics in attitude, behavior, and speech as the Lord has. It doesn't happen overnight, of course. But, as we move farther and farther away from personal sin, such a lifestyle will evidence itself more and more in the eyes of those around us.

To those profoundly weak in spiritual desire and determination, I offer this piece of advice. Maturity most likely will never arrive in anyone's life through miraculous deliverance, though God has sovereignly done so when necessary. However, it will probably come by way of learning to avoid the ugly consequences of sin. Such learning comes by grasping onto the truths found in the Word of God and taught by the Holy Spirit through life failure and success. For, as we more deeply discern and understand God and his will, such conviction ultimately *transforms* our inner person, bringing freedom from fleshly and/or satanic enticement. We'll have everything we truly need to overcome evil (see Phil 1:9-11). Look at it this way:

> *"Understanding God's Truth is the well from which spiritual desire and determination is drawn. The deeper the well, the more life transforming the result. So, discern the Truth of God as revealed to us in the Bible."*

CONVICTION #9

I Believe That Mercy Restores

―――◆―――

> *"The LORD is compassionate and gracious,*
> *slow to anger, abounding in love.*
> *He will not always accuse,*
> *nor will he harbor his anger forever;*
> *he does not treat us as our sins deserve*
> *or repay us according to our iniquities.*
> *For as high as the heavens are above the earth,*
> *so great is his love for those who fear him;*
> *as far as the east is from the west,*
> *so far has he removed our transgressions from us."*
> Psalm 103:8-12

I have a friend who recently lost his thirty-two-year-old son, Greg, who had struggled with drugs and psychological issues most his life. He found and lost several jobs, trying to find some regularity and career stability, and sought comfort in sexual relationships outside of marriage. In all this, his father stayed close to him, meeting for lunches, going to ball games and retreats, and generally hoping to reach out to him with the love of Christ.

In his final year, Greg started seriously searching for spiritual truth, and he renewed the simple faith commitment to Christ that he had made as a child. Though renewed in faith, however, he still battled depression, a brief drug relapse and loneliness at times. But four months before he took his own life, he joined Franklin Graham's team as a volunteer in Texas, 3000 miles away from his apartment in Buffalo, NY. It was the Christmas season, and he was involved in provided hurricane relief to storm damaged areas. Yes, he struggled daily with temptation, successfully so, and reached out to serve as best as he could, hoping to bring some order and meaning to his seemingly purposeless life. Then, one day, his father got the unexpected call telling him that his son had taken his own life. Apparently, the inner voices of discouragement and emptiness became too loud to endure any longer.

I know that his son is in heaven today, because of the sincerity evidenced in his struggle to stay sober over the past year and live a pure life for Christ, as well as serving Jesus with the Graham team in Texas. Though beset by tenacious difficulties, he *genuinely* tried to meet the challenges of his life with faith, family, friends, and with a good sense of humor.

But his father still hurts deeply, questioning and looking for assurance that his son had genuinely come back to the Savior. It's not easy for him to find such confidence, because his son had for so many years struggled with repetitive habits and doubts. Nevertheless, as we looked together at his son's life in recent months, we saw genuine points of spiritual turn-around and real commitment to the things of Christ. We also know that the Graham team found him reliable and committed, serving well in the tasks that they assigned him. In my friend's own life in all this, he remarked that only his own faith got him through it, as he surrendered to Jesus the pain and anxiety regarding Greg's situation. He recently sponsored a church and community outreach race (5K), helping to bring attention to those struggling with depression.

God is compassionate and merciful to those who reach out to him even in the thinnest energy of trust and obedience. It's not about how wicked or how distant from God one is, it's about coming close to God in the "now" through the washing and atoning blood of our Lord Jesus. God looks at the heart and especially answers prayers cried out from a wounded but sincere heart of faith in Christ as Savior and Lord. Greg's faith was real, and his commitment true, but the damage done to his inner person over the years probably overwhelmed him in a moment of unguarded pain and temptation. He reached out to God in a final act of desperation, hoping perhaps that God would free him from his struggle and receive him into a painless and hope-filled eternity...and I'm sure God did just that.

Is it right to take one's own life? Of course not, no more or less than it is to commit adultery, steal someone's wallet or have a hateful grudge toward someone who offended you. But, Greg's cry for peace reached the ears of the Lord, and the merciful arms of his Savior embraced him that day, when he saw Jesus on the other side. No doubt he will also one day greet his earthly father, too, in a warm, heavenly embrace, when my friend's door to eternity is opened up for him to walk through. All sins will have been forgiven, all longings forgotten and nothing but God's love will surround us, when we stumble through faith's door into the arms of Jesus our Lord.

I share this story because it so graphically speaks to the loving mercy of our Lord. We desperately need the mercy of God in our lives, not just at point of salvation, but beyond. Each day brings new challenges and along with it, either failure or success. Wrapped around each day are the truths we're supposed to be learning about God, ourselves, and life, which we store away in our minds. Unfortunately, we often make wrong assumptions, hide inner sins, and miss keys truths, which move us away from what we should be learning and doing. Without the wonderful mercy God provides for us on a daily basis in Christ Jesus, we would be hopelessly lost and subject to unceasing discipline and punishment. God's standards are crushingly heavy, and his judgments unyielding for those who *only* approach him with self-achievement and self-effort. I believe that's why Hebrews 4:16, emphasizes our need to seek God's mercy.

> *"Let us then approach God's throne of grace with confidence, so that we may receive mercy and find grace to help us in our time of need."*

MERCY IS A FRIEND TO ACCOUNTABILITY

> *"Mercy there was great, and grace was free;*
> *Pardon there was multiplied to me;*
> *There my burdened soul found liberty, at Calvary."*
> (William R. Newell, 1895)

Yes, our God is a merciful God. That's why I love the above song so much, for we used to sing it often as teenagers in our youth group in my local church. It speaks so wonderfully of the depths of God's love in Christ, that he mercifully provided salvation as a free gift to mankind, though at the cost of his own Son. No greater love exists, Jesus said, than if a man lays down his life for another. So, we must begin by understanding that the author of mercy is God. It is a core part of his nature, and no one else more deeply demonstrates it than he himself by sending Jesus to be our Savior.

It is so easy to be judgmental, even as believers, isn't it? We hate evil attitudes and actions, so when we see it in others our feathers get ruffled quickly. Then, we mouth off to those around us about the shamefulness of who they are or what they did. The thing about mercy, however, is that *it forgives*. In other words, though there is true wrong, failure or sin involved, the offended person chooses to "let it go." Merciful people do not condemn, they forgive. Even though the sin is inexcusable, they still are willing to forgive.

A young woman, Mary, attended a church I used to go to and worked in a small, satellite bank as a teller. One day a young man with a gun entered the bank near closing time, locked the doors and brought her and two others into a back room. There he abused them, raped Mary and ran off with stolen funds. He was later caught, but she decided that she needed to visit him at prison and share the salvation message offered to him in Christ. Though he legally needed to pay society for his horrible crimes, she still forgave him, seeking only to bring God's mercy into his life. I don't know whether or not he became a Christian, but the love, grace and mercy she showed to him must have been overwhelming to him, if he had any sense of conscience at all.

Two things enter my mind when thinking about such mercy. First, sin brings accountability and judgment. That young man, regardless of whatever hardship he endured in his upbringing, could never justify his actions. It would be wrong to not hold him accountable for what he did, or people would think that such things are just unfortunate issues, which mercy simply disregards like gently brushing off a fly that lands on one's arm. No, sin is serious. God could have forgiven all sin for which each of us is accountable, let us off the hook and never have felt compelled to send Christ as our mediator. But, he didn't, preferring to allow for accountability, knowing that *"people are destined to die once, and after that to face judgment"* (Heb. 9:27). My point is that mercy is not a "get out of jail free" card to be used and expected in every situation.

Beyond that, I also realize that Mary was not *"bound"* to offer him freedom from prison. However, she was merciful in giving him opportunity to find ultimate freedom from the eternal prison of hell. Again, mercy was not in any sense something that *she had to do,* just as God doesn't have to save anyone...though he chooses mercifully to save all who hear the Gospel and receive Christ.

In addition, one may not be able to fully forget an offence, though still able to show genuine mercy. A good example of this is how punishment for a crime is adjudicated. The type, length and severity of punishment is very much "mercifully" taken into account, when the punishment is given. It is often there where criminal history, understanding, forgiveness and mercy find a place to exhibit themselves. God works this way with us, too. There are times where sins are stupid and unplanned, while at other times they are willfully intentional. At other times, some sins are few, while at other times they are habitual and repetitive. Some sins have greater impact, and, therefore, are far more egregious than others, earning for themselves greater condemnation.

In summary, God is rich in mercy, as shown by his sending Jesus Christ. Also, mercy is often shown by an act of forgiveness, but must never to be expected or demanded, for accountability and guilt can still rightly be exercised at some level.

MERCY IS A GIFT

"Do not judge, and you will not be judged. Do not condemn, and you will not be condemned. Forgive, and you will be forgiven." (Luke 6:37)

Okay, let's look at the practical, everyday type exercising of mercy. The other day, my wife and I were driving to a restaurant after church on a two lane, 40 mph country road. I was about to pass the guy in front of me but noticed 4 or 5 motorcycles coming up from behind. I signaled to enter their lane in order to pass the person in front of me, but the bikers seemed to not want that to happen, so I sped up and turned into the left passing lane at the last moment to get around the guy in front of me. It was close, and I was impatient, causing the biker to quickly apply his breaks in order to avoid hitting me from behind. He was quite scared but jostled the bike to a quickly reduced speed. He, of course, then rounded me on the right side, and his female partner shared a well-known pointer of marked disapproval, and they sped away.

However, one of the other bikers followed behind me for about a mile. I really expected him to get out somewhere and start a fight. Well, we did come to a stop and he moved his bike at the stop light a bit into my lane and started to give me a different sign, so I rolled down my window. He was dressed in typical biker's leather, had an earring or two, a couple of large tattoos and a full beard. He did the "two fingers to each eye," sign, indicating that I needed to better watch out for things going on around me. I apologized, and he then told me, "Watch what's going on around you, okay?" After a couple more "watch" signals to his eyes, he sped off. I thought, "Now, that guy gave the appearance of being able to yell, scream and do a lot more to me....and I deserved it for being so impatient. But, instead, I got a very calm, yet serious look from someone who was simply concerned that I should straighten out my driving habits. To me, that was good and godly mercy, well-modeled. I was impressed and humbled... and I was truly sorry, enough so to slow down and think before doing something again that could really kill someone. However, condemning people is not at all a lost art, for most of us are quite adept at it. Here's a few other examples:

- "You cut me off, you *#$% idiot...where's the race!"
- "Can't you remember to put your shoes in the closet, Bobby. You're such a jerk!"
- "That guy couldn't put a golf ball in the fairway in a year. They shouldn't allow him on the course, he's such an idiot!"
- "Okay, Sue has got a difficult marriage, granted. But, that's no reason for her to stop going to church? God's going to judge her severely for that.
- "I'm never going to forgive Pete...he's just annoying and critical, and he won't change."
- "That pastor is crazy...he can't possibly believe what he just said. He's got something missing upstairs...what a dummy."
- "I'm not going to hang around with Bill any longer, Mary. He's got too many issues and problems...and he never solves any of them!"
- "Joe's just a complainer, that's all. He's not much of a Christian!"

The common thread in all of this stuff is condemnation without justification. In every case, complaints were made where the complainer really doesn't know what's going on in the life and mind of the annoying person. You've heard of the phrase, "There but for the grace of God go I?" Well, giving a person some "slack," as another saying goes, is good spirituality and comes close to everyday mercy in action. We don't fully know what's going on in the life and mind of another brother in Christ (or non-believer), and mercy is giving them a gift of forgiveness and understanding, instead of "know-it-all" judgmentalism. Let's put some mercy in our back pack and dispense it throughout our day to those who show a need it...people like us! Then, perhaps, it will come back to us someday.

> *"Cast your bread upon the waters, for you will find it after many days."* (Eccl. 11:1)

MERCY ISN'T SELF-SEEKING
The Parable of the Unmerciful Servant (Matt. 18:21-35)

> *"Then Peter came to Jesus and asked, 'Lord, how many times shall I forgive my brother or sister who sins against me? Up to seven times?' Jesus answered, 'I tell you, not seven times, but seventy-seven times. Therefore, the kingdom of heaven is like a king who wanted to settle accounts with his servants. As he began the settlement, a man who owed him ten thousand bags of gold was brought to him. Since he was not able to pay, the master ordered that he and his wife and his children and all that he had be sold to repay the debt.*
>   *At this the servant fell on his knees before him. 'Be patient with me,' he begged, 'and I will pay back everything.' The servant's master took pity on him, canceled the debt and let him go.*
>   *But when that servant went out, he found one of his fellow servants who owed him a hundred silver coins. He grabbed him and began to choke him. 'Pay back what you owe me!' he demanded. His fellow servant fell to his knees and begged him, 'Be patient with me, and I will pay it back.'*

> *But he refused. Instead, he went off and had the man thrown into prison until he could pay the debt. When the other servants saw what had happened, they were outraged and went and told their master everything that had happened. Then the master called the servant in. 'You wicked servant,' he said, 'I canceled all that debt of yours because you begged me to. Shouldn't you have had mercy on your fellow servant just as I had on you?' In anger his master handed him over to the jailers to be tortured, until he should pay back all he owed.*
>
> *'This is how my heavenly Father will treat each of you unless you forgive your brother or sister from your heart.'"*

Great example. So, how do we become merciful in heart? We start thinking about how we want God to deal with our issues... in this life and in the next. Each of us has sins that seem to hang around our necks and choke us from time to time. Wouldn't we want God to be forgiving toward us? Each of us as weaknesses and shortcomings that are visible to others at times, which annoy them and are probably inwardly embarrassing to us. Wouldn't we want those around us, who see these things, to "give us some slack" and show Christlike mercy? You bet we would, so let's start giving out some of it so that God will not withhold it from us because we withhold it from others.

> "Blessed are the merciful: for they shall obtain mercy." (Matt 5:7)

MERCY IS HUMBLE

> *"A certain moneylender had two debtors. One owed five hundred denarii, and the other fifty. When they could not pay, he cancelled the debt of both. Now which of them will love him more?"*

> *Simon answered, "The one, I suppose, for whom he cancelled the larger debt." And he said to him, "You have judged rightly." Then turning toward the woman, he said to Simon, "Do you see this woman? I entered your house; you gave me no water for my feet, but she has wet my feet with her tears and wiped them with her hair. You gave me no kiss, but from the time I came in she has not ceased to kiss my feet. You did not anoint my head with oil, but she has anointed my feet with ointment. Therefore, I tell you, her sins, which are many, are forgiven—for she loved much. But he who is forgiven little, loves little."*
> (Luke 7:41-47)

This story was told by Jesus on the occasion of being invited to dinner at Simon's house, a Pharisee. At the festivity a woman of ill repute heard that Jesus was there and brought a flask of alabaster ointment to anoint his feet. She must have had the eyes of everyone on her, for Simon told the onlookers that if Jesus really was a prophet, he would have known her background and sent her away. Of course, Jesus did know her background, which was precisely why he let her generously anoint him in this loving display of worship. Simon was so stuck in his streak of pride and position, that he could only see her failings and sins, but completely missed her humility and cry for merciful love. But Jesus saw it, and corrected Simon's condemning attitude, probably in front of all his friends.

It's very hard for our hearts to hold an abundance of mercy, when they are filled to the brim with pride, popularity, and position. So puffed up are we at times, that we forget the great price Jesus paid for *our own* salvation, let alone the exceedingly great mercy he showed...and continues to show...to us, who can sin so repeatedly. As James reminds us:

> *"From the same mouth come blessing and cursing. My brothers, these things ought not to be so."*
> (James 3:10)

Understanding how much God has forgiven us in Christ, and continues to do so daily, is a critical step in being able to forgive others. It is much easier to offer them acceptance, forgiveness, kindness, patience and "slack," as the saying goes, after we've honestly reviewed our own sinfulness.

MERCY IS PRACTICAL

> "But a Samaritan, as he traveled, came where the man was; and when he saw him, he took pity on him. He went to him and bandaged his wounds, pouring on oil and wine. Then he put the man on his own donkey, brought him to an inn and took care of him. [35] The next day he took out two denarii and gave them to the innkeeper. 'Look after him,' he said, 'and when I return, I will reimburse you for any extra expense you may have.' "Which of these three do you think was a neighbor to the man who fell into the hands of robbers?" The expert in the law replied, "The one who had mercy on him." Jesus told him, "Go and do likewise." (Luke 10:33-36)

The good Samaritan above, viewed with compassion the broken and beaten body of a Jewish traveler, who was robbed on the road to Jericho. He wasn't recalling the hatred and bigotry that the most Jews held for Samaritans...and for him. He had every reason to return that hatred toward this fellow, but he didn't. In a moment of genuine compassion, this godly Samaritan forsook any hatred, forgave any thoughts of retribution, and helped him back to health. And we, too, should hold to the same convictions in our walk with Christ! [Samaritans were a "mongrel race," a mixture of Gentile and Jewish heredity, culture, and religion, who were thrown together initially by the conquering king of Assyria after Israel's defeat hundreds of years before Christ.]

MERCY IS A WISE

When I was about 4 or 5 years old, my father had a big old easy chair in which to lay back and watch TV in the living room of our small apartment. It had no electrical components or even a handle to release it backwards. But there was a foot rest or stool that he would put his feet onto and stretch out comfortably. There was always a small place between the foot stool and the chair that I could easily fit into. I would rest my little arms on his knees and kick my feet up onto the stool between his. I called it the "hole." It was my spot to just relax and watch television with my Dad. When mercy is given, the recipient feels comfortable in having experienced it. James 3:17 reminds us that,

> *"But the wisdom from above is first of all pure, then peaceable, gentle, accommodating, full of mercy and good fruit, impartial, and sincere."*

Mercy received is spiritually "comfortable" because it's love in action. Notice the "feel good" adjectives...peaceable, gentle, impartial, sincere, etc. Mercy is just a nice place to sit down at the feet of Jesus and know that you're forgiven, accepted and loved. It also feels just as good to the person giving it out, I think, as to the person who is receiving it. Try it...you're like it!

CONVICTION #10

I Believe That Grace Rebuilds

"Therefore, since we have a great high priest
who has ascended into heaven, Jesus the Son of God,
let us hold firmly to the faith we profess.
For we do not have a high priest who is unable to
empathize with our weaknesses, but we have one
who has been tempted in every way, just as we are
- yet he did not sin. Let us then approach God's throne
of grace with confidence, so that we may receive mercy
and find grace to help us in our time of need."
Hebrews 4:14-16

Case #1: Bob is 29 years old and sitting in a divorce court, his wife, Mary, is seeking separation, because of his unfaithfulness. The judge hates to see young marriages broken up because of stupid or immature choices, so he pleads with the two of them to reconsider and give it one more try. They do love one another, despite his foolish one-night fling, so they decide to follow the judge's advice. One year later, along with the help of their pastor and a group of close church friends, their marriage is stronger than ever before.

Case #2: Kathy is a student at a local high school, who has been hanging around with the wrong crowd these days. Her father died a year ago, and she's been acting out her anger to her mom, her teachers, at God...to just about anybody. She's already been in trouble for smoking, stealing and generally rebellious types of behavior. Other than ending up in detention or getting suspended, she's never gotten in trouble with the law...until today. She saw the opportunity to steal an attractive sweater from a local department store and took it. The store manager happened to be passing her at just the right time, saw her do it, and sequestered her.

At court, the judge said, after looking at her record, "Okay, young lady, time to get tough...six months in the juvenal detention prison." But her uncle stood up an addressed the bench.

"Sir, I believe underneath it all that Kathy is a good kid just needing to get away from the wrong kids at school, that's all. I've got a ranch just outside of town up in the country. Could you to assign her there, to be with me and my wife, instead? I'll pay the fine, if any, and my wife and I'll take her in, and give her one last chance to change. She'll have everything she needs...freedom from temptation, a room to herself, horses to ride, etc. But, most of all she'll have plenty of chores to do on our ranch...milking, mending fences, cutting corn, bailing hay...all kinds of things that will help her straighten up. Sir, I'll give her every chance she needs to turn the corner. I'd like it greatly, if you would give her the opportunity?"

The judge was amazed at the uncle's faith in Kathy, so he looked at her intensely at first, then began to speak. "If I do this young lady, they'll be no other opportunities...no other grace will be extended to you. It would be for six months, along with a $500 fine...and I want a monthly report from your uncle on your progress. He glances at the uncle who nodded approval, then turned back to Kathy. She was fighting the tears, for she really did like her uncle and aunt. But, could she make the commitment? Would she make the choice to end all the nonsense and the bad relationships, and then straighten out her life?

She paused, then spoke through a flurry of tears. "Yes...I will. I love you uncle Pete!" Six months later found Kathy on the straight and narrow, and everyone knew that she was done with her former life of rebellion and anger. She found genuine love and those willing to show it to her.

In each of these situations, forgiveness might have been somewhat involved, but it was grace that both Bob and Kathy needed. Grace for Bob was a second chance to show genuine and committed love to his wife, who really loved him. She gave him the opportunity, and he took it to heart. Kathy also found something she couldn't deny or run from...genuine love and care from someone who was also willing to offer her another opportunity. She took it, too, realizing that this was it... the time was *now* to turn things around. So, she seized the opportunity and found that her uncle's love was enough to keep her on the right path. Grace is like that, it provides opportunity for people to change. It's not earned and most often it's unexpected, but it's got the power to heal people from the inside out.

Let me take an initial moment to discuss the differences between mercy and grace, which are similar, but not identical. Mercy is forgiveness and grace is favor, both of which are undeserved, due to the state of sin that envelopes us as fallen descendants of Adam.

> *"For he says to Moses, "I will have mercy on whom I have mercy, and I will have compassion on whom I have compassion."*

> *"All have sinned and fall short of the grace of God."* (Romans 3:23)

However, God has made *some* opportunity for mercy and grace to be *earned*, though salvation in Christ is clearly *not* one of those ways. Look at Manasseh, the son of Hezekiah, who was known as one of the most wicked and idolatrous kings ever.

> *"Manasseh led Judah and the inhabitants of Jerusalem astray, to do more evil than the nations*

whom the LORD destroyed before the people of Israel." (II Chron. 33:9)

But his tearful repentance found God's forgiveness and favor, and he had a gloriously repentant turnaround.

"Therefore, the LORD brought upon them the commanders of the army of the king of Assyria, who captured Manasseh with hooks and bound him with chains of bronze and brought him to Babylon. And when he was in distress, he entreated the favor of the LORD his God and humbled himself greatly before the God of his fathers. He prayed to him, and God was moved by his entreaty and **heard his plea and brought him again to Jerusalem into his kingdom. Then Manasseh knew that the LORD was God."** (II Chron. 33:11-13)

Jonah found that it is not a good idea to turn from the will of God. Nevertheless, he ultimately found that God's favor in his life was found in obedience to the faith he possessed. He learned to never run from the will of God, no matter what his prejudices and feelings might be. To do so always means losing the good things and blessings that God wants to provide for us.

"Those who worship worthless idols forfeit the grace that could be theirs." (Jonah 2:8)

Godliness was always a contingency for the Israelites to find grace from Jehovah. In this sense, then, there were always responsibilities necessary for the people of God, if they wanted the blessing of God upon their lives as a people and as individuals. Through spiritual obedience they could to a degree "earn" God's mercy and favor, particularly in securing and guiding Israel in the presence of its enemies. Yes, they needed faith, but it was an *obedient* faith that was required.

The same is true in the New Testament, but again, in a *limited way*. Godly obedience on anyone's part can *effectually engage* God's mercy and/or favor toward anyone, if God chooses to accept it. Jesus even says that God provides certain levels of grace to all... *believer or not, for "...he causes his sun to rise on the evil and the good and sends rain on the righteous and the unrighteous."* (Matt. 5:45b)

Obedience is a key factor when approaching God, even when believers seek the blessing and guidance of God. It is important to show the Lord our sincere faith and commitment to him, if we expect blessing and favor to follow.

> *"Whoever would love life and see good days*
> *must keep their tongue from evil*
> *and their lips from deceitful speech.*
> *They must turn from evil and do good;*
> *they must seek peace and pursue it.*
> *For the eyes of the Lord are on the righteous*
> *and his ears are attentive to their prayer,*
> *but the face of the Lord is against those who do evil."*
> (I Peter 3:10-13)

Now, that's pretty clear, and, again, it's an O.T. quote addressed to N.T. believers. God is looking for believers who are obedient, and *his ear is open to their prayers*. Now, please remember that for New Testament believers, godliness or good works have *no efficacy* or *atoning worth* before God, for they are always imperfect and tainted by sin. They cannot earn salvation, for faith in Christ alone as Savior brings forgiveness of sin and eternal life. *However, godly obedience can move the heart of God, no matter who you are.* It can bring *a measure of mercy or grace (undeserved favor)* this side of heaven at any given time to a needy person, depending upon the genuineness of his/her heart in seeking it, as well as God's sovereign purposes for allowing it. Okay, let's look more specifically at how grace brings healing.

Grace Heals Broken Hearts

*"Now when David and his men came to Ziklag on the third day, the Amalekites had made a raid against the Negeb and against Ziklag. They had overcome Ziklag and burned it with fire and taken captive the women and all who were in it, both small and great. They killed no one but carried them off and went their way. And when David and his men came to the city, they found it burned with fire, and their wives and sons and daughters taken captive. Then David and the people who were with him raised their voices and **wept until they had no more strength to weep**. David's two wives also had been taken captive, Ahinoam of Jezreel and Abigail the widow of Nabal of Carmel. And **David was greatly distressed**, for the people spoke of stoning him, because all the people were bitter in soul, each for his sons and daughters. **But David strengthened himself in the LORD his God.**"* (I Sam. 30:1-6)

This is one of the saddest situations in David's life. He probably had been out-maneuvered somehow and, therefore, had forgotten to take precautions for His camp against the Amalakites. When he and his men came back to their camp, it had been ransacked and everyone's wives and families taken hostage. At that precise moment David was finished, stuck in a quagmire of sorrow and self-doubt. Some of his people were ready to kill him, because they were also deep into self-pity and sorrow.

So, what does one do when stuck in such a seemingly hopeless situation? Well, David finally got himself out of his funk and started re-evaluating his situation.

- Was God taken by surprise regarding this raid?

- Is there any reason to blame Almighty God for this?

- Has God every let me down before?

- Should I avoid God and not let him work this situation out for his glory?

Of course, the answer was "no" across the board! So, he rekindled the embers of his traumatized faith, put one foot in front of the other and got up, reassuring himself God was sovereign and able to meet this crisis like any other he had faced along the way. This "self-encouragement" pep talk was from the Lord, and he found new courage in Jehovah. He found healing by re-activating his faith.

Broken hearts are the result of utter loss of hope in some area of one's life. It could be the loss of a loved one, loss of a job, loss of friends, an oppressive personal sin, etc. Or, it could be a lingering sickness that appears to be never ending. Sometimes it's being let down by another person in whom you placed great trust. Broken relationships can cause severe depression and discouragement as well, which adds loneliness to the feeling of hopelessness.

By getting into the Word, being faithful in prayer, seeking supportive relationships with other believers, and worshiping him with praise and song, hope can be restored. Ultimately, of course, it is hope in the person and power of the Lord Jesus that must spiritually reinvigorate us. But this will only come through the daily renewal of our relationship with Him through the above avenues of grace. God is more than able to walk with us through the difficult times of broken heartedness, *if we are also willing to seek him in the midst of them*. Life can hurt at times, but he is able to bring timely healing to situations that seem hopeless to us. Let's be like David, who "strengthened himself in the Lord," and found that God's favor soon brought victory and the return of all of the families involved. God cares, folks, if we remember to seek his grace in the midst of our suffering.

> *"Let us then approach God's throne of grace with confidence, so that we may receive mercy and find grace to help us in our time of need."*
> (Heb. 4:16)

Grace Heals Broken Relationships

I have a good friend, whom I'll call Brad, who was a Pastor of our church for about two years. Brad was not a seminary trained pastor, but a local guy who worked on an assembly line in a nearby factory. He was an Elder in our small church for several years, but felt called to in the ministry. He approached the church, and because of his commitment and reputation, was given the opportunity to Pastor our church. He did well and was loved by many folks.

One day during the week I was at the church running off some copies for something I was working on (I was only a layman, teaching men's Sunday school classes/bible studies, etc.). Now, Brad and I were very good friends, who had worked together in a side business and on various church activities. Without going into the details of the disagreement, we had a strong verbal fight, which almost went physical. We even had to go before the Elders in a meeting to resolve it. However, once the dust hit the floor on it all, the two of us decided to meet together at a local restaurant and "talk it through" without any accusations or anger...just talk about how we felt. We prayed, used Scripture, and focused upon forgiveness, instead of trying to 'win our case." It was one of the most powerful and beneficial things I have ever experienced, because it was first of all honest, then spiritually positive and proactive. Our relationship found healing, though it did require some time for both of us, I think, to really release the negative feelings that were deeply embedded. But God's grace was truly there, and we've had a good relationship since.

For our discussion, I see God's grace as something often available, but not always experienced. For Brad and I, it was the commitment both of us made to each other to seek reconciliation by sitting down together and inviting God to be there in the midst. I think God enjoys and, frankly, demands that we include him in all such serious relational matters, if we expect to see positive results. Otherwise, how can we expect healing, if we leave out the healer?

What makes the church special is that we have the Spirit of God within each of us, we have the Word of God as our guide, we have wise and gifted counsel, and we have direct access to God through prayer. But we must apply these relational avenues and tools, if we expect to access God's healing grace in life problems.

So, let's avail ourselves of the gracious mercy, love and spiritual healing that God's has for us. It's not always easy to heal broken relationships, but in Christ it is certainly possible, when we seek him in the midst of our efforts. Remember:

> "...where two or three gather in my name, there am I with them." (Mt. 18:20)

Grace Heals Broken Families

Bill was a member of the church where I ministered while going to seminary for my Christian Education degree. He and his wife were fine Christian people in good standing within the church and were involved in various lay ministries. However, his family – 3 grown up children in their twenties – did not know the Lord and didn't attend church except on rare occasions. They often heard the Gospel from their father and mother, but they were antagonistic toward making a decision for Christ.

On a late, Thursday afternoon in Boston, Bill saw someone stopped by the road side of this busy highway in rush hour traffic. He pulled up his car about 5' behind the person's car and offered to help someone change a flat tire. The driver was a single woman, who just didn't know how to change a tire. As he opened her trunk and reached for her spare tire, another car slammed into the back of her car and sandwiched him in between the two cars...he died instantly.

It was a sad funeral service two days later, because there were so many people who just loved Bill and his family. As is often the case, many questioned why God would allow such a horrific accident to occur and end the life of such a faithful and beloved man of God. Of course, everyone in the church encouraged Bill's wife and family, hoping that his adult children would not be angry at God.

On Sunday, the pastor delivered a good sermon about faith and commitment. At the end of it, he gave an invitation for anyone to come forward who wanted to receive Christ as Savior and Lord. There was no delay, for Bill's adult children...all of them...

attended church that day and came forward in response to the Pastor's invitation! Bill's wife cried joyful tears, and the whole church rejoiced over the wonderful grace of God, even knowing that Bill's life was the unique sacrifice necessary for reaching his kids with the Gospel.

> *"For as "For My thoughts are not your thoughts, neither are your ways My ways," declares the Lord. As the heavens are higher than the earth, so My ways are higher than your ways and My thoughts than your thoughts...."* (Is. 58:8, 9)

Sometimes, we might want God's grace to accomplish things the way *we* think it should be done, but that is seldom the case. Nevertheless, God is always working behind the scenes in ways that will often surprise us, providing us with a measure of grace that is overwhelming to our thinking. It may or may not have some degree of loss or pain associated with it, but we can believe that there is a gracious purpose being knit together around it, which brings glory to his name.

Grace Heals Broken Ministries

Elijah was quite a guy!

When he was called of God to go to Ahab and Jezebel, he did so with everything he had...full commitment and complete trust in Jehovah. The Lord was about to chastise this wicked royal duo, and Elijah was the center piece of his plan. This couple was sheer evil and led Israel down the path of idolatry and immorality so corrupt that it seemed to make past kings look like angels!

After a period of time for Elijah's training and a time of famine to get Ahab's attention, God set up a single battle on Mount Carmel for Elijah to face several hundred of Ahab's false prophets. It was quite a scene, I'm sure, and the crowd of Israelites in the stands were restless and excited to see what the outcome would be. Who could start the fire on the altar, Jehovah or the prophets of Baal?

> "Elijah said, "I am the only prophet of the LORD here, but there are four hundred fifty prophets of Baal. Bring two bulls. Let the prophets of Baal choose one bull and kill it and cut it into pieces. Then let them put the meat on the wood, but they are not to set fire to it. I will prepare the other bull, putting the meat on the wood but not setting fire to it. You prophets of Baal, pray to your god, and I will pray to the LORD. The god who answers by setting fire to his wood is the true God." All the people agreed that this was a good idea."
> (I Kings 18:22-24)

First, there was Team A...the Lord God and Elijah, who was sitting comfortably to the side as the false prophets spent several hours dancing themselves into a frenzied bunch of blood-letting baboons. Even Elijah saw the ridiculous and hopeless antics so laughable that he yelled out to them in sarcasm, "Hey, call out to your god a bit louder...perhaps he's gone to the bathroom for a while!" (the Hebrew actually implies this). This, of course, only made them jump around and cut themselves more in a crazed display of demonic worship.

Finally, Elijah takes the stage and God greatly empowers him, such that he calls down a fire from heaven that not only sends the previously water-soaked wood up in flames, but it actually burns the stones into ashes! Then, he chases the 450 prophets away and takes their lives, thus purifying the land from Satan's idolatrous grip upon its religious leadership. The people in the crowds repented and went back to their homes with a renewed faith in Jehovah. What a fantastic victory, what a wonderful ending. But, hold on, the next chapter is *not* so great.

Elijah makes it back to Jerusalem, but before the embers have cooled down to nothing, he runs amuck. Ahab's power has been dealt a decisive blow, but he hears that Jezebel is out for revenge. She sends out a death warrant for Elijah, and he is so upset and fearful, that he runs to the desert to get away.

> *"He sat down under a bush and asked to die. "I have had enough, LORD," he prayed. "Let me die. I am no better than my ancestors." Then he lay down under the tree and slept."* (I Kings 19:4,5)

Elijah! What are you doing! Get up and go face her down just as you did on the mountain...why are you so afraid?" Well, we're not told why he was so intimidated by Jezebel, especially right after his colossal victory. The point is, however, that he was done... finished...depressed...ready to die in shame.

God, however, had different plans, those which didn't involve wallowing in guilt and the chastisement of death. In great mercy, he sends an angel to resuscitate him and sends him to a lonely cave in the hills, where he licked his wounds. But God explains that he has better plans for him, and tells him of a powerful assistant waiting in the wings to help.

> *"The LORD said to him, "Go back on the road that leads to the desert around Damascus. Enter that city, and pour olive oil on Hazael to make him king over Aram. ⁱ⁶ Then pour oil on Jehu son of Nimshi to make him king over Israel. Next, pour oil on Elisha son of Shaphat from Abel Meholah to make him a prophet in your place. ⁱ⁷ Jehu will kill anyone who escapes from Hazael's sword, and Elisha will kill anyone who escapes from Jehu's sword. ⁱ⁸ I have seven thousand people left in Israel who have never bowed down before Baal and whose mouths have never kissed his idol."* (I Kings 19:15-18)

We can learn a lot about grace from this grand Scriptural event. First, I believe Elijah was such a "gung-ho" and achievement-driven guy as a person, that he just couldn't understand why Jezebel was still in the hunt. He had always put his full faith in Jehovah and fought bravely. Why, then, was God not silencing her? His emotions got the best of him, which made him doubt God and run for his life.

When a powerful leadership person emerges, his all-out commitment is loud and obvious. Similarly, when he stumbles and falls into significant sin, his fall can be just as loud and demonstrably destructive. Yes, when Pastors and/or church leaders fall there's a loud "thud" that can be heard far away!

Second, to those around him and who saw him run away to hide, the word could have spread quickly that God had left him for some reason. Perhaps this premature accusation would be passed around and lay the ground work for a resurgence of idolatry and rebellion. But, no...God had other plans!

Yes, there may have been some repercussions (Scripture doesn't say), but the point is that Elijah's ministry *wasn't over*. God met him, restored him, re-sent him and supported him with Elisha coming on board. Failure, sin, death, resignations, people problems, church fights and squabbles – all these can occur in the ranks of the church today, but it doesn't necessarily mean the end of ministry. God's grace is always available, *if we are willing to repent, seek and receive his mercy, and then embrace his favor as he leads.*

Yes, difficulties and loss will follow wrong choices and failure, that's part of the "sow-reap principle," which must be understood by all of us. But God isn't *necessarily finished* with any person, program or purpose in the wake of such things...if we do the right thing and allow him to restore us. That restoration may personally be in another form of ministry, or it might be in the same ministry with a few wise changes. But grace is a pathway God uses to refurbish one's personal or corporate call to serve and minister. Hiding in the desert only gives Satan time to brutalize us unnecessarily, for God seeks to forgive and favor the truly repentant soul, the one who returns to him in contrition and love. Listen to the Psalmist commenting upon the graciousness of the Lord after bringing the Israelite people back into their land after the Babylonian captivity.

Praise the Lord.
How good it is to sing praises to our God,

> *how pleasant and fitting to praise him!*
> *The L*ORD *builds up Jerusalem;*
> *he gathers the exiles of Israel.*
> *He heals the brokenhearted*
> *and binds up their wounds."*
> (Ps. 147:1-3)

The Israelites, who God continually called a "stiff-necked" people because of their bent toward following the sins of the surrounding nations, were now graciously being restored. Notice how compassionately it speaks of God's healing grace, which seeks to re-establish relationship with his people, even after years of judgment. The Psalmist is rejoicing in this and gives praise to God for it.

Let's be thankful, knowing that it is God's immeasurable mercy, which brings forgiveness, but it is his boundless grace that restores wanderers like you and I. It's so easy, isn't it, to falter and fall into sin, when evil comes knocking at the door of our minds and hearts. And, there should be no excuses given, when we listen to it and invite it into our lives. But, with the same certainty, we should also rejoice in the knowledge that Christ's blood cleanses us from all sin and seeks to restore us to a place of spiritual health and purpose...in God's time, of course.

In addition, let's never doubt the eternal, inseparable and unbreakable love of our God in Christ, who is not only about holding on to our soul, but intimately involved in making us whole. Let's recall a few verses about this wonderful grace that is available to each one of us, just as it was available to the prophet Elijah.

> *"Let us...approach God's throne of grace with confidence, so that we may receive **mercy** and find **grace** to help us in our time of need."*
> (Heb. 4:16)

> *"For I am convinced that neither death nor life, neither angels nor demons, neither the present nor the future, nor any powers, neither height*

nor depth, nor anything else in all creation, will be able to separate us from the love of God that is in Christ Jesus our Lord." (Romans 8:38-39)

Finally, remember, too, that grace is a daily thing, something we need and must seek out moment by moment. It takes more than a single cup of water for a dehydrated desert wanderer to be restored and strengthened enough to continue on. Such a person needs repetitive times of refreshment in order for him to cross the long, barren and burning sands of a spiritual desert. Similarly, grace is something to live by, to seek out for refreshment and to do the required tasks God gives us to accomplish. The Holy Spirit longs for us to continually invite him into every situation and assignment in life in order to find the grace to truly be an effective, kingdom worker. His grace is sufficient and satisfying for those who seek it with humility and consistency.

So many problems and pressures to meet;
Enable me, Jesus, to rest at your feet!

CONVICTION #11

I Believe Faith Overcomes

"For this reason I bow my knees before the Father, from whom every family in heaven and on earth is named, that according to the riches of his glory he may grant you to be strengthened with power through his Spirit in your inner being, so that Christ may dwell in your hearts through faith..."
(Eph. 3:14-17a)

There's a wonderful song of praise that worship leader Don Moen sings, entitled "We Give You Glory." The words of the refrain go like this:

*We give you glory. We give you honor.
We give you everything we are
lifting our hearts and heads before you.
We give you glory. We give you honor.
We give you everything we are,
lifting our hearts and heads before you, Lord.*

Would you not agree that such words of praise and worship offer great encouragement to any of us who are facing various kinds of difficulty or trouble? But in those times, it's just so good to trust in the Lord. Christians can lose jobs or struggle financially, for instance, just like anyone else, for Adam's sin has harmed this world, shoving us into various times of physical hardship, emotional trial, or spiritual turmoil. The difference, of course, is that believers have invited God *into those struggles* as Savior and Lord, and that brings us the joy of seeking his mercy and grace in the midst of it all. Here are two encouraging Scriptures.

> *"No one will be able to stand against you all the days of your life. As I was with Moses, so I will be with you; I will never leave you nor forsake you."* (Joshua 1:5)

> As believers, we do not live our lives out alone, for Jesus said, *"... and surely I am with you always, to the very end of the age."* (Matthew 29:20)

What we're talking about here is our faith conviction, and, as the apostle John reminds us, it overcomes the world (I John 5:4, 5). But faith at times is itself hard to maintain, leading the writers of Scripture to remind us of our need to *re-consecrate ourselves continually* to the Lord. We do this by renewing our spiritual posture, our faith conviction and commitment to God. It's where we re-focus ourselves upon Jesus, upon the Gospel, and upon our faith relationship with the Lord.

> Satan says, "God is not real, so ignore him." Faith replies, *"God is alive in Christ, and I will follow Him!"*

We do this as we listen to Him speak to us in the Bible during our daily devotions, during fellowship at Bible Studies, in worship services, in Sunday School classes, at retreats, etc. It's both a *point-in-time act,* as well as a *process (more on this later).*

> *Consecration follows conviction and is the foundational goal of spiritual life in Jesus Christ. Because we believe, we set apart our inner person (beliefs, motivations, will, attitudes... whatever) as a sacrificial offering to God in complete, unreserved, undivided, and fully surrendered faith commitment to God (Mark 12:30). This necessitates an "in spite of all and no matter what" spiritual posture, an unmovable primary conviction, and an ever-deepening heart relationship with God.*

The Word of God is our resource in all this. Practically speaking, faith needs to be continually refurbished, if you will, just like taking an older room of your house and repainting it. Just as that room's color fades a bit or acquires some scratches and imperfections along the way, so our faith also experiences the daily wear-and-tear of normal living. So, we must regularly isolate those issues and repair them, so that faith bears all the versatility and beauty of what it is meant to possess.

Let's take a few moments to review this "conviction of faith" that forms the necessary foundation for all of us in Christ Jesus. First, we'll isolate some common issues that can mar it and then look at how to successfully repair it.

DOUBT

Doubt wears many hats, but the most common has to do with intellectual concerns over the reality of Jesus, the Gospel and/or the existence of God. Now, some of this we touched upon in chapter one, understanding that our intellectual trust in God and his Son, Jesus, is well-founded and intellectually sound. Furthermore, we also discussed the substantive and historically trustworthy foundation we have in the Bible, God's written Word.

However, let's look at another part of this for a moment... *how* we should handle doubts that come when our prayers seem unanswered or when life becomes almost too stressful to bear. That's when Satan loves to whisper in our ear, "Don't believe in God and his love for you. All this "mess & stress" of your life wouldn't be happening to you, if he really loved you, right?"

Mess and stress? And, may I ask who's the author of all that stuff? You guessed it...Satan is. He already rebelled against God in full knowledge of the consequences and continues to willfully fight him, even though it's impossible to win against God's will. He also enticed Adam and Eve to doubt the God who gave them life, saying, *"Surely You will not die."* (Genesis 3:4 ESV). In their freedom and ignorance, they swallowed the bait, and *that's* why we have all this "mess and stress" in the first place. Here's a helpful way of dealing with doubts that arise out of impatience and/or disagreement often associated with God's Will:

Don't let what you don't know keep you from doing what you do know

You see, doubt always surrounds us when we lack understanding about something that's important, but which we can't resolve intellectually (a common experience, by the way). But what we do with those *"unanswerables"* is where wisdom and spiritual responsibility comes in, rather than doubt. Will we allow such questions to dull our commitment or derail the faithfulness of our walk with God? Hopefully not. Rather, it's in the midst of these unanswerable questions that we must "faith up" and continue to trust in God, praying that he will fill in the blanks sometime in the future, if it is his will to do so. *"Understanding God fully isn't necessarily his will; but obeying God's will completely... well, it always is."*

Remember that human reasoning is always looking for "answers" upon which to build its conclusions and a logical framework. Questioning is a way we accomplish this and how we build stability into our mental responses to life. But God desires...in spite of our rational limitations...that we believe in him, trust in him and continue to seek his will for our lives. When such questioning is positive and genuine, it won't harm our spiritual foundations...God, His Spirit, and his Word can handle it well.

But, if you let it morph into *obsessive* doubt, then one's mental foundation can gradually lean in a dangerous direction and eventually topple. That's not good, so, keep your faith focused on Christ, regardless of your doubt, and God will see you through. He will either fill in your intellectual blanks over time, or enable you to live productively with a few empty ones, here and there. Guess what...if we knew everything about everything, we still couldn't handle it anyway! Let's resign as "Master Designer of the Universe," and ask God for patience and intellectual peace. I know it may not be easy, but it's still our responsibility to go forward, trusting the Lord to resolve our issues and answer our prayers *in his time*.

DESIRE

Desire is built into us in many areas, though the objects of desire mostly come from experience and the environment in which we live. For instance, a male physician deals with naked female bodies all the time and finds little that may attract him sexually. Yet, in his marriage, he is still sexually attracted to his spouse. This is because the *context* guides his physical and mental reactions in either situation.

Similarly, Jesus said that we are called to live our lives in the *context of faith*. It's in this sense that everything we desire should be put under the umbrella of holiness, godliness, and self-control.

> *"Love the Lord your God with all your heart and*
> *with all your soul and with all your mind and*
> *with all your strength."* (Mk 12:30)

All of us have desires for many things...sex, food, relaxation, fun, social interaction, excitement, competitiveness, adventure, among other personal needs and wants. It is not that God doesn't want us to find fulfillment or satisfaction in these areas...for he created the capacity to seek out and enjoy them. But faith and commitment to Christ demands that we always keep the *context* in mind, when seeking to satisfy the many desires of our lives. And, the context is to show patient, resting, and trusting obedience to his will in the midst of it all.

Practically speaking, we are to filter every desire of our lives through the lens of God's Word, as God's Spirit within urges us forward in spiritual obedience. For example, if you slide your hand sideways back and forth in front of your face, that gives you an idea of what I mean. We look outwardly and see the world, but just as our hand passes in front of our eyes, so God's Word must continually pass in front of our spiritual eyes, filtering out worldly thinking or *anything that stimulates ungodly desire.*

It is oftentimes the case that believers are caught in a sinful desire or chained to a habitual weakness. How do we break that cycle? We break it through developing a more powerful, pervasive, and deeply rooted desire for God and his will instead. Romans 8:5-6 tells us how:

> *"Those who live according to the sinful nature have their minds set on what that nature desires, but those who live in accordance with the Spirit have their minds set on what the Spirit desires."*

Fleshly desire comes from within...our fallen nature...and brings to mind lustful pleasures and ungodly thoughts. Spiritual desire comes from within as well...the Spirit's nature...and brings to mind godly pleasures and godly thoughts. The one we listen to and lean our minds toward will drive us to eventually embrace it with impassioned commitment. Listening to the flesh brings carnal capitulation and possible captivation, if we repetitively yield to its desires. Listening to the Spirit brings spiritual security and godly character to those who yield to God. These two passions sometimes whisper, but often shout to us from within for attention and submission. But only those who listen and yield to the Spirit's desires will be unleashed to accomplish great things for God. In the meantime, let's *"clothe yourselves with the Lord Jesus Christ, and...not think about how to gratify the desires of the flesh."* (Romans 13:14)

DEATH

Death is not good. It's a consequence of an evil choice made several millennia ago, and it fell upon Adam's progeny as swiftly as night follows day. There are two types of fallout that death brought to us all...physical and spiritual. Physical death meant that our bodies and all of creation became subject to eventual destruction. Spiritual death meant immediate separation from intimate relationship with God, which in turn also meant that we would be corrupted within...in our minds and hearts. Thus, we were no longer able to fully comply with God's Will. Instead, we rebel and seek to do things that satisfy our own misguided inclinations.

Faith, however, is the conviction that rejects such a way of life. Instead, by repentant belief in Jesus as Savior and Lord, we choose to follow God. This permanently restores our spiritual relationship with God, though physical death will remain a spiritual thorn until Christ's 2nd coming finally eliminates it. Faith is the spiritual platform upon which our entire life exists and finds purpose and blessing.

For believers, however, death remains an expected reality. Though our eternal destiny is secured in Christ, our daily surroundings still remind us that earthly temptations and difficulties remain. Always be looking forward to what we have in Christ and dying to what we've left behind, for *"those who belong to Christ have crucified the sinful nature with its passions and desires. Since we live by the spirit, let us keep in step with the Spirit."* Gal 5:24-25

DEBRIS

This fallen state of sin brings unwanted results into our lives that can harm the spirits (and bodies) of believers trying to live a life of faith conviction. For instance, physical difficulties and diseases cause us to often struggle in our ability to trust God. The pain and stress we endure until we arrive in heaven causes us to sometimes give up and surrender ourselves to haughty spiritual antagonists like fear, lust, pride, anger, jealousy, discontentment, discouragement, depression, etc. In fact, it's often like walking through a spiritual minefield with explosive debris scattered all over, causing us to stumble and hurt ourselves. More mature believers may have less casualties in such battlefield conditions, but many a young believer's faith can be disabled in the midst of it all.

I have a golfing buddy, who's had a fair amount of spiritual debris in his life. It's obvious to many around him that after coming to Christ later in life, there remains a lot of "rough edges" in his spiritual walk with Jesus. He missed the blessing of having a solid Christian family in his early years, so he has some issues that dog at his spiritual feet. His language can be coarse at times, though not in any way vulgar or dirty minded, and his professional attitudes are still too accomplishment driven and, perhaps, lacking sufficient compassion toward others who aren't the "type A" personality he is. I also know he had some serious bouts with soft porn years ago, which probably raises some difficulties for him at times. Nevertheless, he's serious in his faith conviction and continues to grow in his commitment to the Lord. He visits homeless folks, works as a youth sponsor, and generously gives to the financial needs of individuals and the church at large.

My friend's situation is not all that unusual in the church. If you think it is, please revisit this topic in the Scriptures or have a chat with a few pastors. You'll soon realize that discipleship is a difficult road to follow at times, and it takes time for the debris of our former life (ungodly lifestyle choices) to get cleared away this side of heaven. *That's not to excuse sin,* for all of us must remain repentant and continually vulnerable to the Spirit's leading in our lives.

DISCOURAGEMENT

Let me refer to an experience I recalled in my book, *"Reaching Teenagers For Christ."* We had a large outreach youth program in my local church during my teenage years, which reached many teens with the Gospel. One such person was Sue (not her real name). About 15 or so years ago, we had a reunion for all of the teenagers, and one of our get togethers was at Sue's house in Connecticut. It was fun talking about all the crazy things that happened at Winter Retreats and Summer Camps, as well as at our weekly Saturday night meetings...the skits, the singing, the music, the talks...all the memories. We munched on a ton of snacks, while continuing to catch up on the more intimate details of everyone's situation, since being away from Cheshire Teens for over 35 years. Toward the end, I was chatting with Sue, and she became very quiet and vulnerable in her conversation about how her life had turned out so far.

> *"So, how are things with you, Sue?" I asked.*
> *"It's been rough, Ed. My husband left me for younger woman over 2 years ago, and it's been terribly difficult. Without the Lord...well, I just don't know how I'd get through it."*
> *"That's tough, Sue. I'm sorry, really I am. I didn't know."*
> *"Well, I've taken a new job, but I barely have enough to pay the bills for the kids and me. There's not much left over after that."*

I could only imagine her pain. We talked about the fun times we had at Cheshire Teens and continued to discuss the important lessons we learned as teenagers from Al, Rollie, Charlie, Jorie, Margaret and the other leaders. The Scriptural truths they had taught us had never left our minds. They formed the character expectations with which God guided all of us even into our adult years.

I was hurting for Sue. Still, her message to me was very encouraging...Christ is sufficient and God's will is always best. As I listened, I knew that she would survive and go on to find the next steps in God's plan for her life. I knew this would happen, because hurting or not, discouraged or not, struggling or not, she had the *faith conviction* to keep going in Christ.

In looking back, not all of those who *claimed* to be Christians were still walking with the Lord. On the other hand, all who had really made what I would call a serious and decisive commitment to Christ as Savior and Lord were still very much "staying in the faith." Yes, all of us have faced times of great difficulty and discouragement, and that's not going to change. But, the cutting-edge difference in various believer's lives was their *faith conviction*. A sufficiently rooted belief in Jesus Christ as Savior and Lord doesn't guarantee a perfect life this side of heaven, but it does enable one to find hope and spiritual growth along the way.

> *"No one born of God makes a practice of sinning, for God's seed abides in him; and he cannot keep on sinning, because he has been born of God."*
> I John 3:9

HOW TO DEEPEN THE WELL OF FAITH CONVICTION

Okay, we've looked at some of the issues and challenges of faith. Now it's time to summarize things a bit and look at how to fight these and to develop a deeper conviction for Jesus Christ.

Register First!

It almost goes without saying that spiritual convictions come from a spiritual source, which happens to be the Holy Spirit. And, of course, the Holy Spirit only indwells and ministers to hearts that he has previously awakened through the new birth of salvation in Jesus Christ. Though anyone can have convictions, salvation in the name of Jesus can only come through God's Spirit by what we call "unction." That's a theological term for the influencing and convicting work of the Holy Spirit upon our hearts and minds. This faith stirring unction can only happen as we align ourselves with Scriptural Truth from the heart.

But, since we're talking about our faith conviction, let's remember that this is how we sign up for eternal life. Our names must be registered in the Lamb's Book of Life, which happens when we place our faith in Christ's sacrifice upon the cross to expiate (or atone) for our sin...that is, to wash away the guilt. If you, by chance, have not yet wholeheartedly *"signed up"* by faith (asking Jesus to forgive you and become YOUR Savior), I pray that you will do so soon. Eternity in heaven or in hell is literally only a breath away.

Restore Relationship

Okay, assuming we've done the above and are "registered believers" bound for heaven, then let's understand that our faith conviction needs "daily gardening," if you will. In other words, we tend to get spiritually lazy, and don't always have the *deep* faith we once had (which conversely affects our attitudinal and behavioral consecration as well). Again, we know Christ and are bound for heaven, but sometimes we become a bit cold to God's indwelling Spirit, usually because of some sin, for instance, or because we're not staying in as close a relationship with Christ as we did before. Such spiritual dullness may be seen by our lack of faithful attendance at church activities, or just generally by the things we say and the entertainments we allow. Whatever the cause, before long close friends might even describe us as controlled by carnal *compromise* instead spiritual *conviction*. So, how do we get it back?

We need to restore our relationship with God's Word. That relationship begins, of course, in our daily devotional time with God in the Bible. But it also means getting into the Word at Bible Studies, Sunday School classes, men's/women's groups, fellowship times with Christian friends...whatever avenues brings the precious Word of God through our ears and into our hearts. Christian music, television, and radio, can do the same, as well as a good Christian book. We can't hear God speak to us unless we give him the platform to do so in these various ways. Not disciplining our lives in these things will dry up our spiritual conviction, and we'll fade into the woodwork of spiritual lethargy, moral looseness and non-productivity for God. Convictions always begin in the mind, where our ***perspectives*** begin to take root. With the proper nutrients (above), they will grow deep and become life-changing habits, but ***only*** if we cultivate them prayerfully and persistently.

Relinquish Your Rights

John was a reporter writing a story on a circus act for his newspaper. He was standing alongside the center ring in the main tent chatting casually with someone involved in the trapeze act.

"Awe, the high wire trapeze stuff ain't really so tough. As a matter of fact, I think just about anyone could do it," John said to the fellow nearby.

"No kidding," he replied, "and I suppose you could do it with no problem?" John looked at the two persons practicing high above and smiled.

"Yeah...no problem. What's so difficult about it, anyway? The guy in the blue shorts is the "catcher," I guess you call him...and he never seems to miss. The flyers flip around a lot, but he always catches them."

"So, again, you would trust that "catcher," as you call him, to catch you, right?" asked the guy. John again responded affirmatively and confidently.

"Let's go, then," said the guy.

"What do you mean?" asked John, a bit befuddled.

"Well, that's my son up there, and I'm the *main* "catcher" – and I agree with you, I don't think I've ever missed anyone. Of course...there's always a first time...but I wouldn't worry too much about it." He started walking over to the ladder where the flyers climbed up to the tight rope. "So...let's go. I'll be a great story for your newspaper!"

John looked up at the 30' drop and the thin rope stretching out about 40 feet long with no net below. His jaw dropped a bit and he smiled sheepishly.

"Well...a...I better not. I don't want to be your first "dropee!"

The man came back over to John and gave him a friendly smile. "That's okay. Up there we're used to each other, and we trust each other. I don't think you trust me. If you did, you'd come on up and enjoy the ride, my friend."

My point is that intellectual belief alone doesn't go very far with the Lord. We can't "enjoy the ride" with God either, until we're genuinely willing to trust Him, which means fully surrendering to his will instead of ours. But, when we do, we'll start flying higher in our faith than ever before.

> *"You see that his faith and his actions were working together, and his faith was made complete by what he did."* (James 2:22)

James says it so well, doesn't he! There's an important part of the process of sanctification, which involves you and I choosing to do right things right. Right actions can't save us, of course, but they are the *responsibility* none-the-less of every believer. Spiritual maturity will never be the result of lazy living, for it demands a personal faith, rooted in deep conviction. If we truly believe in God and in his Son, Jesus, then we are inherently and inwardly motivated to act upon that faith, saying "Yes!" to God's Spirit as often as we can. The results of such a life are literally *"out of this world!"*

CONVICTION #12

I Believe God Heals

*"God saw all that he had made,
and it was very good."*
(Genesis 1:31)

When God does something, he certainly does it right, doesn't he! Creation is a model of his awesome power, and we have been given it to rejoice in who he is. He's so worthy of our praise!

However, we aren't living in that perfect environment any longer, since the day Adam and Eve sinned by partaking of that forbidden fruit. It's been marred with decay and corruption by spiritual forces of evil, awaiting the day when Christ will reverse this curse and restore the world to its original beauty and majesty.

> *"For the creation waits in eager expectation for the children of God to be revealed. For the creation was subjected to frustration, not by its own choice, but by the will of the one who subjected it, in hope that the creation itself will be liberated from its bondage to decay and brought*

into the freedom and glory of the children of God. We know that the whole creation has been groaning as in the pains of childbirth right up to the present time." (Rom. 8:19-22)

The world in which we live, therefore, exists in what theologians call the "state of sin," which means that the life situation and environment around us has been corrupted. Therefore, we experience the debris or fallout of this rebellion against God's will that Satan ultimately caused, bringing disease, destruction and death into the world. Sickness, calamities, suffering, loss, danger...all these are realities we must now face in the physical "jungle" of this fallen world.

Let's not forget that we are part of his glorious creation. So, *we also* have also been *personally* marred by sin and corrupted in the following ways:

- **Personal Sin:** We have acquired a fallen nature, where sin has separated us from God. This spiritual situation has corrupted our inner person in a way that feeds selfishness and carnality into our soul, such that we persistently fail to do God's will.

- **People Sin:** God is a triune God and relationship between the Father, Son and Holy Spirit is something that God modeled in his creation as well. Loving kindness and relational harmony, however, are no longer the norm for human beings. Relationships have been corrupted by jealousy, hate, anger and many other destructive attitudes.

- **Political Sin**: It doesn't stop there, for nations fight against one another, and political conquering systems and/or religions have emerged throughout history like Islam and communism. For instance, it has been estimated that over 200 million souls alone have died in the name of Mohammed's world conquering agenda (https://www.americanthinker.com/ .articles/2014/05/the_greatest_murder_machine_in_history]

Over the years, I've been involved in many Bible studies, conferences and classes. I've also known a lot of Christian people, some of whom are leaders and Pastors, while others are just regular church goers and workers in the kingdom of God. But one thing describes all of them and myself – we are all damaged people. Each one of us knows what is right and godly, yet each one of us does the opposite at times...not continually, not necessarily with rebellious intent, but still in cognizant disobedience to the will of God. Each one of us has suffered with unwanted physical sickness or disease, each one has been nasty and unloving to others on occasion, and each one has at times had thinking that is antagonistic to the Word of God. In other words, we're broken people, who have been damaged in greater or lesser degree by sin. So, how can we live for Christ with this broken frame of ours and in this broken and damaged environment all around us?

------- Accept That We Are A Broken People -------

God wants to bring positive, healthy, and lasting change into our lives this side of heaven. But like any experienced doctor, we've got to first identify the symptoms of the disease before healing can take place. Some people, however, have a theology that's a bit off on this issue. They reason that, because Christ died and the Spirit dwells within us, we can no longer be overcome by any sin. We have restored minds and refurbished hearts, such that we simply can't be caught up in such things. They acknowledge that believers aren't perfect, but they believe that they no longer struggle with sin or become stuck in a nasty habit or addiction. In effect, they do not recognize the remaining, ugly state of affairs in which all of us find ourselves living in this damaged world.

Their thinking is somewhat askew from Scripture. God's Spirit is powerful and able to address our needs according to his awesome, sovereign grace. But Scripture also warns us about the power of sin in a believer's life, that it must be wisely dealt with, or it can wreck-havoc in our spiritual lives as well.

> *"Therefore, since we are surrounded by such a great cloud of witnesses, let us throw off everything that hinders and **the sin that so easily entangles**…*let us run with perseverance the race marked out for us…" (Hebrews 12:1)

> *"Therefore, strengthen **your feeble arms and weak knees**. Make level paths for your feet," **so that the lame may not be disabled,** but rather healed."* (Hebrews 12:12, 13)

> *"My dear children, I write this to you so that you will not sin. **But if anybody does sin,** we have an advocate with the Father—Jesus Christ, the Righteous One."* (I John 2:1)

> *"When they had preached the gospel to that city and had made many disciples, they returned to Lystra and to Iconium and to Antioch, strengthening the souls of the disciples, encouraging them to continue in the faith, and saying that **through many tribulations we must enter the kingdom of God…**"* (ERV Acts 14:21-22)

> *"Brothers and sisters, I could not address you as people who live by the Spirit but **as people who are still worldly**—mere infants in Christ. I gave you milk, not solid food, for you were not yet ready for it. Indeed, you are still not ready. **You are still worldly**. For since there is **jealousy and quarreling among you,** are you not worldly? Are you not acting like mere humans?* (I Cor. 3:1-4)

We need to maintain a perspective of Christian living that recognizes…as a good friend has reminded me…"trials, temptations, tribulations and testing." She was somewhat kidding about it, but nevertheless it is true. There are temptations and difficulties emerging from within and without, all because of the catastrophic results of sin upon our fallen world, which we highlighted at the beginning of this chapter. And, because of this, we can at times struggle with a sin, yes, even as believers. All of the Scriptures above point to the reality that believers can and do become entangled at times with a sin or sins (directly or indirectly), which can have a disastrous effect upon them physically and spiritually. This doesn't mean that God will let them reject him and be lost. Nevertheless, the sanctification process can be very frustrating and trying at times. Listen to David share the physical and spiritual pain he was experiencing, because of his sin with Bathsheba, exposed by the prophet Nathan:

"Because of your wrath there is no health in my body;
there is no soundness in my bones because of my sin.
My guilt has overwhelmed me
like a burden too heavy to bear.
My wounds fester and are loathsome
because of my sinful folly.
I am bowed down and brought very low;
all day long I go about mourning.
My back is filled with searing pain;
there is no health in my body."
I am feeble and utterly crushed;
I groan in anguish of heart." (Ps. 38:3-8)

Bottom line to all this is that spiritual maturity is a rough road to follow, though I believe God's Spirit ultimately keeps us moving forward. The Spirit saves us and sanctifies us, but the sanctifying process can often be painful and filled with potholes for the naive believer and/or the "slow-to-learn" disciple of Christ. Life will have its share of unrealized dreams, bruised spirits, guilty feelings, habitual struggles, relational issues, occasional hardship, and other "nasties." To deny this is to deny spiritual reality and Biblical truth. That's why Paul says to the Romans in chapter 8, verse 28, that God doesn't always keep believers free from stress and struggle, but he **does** promise to be working *"in everything"* for good.

Now…put these truths together with another reality of life; people coming to Christ **already have** some degree of brokenness and or disfunction, which only adds to struggle to become mature believers. To a greater or lesser degree, they may have been involved with sexual habits, substance abuse, broken homes, job loss, financial difficulties, psychological issues, etc. God's healing grace is of course available and working to bring comfort and healing to them in any or all of this. But spiritual living is not going to be an instantaneous cakewalk, either.

Regarding this, I asked a teacher friend a question at lunch yesterday. He recounted a recent incident where one of his students (a 6th grader) got upset over something and shoved a pen into his own scalp, which bled profusely.

I asked, "Why? I mean, that's kind of a crazy thing to do… harm yourself?"

"Well," he explained, "he's been diagnosed with juvenile schizophrenia and sometimes has these types of fits, if overwhelmed by some task or class issue." He comes from a home where the father is incarcerated, his mother is a cocaine user and… well, it's just not a good place to live. When this happens, as it has in the past, I immediately call the office. Others trained to handle this behavior come and assist me, and things usually get back to normal fairly quickly."

"Do you think a kid like this could come to Christ? If so, how would the Holy Spirit help or bring some kind of healing to the situation?" I asked. He didn't have a polished answer, nor did I. Now, I'm sure folks with serious psychological issues can find salvation, of course, and God can give them healing grace and spiritual growth. That help, though, may require a period of time for such a person to learn how to manage both his or her emotional/mental health issues and spiritual needs as well. However, it's not as hopeless as it may seem at first.

Okay, my point is that all of us are broken individuals to some degree, because of the life difficulties in our early childhood or family situations. This brokenness brings into our Christian life many issues that require God's Spirit to gently "rebuild" us from within, establish new ways of thinking and form new and Christ-like habits. All this takes time and requires patience on the part of all of us. All of us need lots of love, compassion, forgiveness and grace in order to *"grow in the grace and knowledge of our Lord and Savior Jesus Christ."* (II Peter 3:18)

------ Allow God's Word to Rebuild and Heal Us From Within ------

Okay, now let's look beyond the problem and see how God can take that which is broken and bring his healing grace. It starts within and continues to heaven!

First, brokenness has a positive side to it.

In fact, you can't fix something unless it is broken first. Here's what I mean. I've been told that an individual lamb, which tends to wander too often away from the fold, will find the Shepherd purposely breaking one of its legs. The crippled lamb is in this way kept from wandering too far and getting eaten by predators or falling into other harm. The leg heals, of course, but the little wanderer has learned to respect its boundaries and act the way it should.

Similarly, broken people need to face their weaknesses, accept them and repent of them before their loving spiritual shepherd. As they humbly allow the Spirit into those painful areas of their souls in faith and obedience, he can bring gradual, but forward-moving grace into their Christian walk. Such a path of healing can widen into a highway of peace over time, if one is willing to be spiritually obedient and vulnerable. But it requires a genuine faith and serious surrender to the things of Christ gained over time and after surviving some annoying spiritual potholes along the way.

Second, brokenness needs the corrective medicine of God's Word.

Usually, I get a cold at least once a winter season. When I do, I'm pretty much aware of how to deal with it, which includes taking appropriate vitamins and seeking antibiotics when necessary. I know my body well enough to recognize when my cough gets deep enough into my lungs that I need some bacteria fighting antibiotics, so I give a shout out to my doctor. Unfortunately, what usually follows is a series of delayed steps, where one is caught in the medical system longer than necessary. There's the initial phone call to the doctor, then you wait for a week or so to see the doctor. Finally, you go only to be told that they're not sure whether it's bacterial or viral yet, so it's best that no antibiotics be described. Just wait another week and call back...then, if necessary, they'll write you a prescription. Not very efficient or customer focused, right?

Well, I told the Doctor a few years ago that I most often know when it's viral or bacterial (which can be treated with drugs). I further explained that, because of my business trips, I can't be waiting for two weeks to make this thing go away. I need to correct it as quickly as possible, for I'm a trainer and I'm in front of people all day. Only antibiotics will ultimately keep a bacterial infection – if it is one - from deteriorating into an upper respiratory issue, or even pneumonia.

So, I asked affirmatively, "It's not going to hurt the environment, or anything else...everyone knows this...if I take the full dose prescribed, even for a mistakenly diagnosed viral cold. So, let's do it, okay?" He saw the wisdom and the need, and now I've always got the right medicine, if and when I need it.

Spiritually speaking, having the right medicine for a broken life is critical. Essentially, this means applying the Word of God to our spiritual wounds with regularity and consistency. Our personal weaknesses, wounds and issues can be deeply rooted and are often quite resistant to any attempt to bring healing grace, so it requires more than reading a verse or two at night or saying a few prayers.

However, God's Word really can cut through all our pain and disablement over time. Broken people are usually folks wrapped in a world of unspiritual and/or skewed thinking, as well as being buried under a lot of painful emotions. As we come to understand the truths of God's Word more deeply and start thinking right, change comes. Emotions will begin to heal and calm down, while one's life starts moving forward toward more healthy attitudes and behaviors.

> *"For the word of God is living and active. Sharper than any double-edged sword, it penetrates even to dividing soul and spirit, joint and marrow; it judges the thoughts and attitudes of the heart."* (Hebrews 4:12)

Please remember that God's Scriptural medicine must be taken faithfully, but it must also be applied in its various forms. So, Bible-based teaching, counseling, personal devotions and fellowship all are necessary in various doses to correct one's mental and spiritual perspectives. And, just as in the case of physical brokenness, healing always takes time. But God is faithful and longs for us to take our hurts and problems to him in faith so he can help to restore our spiritual health.

> "Spiritual maturity hinges upon our ability to discern, hold onto, and focus upon God's Word and its inherent Truth."

Third, brokenness needs the soothing peace found in personal worship.

A few years ago, I was experiencing a season of unusual discouragement and testing. I seemed to have lost the "spark" in my relationship with the Lord. I went to church regularly, taught a couple of Bible studies, led and/or spoke at special events, etc., but I was lonely and distant. A friend of mine at church mentioned that he knew of a great worship leader, who's music might step things up for my somewhat "boring" and "routine" Christian walk. The worship leader's name was Don Moen, and I can tell you that

God used him greatly in my life to bring meaningful worship into my daily life with Christ.

It seems that many folks struggle to find what Don already found in worship. Such folks think they have to jump up and down, and get into a loud, amen-shouting frenzy to worship God. On the other extreme are folks that think "Rock of Ages" and old-time hymns are the only answer to having true worship. Well, I love old hymns, I really do, mostly because of the spiritual depth of their words, and some of them have beautiful musical themes as well. But, much of the new stuff today is "off the charts," when it comes to good worship. It's feeling-focused lyrics and shallow spirituality only offers entertainment stuff that is gimmicky, not genuinely pleasing to God. Don, however, struck a center to it all...beautiful harmonies, gentile sounds, meaningful words, and controlled rhythms that honor God and anyone who seeks to experience genuine worship.

My point is that broken people can find great personal release and healing as they praise God through non-manipulative methods in worship. And, you don't have to be in church to find such joyful and peaceful times either, just download a song appropriately and legally on the internet, and you can have your own church service in your home! You'll find more than a spiritual bandage there, believe me. You'll begin to find a renewed intimacy with God, rich in mercy and grace, that will rebuild your tired and struggling inner person. Yes, worship really does help to heal the broken-hearted soul!

Fourth, brokenness finds grace in loving relationships.

How often do you meet with Christian friends at a lunch or breakfast? Let me introduce to you my friend, Mike. He's a former cop, who left law enforcement to eventually do what he loved best... carpentry. He made some of the finest kitchen cabinets you could find. But, starting his own business wasn't easy nor was making it profitable a simple task either, particularly when one is up against large companies providing the same service for less.

Because I was also starting my own training business at the time, we often met at breakfast or lunch to encourage one another.

Sometimes we'd talk for as much as 2 hours about church, personal growth or business, and often we'd have prayer outside by his truck. In those special days, we developed a deep trust and loyalty for each other in the Lord, which kept us going forward. Even when there seemed to be *more month than income*, God enabled us to provide for our families. You just can't beat that kind of friendship, when it's based around God.

Most importantly, the fellowship we shared together brought great peace in the midst of difficulties, personal losses, and the struggle to let Christ become the helping resource he wants to be. Oftentimes, it is the ministry of fellow believers and Christian friends that can have a significant impact in our lives.

Mike has since gone to be with the Lord. But I greatly miss our "executive meetings" together in those small, corner restaurants he knew so well throughout the area. *Do you have "a Mike" within your circle of friends at church?* Broken people need others to help them find healing and grace.

Lastly, there is no brokenness that God can't fix!

Most of the time, we stay *unnecessarily* broken, because we don't step up to the provisions God has already given us to find mercy and grace for meeting our life needs. We tend to be long on sermonizing, but short on action, right!

In closing, it's always spiritually invigorating to bask in the sunlight of God's love. We hear about his love, we understand it to a point, but seldom are we pursing it aggressively and genuinely enough. Nevertheless, James tells us to, *"draw near to God and He will draw near to you."* In other words, serious everyday action is necessary to step out and seek the love of God, if we want his love to touch us with a full expression of spiritual warmth and blessing. Certainly, the love of God, like all characteristics of his nature, never diminishes, vacillates or wanes. But again, his fullest favor toward us is measured out *practically* to us based upon one's faith, one's obedience, and also God's perfect will for our lives.

So, let's make a silent covenant today…each of us…to reach out in the coming weeks for God's merciful grace in order to heal our brokenness, however it manifests itself. Let us pursue God's merciful love daily by devotions, fellowship, worship and intimate relationship with the Word of God!

CONVICTION #13

I Believe In Godly Worship

"Therefore, since we are receiving a kingdom that cannot be shaken, let us be thankful, and so worship God acceptably with reverence and awe..."
Hebrews 12:28

It was a weeknight, and I was at a special church service in central Connecticut, where I was raised. My high school buddy had invited me to attend this evangelistic crusade being sponsored by a local church. The primary speaker was a well-known evangelist, whose reputation working with disadvantaged and troubled youth was nationally known.

As I looked around the audience of about 175, I noticed that the pews were stuffed. Everyone wanted to hear this guy speak, as well as hear the three former gang members share their testimonies of how Christ changed their lives from drugs, prostitution and crime. The three testimonies were great and, frankly, amazing to hear.

Then, half way through the service, the evangelist rose to bring the main message. My friend elbowed me, saying, "Okay, now watch what happens when he says, "Let's worship the Lord." I didn't understand what he meant by that comment, for my background was fairly conservative and Baptist. But, after the evangelist said those words and opened up in prayer, the place went wild. His mannerisms and flow of words seemed to excite the crowd. Soon people were literally jumping up and down, while clapping and shouting out, *"Amen...Halleluiah...Praise the Lord!"* It was like a faucet somewhere had been turned on!

As he continued to move the crowd by his words, some folks began running back and forth down the isles with raised hands. All around me, most everyone was mumbling strange sounds and words in sort of a collective outburst of King James phrases. The evangelist let these outbursts continue for periods of time, throughout his sermon. I had never experienced anything like that before and was both unnerved and amazed at the same time.

Now, that evangelist was a wonderful man of God, dealing successfully with inner city youth of the day, those caught in addictions and gang wars. But this was not even close to the picture presented of what I believe is New Testament worship. It was, however, a "Christian sub-culture" created by certain denominational groups and their doctrinal understanding of worship. And, just like any of us, sometimes good people embrace improper or unwise cultural norms and habits. We're human, and get things mixed up at times...right?

In balance, here's another glimpse of a worship style I experienced. My sister lived in California and invited me to visit her during the summer after I graduated from high school. California really was beautiful, sunny all the time and it had a lot of well know places to visit, which we did together. My sister didn't know the Lord and was living a very rebellious lifestyle, spiritually speaking (the good news is that she later came to Christ at the end of her life!). At this time, however, she would argue with me regarding the Bible, salvation, heaven vs. hell, etc. Well, I didn't have too many resources out there in the three months I visited her, though I did work briefly for Bethlehem Steel Corporation, while there. But I had no friends to talk with and find support, so I looked for a church that I could at least attend on Sundays. I found an average sized conservative church and started attending it.

On one Sunday night this church had a special service with a visiting, denominational evangelist. I remember his name as Dr. Jarmon, and his testimony was equally meaningful, though not as dramatic as the other church. He had tried all religions and studied many philosophies through life, but eventually found himself empty and still searching. Through a series of sovereignly led events he came by faith to Jesus and found the peace, hope and purpose for which he so desperately sought. When finishing, he paused to pray and lead the folks in a brief time of worship. Other than just a few "amens," the crowd was quiet and reverent in its posture.

WHAT IS WORSHIP?

Above are 2 types of worship, each very sincere. But which one is more *Biblically accurate?* Well, the essence of worship is *"bowing down"* or giving worth and honor to God, because of an enlightened understanding of his attributes and character. It can be offered alone or in the gathering of God's people on a corporate basis.

In Old Testament times (a span of almost two thousand years), worship was given in a variety of settings. Abraham built an altar as a place for worship, Moses initiated sacrifices and Solomon built a temple for songs and instrumental music. So, worship had specific places necessary for it to occur, and it was accompanied by various practices, including rituals, singing, instrumentation and body movements (ie. raising hands, prostrating oneself, bowing, etc.).

In the New Testament, worship no longer required a specific place or posture, nor did it require sacrificial lambs, due to the finished work of Christ on the cross (although the newly forming church did initially tend to meet in the temple courts, because of its Jewish roots, then later in homes). However, singing, praising, raising hands, musical accompaniment, bowing down, etc., were the methods of worship practiced and approved of even today. Speaking in tongues, which mostly can be identified as personal worship, did *not* have a place for corporate worship, *unless* it was accompanied by interpretation. Only then was it encouraged by the Apostle Paul both for private and corporate *edification*.

> *"I would like every one of you to speak in tongues, but I would rather have you prophesy. The one who prophesies is greater than the one who speaks in tongues, unless someone interprets, so that the church may be edified." (I Cor. 14:5)*

> *"For this reason, the one who speaks in a tongue should pray that they may interpret what they say. For if I pray in a tongue, my spirit prays, but my mind is unfruitful." (I Cor. 14:13, 14)*

JESUS AND WORSHIP

Overall, Jesus added a new *identity* to worship in saying that believers must *"worship in spirit and truth."* In other words, worship is spiritual and personal, not something to be identified as just physical or structural. It is not an act or ritual performed in a temple, accompanied by sacrifices, and it's not to be confined to a place or a building. Rather, it is *understanding and acknowledging the Truth of God*, beginning with acceptance of the Good News. New Testament worship is now an internal thing, made possible by God's indwelling Spirit. It is, therefore, a spiritually intimate and internal relationship of adoration and praise to God through his Son, Jesus Christ. (Heb. 10:11-14 and 19 - 22).

Worship, then, is an attitude or perspective, a way of thinking about God. It's an understanding, an acknowledgement of who God is...almighty, glorious, merciful, loving, etc. Thus, praise filled adoration is usually prompted in response to God's Word, to another's testimony about God, or perhaps by a miraculous manifestation or blessing in someone's life. Regardless, it causes us to **acknowledge** God's greatness and to **bow down** in our hearts before Him (the actual Greek definition for worship is "bowing down" in posture).

So, true worship is *essentially* and *fundamentally* only one thing...a ***perspective of praise*** regarding the greatness and goodness of God. Nothing more is necessarily required or expected. All outward symbols such as instrumentation, music, singing, etc. are personal and changeable choices to honor God. New Testament worship is now housed (or "tabernacled") within our human spirit.

WORSHIPFUL EXPRESSION

However, worship can also be ***expressed*** (acted out) in various ways, none of which is to be confused with worship *itself* (one's inner perspective toward God). These outward things are only the *personal and physical responses* we make as a result of our *inner perspective* of praise and adoration. The ***chosen expressions*** of one's "worship perspective," must be realistically open to honest evaluation, whether individual or within a corporate setting. They can be very inappropriate.

Again, the perspective we hold about God *is* true worship, while the expression of it, frankly, may ***not*** be acceptable or even pleasing to God. So, if I choose to raise my hands, when alone and praising God, probably no one would say that such behavior is wrong. The same would be true for the words I use, the posture I take (on my knees, standing, swaying, etc.), or the music I might be singing in adoration of my Lord. That's because these would be personal choices when alone.

However, *there are limitations to consider.* For instance, I remember a Bible Study group I was a part of in my early married life, attended by about 5 couples. We met on a Tuesday night for study, prayer and fellowship. It was a great source of encouragement and instruction, and very helpful to us all.

But I remember going over to one of the couple's home in the morning to drop off something that the wife had left at our house the night before. Mary (not her real name) came to the porch door after I rang the bell. As the door opened, there was Mary, but she was almost in a trance, softly repeating "praise the Lord" incessantly. She interrupted herself to take what I had brought, then hurriedly said, "Hi, Ed. Thanks…listen…got to keep praising… keep praising. We've got a women's prayer group inside…praise God, praise God…and I don't want to get 'out of the Spirit,' okay? Talk with you later!" She promptly closed the door, and I stood there wondering what in the world she was doing. Later she explained that a handful of her friends had gathered for a time of worship. They were "in the Spirit," which to her meant that all were praising God together verbally and she didn't want to lose the "feeling" of it. So, she kept chanting over and over to keep *in the feeling* of worship.

I would suggest that even in individual worship, there has to be sensibility, not sensuality. In other words, sensual feelings are great, and we all have them at times in our worship settings. *But feelings are never the essence of worship, just responses to it, and* the choices we make to express worship matters to God and should be controlled. Repetitive babblings cheapen worship, foster a feeling-fest, and can easily become self-manipulating. Such "in the Spirit" experiences, I believe, are nothing more than a roller-coaster ride down the track of self-induced emotional indulgence (sad, but often true).

If not watched over, such gatherings can easily morph into a frenzied free-for-all of body movements and ecstatic verbalization, *where no one is genuinely focusing upon God's greatness or his Word*. They're *"in the Spirit,"* they would say, but probably more realistically, *"in the feeling."* In such situations, the *quiet appreciation* and *rational understanding* of the glorious goodness of Almighty God and his Word has, like the well-known entertainer, "left the building." It's not that such feelings are evil, but they certainly are not to be confused with that which is at the core of worship! Distinguishing between the two is critical for spiritual growth.

This type of thing in the early church prompted the Apostle Paul to impose sensible boundaries for the expression of worship, when one finds himself or herself in a corporate setting. Let's look at those next.

THREE CRITICAL BOUNDARIES FOR GENUINE WORSHIP

1. Focusing Upon God's Word

"The Spirit gives life, the flesh counts for nothing. The words I have spoken to you are spirit and they are life." (John 6:63)

"God is spirit and his worshipers must worship in spirit and in truth." (John 4:24)

The foundation for worship is always upon the Word of God, for it is Truth. Remember that Jesus taught us his new plan for worship, that it is "in spirit and in Truth." Within us (our spirits), *worship begins with our belief-convictions about the goodness and greatness of God.* And, inherent in those convictions should reside the precepts and principles of the nature of God revealed to us in the Bible. Without these, our worship, our convictions and our attitudes are just personal feelings wrapped around emotionalized ideas. But, the joy of *true* worship lies in *knowing* the Word of God as it shines upon our daily experiences, enlightening us according to God's Truth. Then, worshipful praise becomes far more Scripture based, emotionally controlled and knowledge based, as it moves our inner person toward faith and commitment...instead of emotionalism.

2. Orderliness

"Therefore, my brothers and sisters, be eager to prophesy, and do not forbid speaking in tongues. But everything should be done in a fitting and orderly way." (I Cor. 14:39-40)

As much as possible, individual activities and preferences, therefore, should never ostentatiously exhibit themselves in the church worship service. Rather, as church body focuses upon the message in a sermon, it purifies one from sheer emotionalism or outbursts of personal pleasure. Godly worship can and should be expressed through music, prayer, or testimony, but it should always be in the context of order and propriety. The Apostle Paul was opposed to displays of uninhibited personal feelings and unbridled actions in a corporate setting, probably because of the craziness involved in the pagan, sensually charged religious groups that captivated so many souls outside the churches.

Unfortunately, it seems today that his wisdom and teaching on worship has again reverted backward to gatherings where people look for "happenings of the spirit." Loud evangelists with pulsating musical backgrounds and personal charisma seem much more focused upon fostering worship "experiences" instead of simple, rationally focused, and praise-filled acknowledgement about the goodness and glory of God in doctrine and life.

Having raised the above red flag, however, there certainly is room for feelings, emotions and experience for worship *in general*. We are a people that express feelings, show our love and share our experiences...of course! But such things should never be manipulated, nor should worship bands and leaders simply provide staged routines for emotional effect. Order, genuine responses, and self-control should always dominate.

> *"...the spirits of prophets are subject to prophets;*
> *for God is not a god of confusion, but of peace, as*
> *in all the churches of the saints." (I Cor. 14:32)*

The **opposite** is also true, as I think back on the second worship experience I mentioned above. Worship without any feelings probably is unnecessarily cold and ineffective, whether individually or corporately focused. Remember that true worship is a conviction about the goodness and greatness of God. If such convictions *never* move an individual to tears or to praise, then I would suggest that it is being squelched.

Some other churches are so entrenched in weekly doctrinal-type preaching, for instance, that worship or praise can't find a seat! People become cold and distant, which is also not pleasing to the Lord, who "inhabits the praise of his people."

Again, there are various forms of worshipful expression in both personal and corporate settings, but everything should also be done *in an orderly fashion.* When the church body is shouting out together and jumping around, no one is listening and learning about the goodness and greatness of God. Faith has been reduced to dancing a jig and discipleship to displays of undisciplined emotion.

So, we must discipline ourselves and choose what we say or do in a service of worship (even in our personal worship). Various factors will affect this choice, too, including our particular personality and proclivities, up-bringing and personal experiences. So will our cultural setting, the social context, the atmosphere of the moment, my health at the time, musical skill, my experiences coming in to the sanctuary, etc. But we must understand that all of these are **experiential factors**...they are not "of the Spirit." Thus, the expression of our worship at any given time can be a matter of personal emotion, staging or cultural comfort. Because of this possibility, worship must be *watched over* continually…personally and corporately… in order to avoid being "out of line" at times with what is spiritually *healthy and wise.* Otherwise, an "anything goes" mentality is the rule, and all kinds of excesses can emerge.

For Goodness "SNAKES!"

Snake handling as a religious rite in the United States, also called serpent handling, is observed in a small number of isolated churches, mostly in the United States, usually characterized as rural and part of the "holiness movement." The practice began in the early 20th century in Appalachia and plays only a small part in the church service. *In 1955, George Went Hensley, the founder of modern snake handling in the Appalachian Mountains, died after being bitten by a rattlesnake during a service in* Florida:https://www.bing.com/search?q=Snake+handling+worship

One quick point...culture is never a reason to tolerate worship expressions that hinder genuine and/or mature worship from taking place. The global church is full of ideocracies and cultural ways of worship that are theologically problematic. As in everything else we do as believers, worship must be clearly identified (above) and kept in sensible harmony with Biblical Truth. Cultural diversity is often an excuse for self-serving antics. Worship, however, is about God, not us.

3. Edification

We call our "get-togethers" worship services, but worship is actually only a part. As mentioned above, our *primary goal* should be *edification* according to the apostle Paul, which is the building up each other in our relationship with God. This is why Paul addresses worship ("coming together") in I Corinthians so strategically. As in many other areas at Corinth, **abuse** was taking place there, too.

> "What is the outcome then, brethren? When you assemble, each one has a psalm, has a teaching, has a revelation, has a tongue, has an interpretation. Let all things be done for edification."

Worship, of course, plays an important role of support in the purpose of edification, but is not an end in and of itself. We meet together primarily *for spiritual growth...not worship*. Yet today, the opposite situation seems to prevail. Many believers meet for an *"in the Spirit experience"* with God, instead of *instruction from God*. Hence, if I *feel good* when walking away from a service, then folks think they have experienced God in that service. But, if I have no overwhelming feeling of happiness, then I haven't truly met God or experienced him.

However, Paul does not at all suggest that "worshipful feelings," pleasures, or emotional highs should be the measure of our fellowship together. The measurement is the building up of one another in the Lord (edification)... regardless of how we feel about ourselves, our life situation, others, or whatever. I should be asking myself, *"Do I understand this truth in **my** life? Am I in need of confession and rededication to the precepts and principles of God's Word? What is God trying to say to me today in this study or service?"* These and much more focuses worship in the direction of **edification:**

> *The root of this Greek word is found in various words and compound words in the NT, i.e., build (Mt 23:29; 26:61), building (Jn 2:20), builder (1Co 3:10; Heb 3:3-4), builds up (1Co 8:1), strengthen (1Co 8:10), edified (1Co 14:5, 17), edification (Ro 14:19). Paul doesn't use the word in the literal sense of "building" a building. He uses it in the metaphorical sense of "building up" the church, and of "building up" fellow believer...Paul uses the words more frequently in the sense of "strengthening, unifying, making for peace." Christians are to build up each other in this sense (1Th 5:11). It is primarily love that "builds up" (1Co 8:1).* (From the NIV Dictionary)

For instance, music should be clear, understandable and **enable** the *message* to come through. Music should enhance our *understanding and adoration* of God. As a form of media, it should not glorify itself nor hinder true worship from happening... inner praise in acknowledgment of the goodness and greatness of God. Music, therefore, needs to be Biblically sound, modern enough to communicate easily, and supportive of its inner message. In message and format, it should avoid focusing upon or fostering experiential feelings (though this not *entirely* possible, of course). Nevertheless, musical preferences differ from person to person, hence the reason to keep it conservative and message supporting, not culturally relevant alone. Musical culture can destroy a church's genuine worship.

Okay, what about physical movements, verbal outbursts, hands, ju mping up and down, etc.? Again, these should not dominate nor distract the corporate worship service, for they are personal, controllable and shouldn't be overly ostentatious. Instead, remember that testimony and teaching should bring out a *calm and controlled appreciation for God*, never a pep rally... which is not the goal of worship, anyway. Such things have strayed way beyond the purpose of worshipful praise. They have morphed into a chaotic, undisciplined and compromised culture...instead of Christ focused praise. "Worship bands" in the main church services can get out of hand with loud, pounding rhythms balancing on the edge of cultural norms and obscuring the humble acknowledgement of who God is. Unfortunately, in too many churches across the nation, Christian worship has been hijacked by emotionalized concerts of cultural entertainment, where the message has been completely overshadowed by method.

In the end, meaningful praise in word and music should always be expressed with **balance, propriety, sensitivity, orderliness,** etc. so that the *priority* goal of edification is attained. In addition, older hymns and choruses may be too "stale" for some, but their words can still be very encouraging and uplifting - if we allow them to speak to us. However, they probably won't form the main diet of a worship service, because their style of expression is more cumbersome for some to enjoy (cultures and forms do change, after all).

In summary, however, our inner perspective of worship regularly leads to various "choices of expression" (some conscious, some not), by which we find personal comfort, when communicating the "height and depth" of our love for God. In corporate settings, these differences can cause discomfort and/or disagreements among believers regarding worship styles due to differing backgrounds and varying personalities. On both a personal or corporate worship level, the truth remains that differing worship preferences can range from good to bad, healthy to not healthy, godly to ungodly, wise or unwise, etc. In other words, just because a person or a group of believers expresses worship in a particular way, doesn't automatically justify its expression before God.

Examples of phony or unmanaged worship would be where people are jumping around "in the spirit;" group praising where everyone is speaking in sort of a "praise stew;" instrumental solos played wildly "in the Spirit" with no reference to Scripture in order to put such in a context for meaningful worship. Paul would clearly call this disorderly, confusing, without a peaceable effect, and certainly without body edification. It's similar to the misuse of the gift of tongues:

> *"...in the church I desire to speak five words with my mind, that I may instruct others also, rather than ten thousand words in a tongue. Brethren... in your thinking...be mature." I Cor. 14:19)*

Now, some would say, "Paul, you're so unemotional, fearful of true worship, restrictive of the Spirit!" Not in the least! Rather, he is aiming for **genuine** worship, keeping his responses **under control** in order that both he himself and others around him **may benefit,** too. He would allow more personal expression privately, perhaps. But even there, it would never be at the expense of worship that **understands** and **acknowledges** *the greatness and goodness of Almighty* God. What about the corporate level? **Balanced, sensible, non-distracting,** and **Word-based,** expressions of worship are best, where music and praise can **build up** the body of Christ.

> "Manipulated worship is staged spirituality; it is rooted in man's emotions and contributes little to lasting spiritual character."

In closing, please let worshipful praise be genuine and richly enjoyed in your personal and corporate settings. Love God by praising him for his sovereign grace, goodness and mercy in your life. Respect him by being sensible and propriety-focused in every method you choose with which to praise him.

> *"Though worship is unchangeable in essential character, it must always be expressed with self-control and order. Expressive context in worship should never overshadow, overwhelm, hinder or*

*hijack its essential character, which is pure and reverent adoration. It is not **entertainment**, nor is it **celebration**, two expressive and popular roads for worship to travel, but which at unguarded times can become harmful baggage for the trip. They can stimulate an emotional or cultural context, instead of focusing upon the convictional character of the message. Genuine worship must always be kept free from the control or dominance of secondary desires and feelings. The message of unadulterated worship must be center stage in adoration for who God is. The methods are just supporting characters who are content to beautify the message, while remaining quietly unnoticed in the background."*

CONVICTION #14

I Believe That Little Things Count

c=◆=o

> *"His master said to him, 'Well done, good and faithful slave. You were faithful with a few things, I will put you in charge of many things; enter into the joy of your master."*
> Matt. 25:23

Jesus was a guest at Martha's house and had just come back with his disciples for a meal. Mary and Martha were very busy preparing food for everyone, but when Jesus passed by her, she stopped helping Martha and went to him. As he was sitting down, she took the bowl of water she had brought with her and sat down next to him. Slowly and lovingly. she began to wash each foot from the dirt he had acquired walking the dusty roads in the neighborhood. This was a custom in Jesus' day, but no one had offered to do it presently except Mary.

Martha caught sight of Mary out the window of her home and came out to find out what she was up to. Martha needed help in setting up the meal for these hungry disciples, but Mary left her to finish up alone. Emerging from the wood framed doorway into the stone courtyard outside her home, she immediately saw what Mary was doing. Martha loved Jesus too, but why wasn't Mary doing what was important...getting the meal ready? Her first thought was to say nothing, but her impatience over-ruled her wisdom.

"Mary...come on, girl, I can't do all this alone, you know," she frustratingly exclaimed. But Jesus immediately turned to her and caught her eye. At that moment Martha was quick to realize that she should have held her tongue and just waited for Mary to return. However, Jesus, decided to use this as a teaching moment.

Jesus replied, "Martha, Martha, you are worried and upset about many things, but only one thing is needed. Mary has chosen what is better, and it will not be taken away from her." (a paraphrase of the events in Luke 10). Martha learned that day that a common and ignoble thing like washing a guest's feet meant more to Jesus that catering to a crowd's hunger.

> *"Whoever can be trusted with very little can also be trusted with much, and whoever is dishonest with very little will also be dishonest with much."*

I know another person in the corporate arena that also models this welcome spiritual quality. Having many people under his authority, he doesn't often get the opportunity to mingle with everyone and know their names, let alone their job responsibilities. Recently, however he started a policy of regularly coming down from his corporate office and walking amidst the cubicles, chatting with his employees and letting them know they're appreciated. It's increased the morale greatly and probably boosted productivity as well. Again, it's just a little thing, not very time consuming really, but it can profoundly change attitudes and relationships.

I believe that most of us enjoy pleasing others in little ways from time to time. But to do so often means stepping away from our day-to-day busyness and investing our time in the lives of someone else. Life brings us many time-consuming activities and responsibilities that we easily forget to do little but meaningful things in the relationships that exist all around us. And, it's in those relationships that little seeds of God's love can be planted, which can make a larger impact for Christ. So, here's a list of "little things" we all can do that can have a bigger impact for Christ in the lives of those around us in the course of our daily routines.

SMILE WITH INTENT

Believers have the same challenges, frustrations and heartaches in their lives, as do non-believers. Traffic conditions still make us angry on the way to work, and airline delays will always frustrate travel plans. Things we buy will continue to break down, and we'll have to stand in long lines to bring the defective product back for credit. Customer care reps on the phone will still be hired from somewhere across the globe and speak in varying degrees of broken English, enough to frustrate clear communication from taking place. Computers continue to have issues, making one feel like throwing it out your office window, and managers at work will continue to ask you to do things faster and more efficiently than you're able to do...or at least feel inclined to do, right?

So, here's the thing...SMILE! It's contagious, especially when it comes from the heart, therefore, proving itself to be genuine. It's low cost, easy to give away, and it brings tremendous results as a rule, because not a lot of folks use it, particularly in annoying situations where impatience tends to rule. But, as believers, we should be modeling the Spiritual fruit of patience, kindness and love by wearing...sincerely so...a warm and inviting attitude. The smile itself means little, but the understanding heart behind it can give a fresh breath of hope to a beleaguered soul briefly overwhelmed, for instance, with their own job and life issues. For example, you might wonder why a customer service person can't step up and be more efficient or resolve your issue. But your "love gift" of a compassionate smile can soothe their particular stress, too. This has nothing to necessarily do with who's right or wrong in a given situation, just common everyday kindness, which all of us need and enjoy in such challenging situations.

Here's another tip: when you give a smile away to someone, look them in the eye at the same time. That communicates sincerity, genuine concern and compassion. You'll find that the "smile habit" resolves issues and cements positive relationships faster than you can imagine.

Be careful, because our human nature wants to replace a smile with a scowl, a smirk, or a sassy put-down. I remember working as a sales person in a store's furniture department, when I was in my twenties. A customer came in and turned rather belligerent after I gave him the price.

"You guys are a bunch of idiots...the price is ridiculously high," he quipped. "You can't fool me, kid, I've been around a long while!"

"That's okay, friend, I don't hold that against you," I responded with a smile, which had nothing to do with kindness. Well, he complained to my manager, and after a few minutes of discussion later on, my manager let me go. I think he appreciated my feelings of being abused by that angry customer, but he couldn't tolerate my nasty remark. A simple but genuine smile on my part to the annoyed customer would have saved me from losing my cool...and my job.

This smile stuff is important for believers, who are trying to keep their "witness" for Christ at the forefront of how they interact with non-Christians. It can make or break one's witness on the spot, given the right set of circumstances. It reminds me of the statement by G.K. Chesterton:

> "The Christian ideal has not been tried and found wanting. It has been found difficult; and left untried."

GIVE A THANK YOU GIFT

When I buy a car, I value the salesperson's efforts putting together all the paper work and just making sure everything works out smoothly. The last time I did this, I sent a large pizza to the dealership, specifically to the 2 or 3 people that helped me out. It's a good gesture and when I've done it, I always get a genuinely given thank you card in the mail (didn't get any more money off the sticker price, however!!). Of course, that's not why I do it any way, and I only do it once the car has been delivered.

Here's another thank you gift. I remember a time when I was California, visiting my sister two months after just graduating from high school. This country boy from Connecticut thoroughly enjoyed visiting with her and seeing the sights around Los Angeles and San Francisco. We went to some shows and visited the well-known entertainment places, such as the Hollywood Bowl, bull fights just over the border in Mexico, and the famous Rodeo Drive. We stopped there just to look, believe me, for amidst all the retail store glitter rested prices for clothing and jewelry that would make your eyes roll!

Unfortunately, my sister was going through a tough time in her life, dealing with alcohol addiction (later in her life she came to Christ as Savior, and the Lord delivered her completely from its grip). However, at that time she would drink too much at times. I don't ever remember her getting falling-down drunk, for she cared enough for me to control herself.

One night she took me to a fine dining restaurant, but didn't appreciate the quality of the food or the service (after a couple of drinks, of course). When it came time to pay the bill, therefore, she made it a point to tell the waiter that his service was not "up to her expectations," as she put it, and she didn't leave *any* tip. I felt so bad for the guy that I slipped a $10 tip into his hand as we left. She didn't see it, but I just wanted to assure him that it really wasn't anything he had done wrong that caused my sister to be unkind. Looking back, I'm sure that an experienced waiter in that type of restaurant understood what too much alcohol can do to some people. But he gave me a strong smile of appreciation, and I felt good that I had acknowledged his genuine service. I learned that little gifts of kindness can bring joy to the giver and encouragement to the receiver.

KINDNESS COUNTS

My wife works at a small, but high-end women's clothing store in the inventory area. She takes in new sweaters, dresses, coats, etc. and enters all that information into the computer...then makes tickets for each item. It's a lot of work, but she really does enjoy it.

Her boss and owner is a single woman in her eighties, who is a very generous type of believer. Over the years she's been very active in church women's groups and workshops, and contributes locally to the Buffalo Philharmonic Orchestra concerts. In response, she has season tickets given to her, and the seating is right up front and quite expense to purchase separately. Occasionally, she'll give out those tickets to a friend, a relative or to someone who just enjoys the symphony.

Now, on that basis alone...just giving to support the orchestra... that's a good thing. But, as one of those people who frequently receives those tickets, I am really grateful for her thoughtfulness and compassion, for my wife and I couldn't have afforded to attend those concerts over the years so regularly. And, to show my appreciation, I'll drop off a small gift of chocolates for her to enjoy in appreciation for thinking of us (she says she's on doctor's orders to cut down on the sweets, but I've heard that those chocolates disappear quickly!)

I can think of another little kindness that someone at our church did for us over the years, when I served as Assistant Pastor. I was primarily in charge of the youth ministry, and two of the older college-age kids under my care worked part-time at their father's custard stand in town. At that time, it was a small, roast beef sandwich and custard restaurant, which was very popular.

At Christmas time, the owner also sold Christmas trees during the holiday season on the business lot. Every Christmas, while I served at the church, they would bring us a large, freshly cut tree for our home to decorate. No one asked them to do it, they just thought it would be a good idea...a little thing...to give to their youth pastor in appreciation for the work he was doing with the kids. Kathy and I really did appreciate it, and it made the holiday extra enjoyable.

Please remember, it doesn't take a lot of money to think of showing love to someone else in a meaningful way. Those who are willing to do so will experience a special joy in return, knowing they were used by the Lord to bless another person.

A GIFT OF FORGIVENESS

The "Merchant of Venice" was one of Shakespeare's brilliant works. According to the wicked Shylock character, if Antonio defaults on a loan, he will have to give Shylock a "pound of flesh."

> *"Antonio agrees to Shylock's brutal terms, although he knows that the usurer despises him. But while Antonio is ultimately forced to default, and while Shylock refuses the merchant's pleas for mercy, the usurer is foiled in the end. Dressed as an eminent judge, Antonio's indirect beneficiary Portia takes Shylock's insistence on the letter of the bond to its absurd conclusion. The bond specified only a pound of flesh, she maintains, but "no jot of blood." Shylock may be demonic but he can't perform miracles; Portia's clever piece of legal hairsplitting carries the day."*
> (https://www.enotes.com/shakespeare-quotes/pound-flesh)

I am reminded of the time some pharisees were berating an adulterous woman in front of Jesus. After hearing their complaints and condemnations, he responded to their attempts to entrap him at her expense."

> *"Let him who is without sin among you be the first to throw a stone at her." And once more he bent down and wrote on the ground. But when they heard it, they went away one by one, beginning with the older ones, and Jesus was left alone with the woman standing before him. Jesus stood up and said to her, "Woman, where are they? Has no one condemned you?" She said, "No one, Lord." And Jesus said, "Neither do I condemn you; go, and from now on sin no more."* (John 8:3-11)

It is wonderful to offer mercy, rather than viciously demand justice. Thank the Lord that in Jesus Christ we have opportunity to experience God's compassion and forgiveness. Perhaps, if believers themselves were more gracious in the way they act toward the passing sins of others, those folks might be more receptive to Christ's Gospel. Justice is real and part of the nature of the world and of its Creator, but little acts of mercy can be profound in their affect upon relationships.

PAY THEIR TOLL

The other day my wife and I were returning from a brief two-day vacation. We waited in line at the toll booth for one car ahead of us that seemed to be taking unnecessary time (perhaps, I surmised, he might be asking for directions). Finally, we moved forward and reached out my hand with the toll money.

"Keep going," said the attendant, "the person in front of you just paid your toll for you." I looked at her totally dumbfounded.

"What?" I responded.

"That's right. He just paid me the $2 toll for you, too. So…keep moving." I found it hard to believe, but I withdrew my money and pulled ahead.

I used to think that it would be great to have a lot of money to help others in big ways, and I'm sure there are wealthy individuals that enjoy that opportunity. But I've found that the little things in which you help people are just as appreciated, like paying a toll for someone. There are many other ways to do this, like offering to make up the difference at a grocery counter when the person in front of you embarrassingly comes up a few dollars short. Or, paying the bill for a friend at lunch, not because he or she expects it, but just because you enjoy showing appreciation for their friendship.

The essence of this whole idea above is that there are times when something is owed, but someone else intercedes to pay, not because he or she has to do it, but because they just want to help out. It's amazing the respect people have for a person who will compassionately step in to offer assistance.

One of the greatest examples of this was something that happen to me years ago, when I was newly married. My wife had worked through college as a part-time governess for a wealthy family living along the shore line in Manchester, Massachusetts. She and I got to know this family very well, often enjoying dinner with them and sometimes just hanging around or going boating with them.

Once both of us finished college nearby, we secured a small apartment in the area, and I set my goal on entering Seminary in the fall. However, expenses for just living, let alone paying for grad school, made it very difficult to plan, but we just trusted that God would bless us.

One night I got a call from "Mrs. Salty," as we liked to call her. She said, "Ed, I just can't sleep, knowing you and Kathy are struggling to get enough money for you to go to seminary this fall. So...now, don't say no...I'm going to pay your way through seminary. Just send me the bills along the way." (I didn't say no!)

To me, that was, of course, far more than a "little thing." But, the idea of wanting to help someone out like that remains a strong model of loving kindness. For her and her husband, it was financially speaking a "little thing," though it wasn't for me. But, for them to think of us and "lose sleep over it," told me that they cared a lot for us. We had become sort of their extended family, for which we've thanked both them and the Lord many times through the years. Whether something is done in a small or larger way, the thought, if genuine, is something special and models the love of God in Christ.

BE WILLING TO LOSE

It was the same argument, just a different occasion. My wife and I had a sharp difference of opinion over something, the specifics of which doesn't matter. My point is that this issue constantly raised its head in our lives from time to time, but we'd never resolved it...just continued to fight over it as to who was right.

I tried a different tactic after a while and decided to just let the discussion end *before it started up again* by suggesting something like this: "Well, I don't see it, but...perhaps you're right." I couldn't believe the sudden rush of silence! Neither of us had reason to continue, for there was no further disagreement to discuss. We both accepted the possibility of being right or wrong, without having to prove either on the spot. In other words, we agreed to disagree!

Paul and Barnabas had a strong disagreement over taking Mark along with them on their missionary journey. Mark had cut out half way along in another evangelistic trip, so the Apostle Paul wanting nothing to do with him. Barnabas was Mark's relative, so he apparently had more compassion and hope for him. They disagreed so much while sitting in Jerusalem and planning their trip, that they could only resolve the issue by Paul agreeing to take Silas and for Barnabas to take Mark.

The point to all this, is that both Paul and Barnabas had to "lose" somewhat, committed somewhat to a constructive, Spirit-led compromise in order to still carry on the Lord's ministry. Was there an actual right or wrong to the specific issue? Probably, but we'll never really know. The best we can garner from it is that Paul must have heard about Mark's increased maturity in Christ and good ministry results later on, for he did ask him to join in on another ministry event.

Opinions are fine to have and to share in situations of relational importance and ministry choices. But differences will most always occur…big or small…and people just have to be willing to lose a little, if they are to gain anything more than a pat on the back for being "right."

In marriage, particularly, couples easily slip apart gradually when continually fighting over differences of opinion and how to handle important issues. Fortunately, as far as marriage is concerned, the Bible is quite clear that the man is the one with final authority in the family decision making. However, that being said, he should be wise enough to consider all other opinions and feelings existing in the family, when making major decisions. Even so, this doesn't mean that the wife or husband will adhere to this standard at all, frankly, especially in today's feminist atmosphere and anti-biblical thinking so prevalent even in the church. Regardless, being willing to at least suggest, "Okay, I could be wrong" on occasion, can go a long way to restoring relationships in the home. It's just a little thing to do, but when done genuinely, it can bring healing and hope to fractured families.

I should also say that this is a good way of achieving positive results in relational difficulties. Eventually, like Paul and Barnabas, a decision has to be made, one way or the other, of course. And, a fair amount of seriously logical, firmly held and loudly spoken persuasion is probably necessary...that's life. However, for believers, keep in mind that head-strong opinions are sometimes born of ego-driven personalities, which is not a good thing to parade around work, church, and other types of environments. Be willing to listen, be open for discussion and have a humility to be corrected, if necessary. This makes for a far better family, church and life impacting attitude.

The Apostle Paul no doubt was a strong leader, powerful in his logic, and thoroughly committed to doing the right thing in all situations. But he was clear in his letter to the Ephesians that we should always, "speak the truth in love" (Eph. 4:15). Often, I've found, it's not a dominating defense, but a soft persuasion that can "win the day."

GO THE EXTRA MILE

Have you ever noticed the types of brand foods often put into the food pantries at church to help the poor or financially struggling? Rarely, it seems, are the major and quality brands there. I don't think that it's an evil thing to give cheaper brands necessarily. But I do think that stepping up to a quality brand, when you give something away, shows a higher sense of care on the givers part. Otherwise, those that ultimately receive the food gift can't help but recognize, subtly of course, that they are less valued..."not quite *worth* the cost of a higher quality gift." How about trying to go the extra mile and spend the extra 25 cents to let people have what you would ordinarily buy for your family. It's good to, "Do unto others as you would have them do unto you."

Here's another suggestion. Go out of your way on occasion to pick someone up more than once for church. My friend, Dave, brought a person we knew (we'll call him Ted) to church every week for quite a while, because he was suffering sight degeneration from a diabetes related issue. He couldn't drive to church any longer, but Dave offered to help him out. On occasion, his friend

Ted could be a little demanding and insensitive to Dave's schedule, frankly, but Dave remained faithful to what he felt God wanted him to do. The extra mile can sometimes be annoying, can't it, but unless we're just "door mats" (such enabling isn't good either), we should try following Jesus' example.

INVEST SOME TIME

The world we live in today has become a very busy one, no question about it. Our business demands more hours just to keep ahead of the driving competition, and because of this, management expects us to put in extra hours for the same pay. If you have kids, you also know how much parents have become "sports chauffeurs," transporting them to practices and games. Transportation issues are even more difficult today, because our kids might be on a "travelling team" that plays against regional schools much farther away. Then, there's all the ministries being offered at church, some with which you or I may be personally involved teaching or helping out.

So, we're busy...understood and accepted. However, you may have a child or grandchild that needs some special love. Are you willing to let the basketball team take 2nd place and meet that need is some helpful way? Perhaps your children are great in sports ... wonderful. But perhaps they don't know much about the love of God or about how to deal with their spiritual struggles. You may recognize it, even pray about it, and perhaps talk with them about things occasionally. But, are you willing open up your schedule to do even a little something with them relationally, that could make an eternal difference in their lives? What a shame it is to have discipled others at church, but to have left your own kids to the world, because you're "too busy" to spend time cultivating a loving and more intimate relationships.

Here's a quick list of additional suggestions:
Offer to pray
Sometimes, just the thought of someone willing to pray – a little thing – can bring great encouragement to a struggling soul.

Overlook an Offense
It's a good thing to overlook a disagreement, a hastily misspoken word, an unkind criticism, a subtle rejection…whatever. It's a measure of mercy and grace that goes a long way. Christ has done so much more for us…can't we give just a little of it away?

Text or Send an Email
In today's fast-paced world, people appreciate a quick update on what's happening, and keeping in communication shows you care. You don't have to be a Twitter or Facebook guru, but it can be an encouraging tool.

Share a verse
"Was just thinking of you and what you're going through. Came across this verse…hope it helps!"

Help out
For an elderly, disabled or incapacitated person, offering to paint the steps, cut the lawn, walk the dog, change the car's brake pads, fix the faucet, etc. can be a big deal, even though it's just a little thing for us.

Touch
Touch isn't a bad thing, though obviously it can be overdone or abused. But, put your arm around your kids once in a while and tell them that you love them. If you're shaking right hands with someone you want to communicate genuine care, put your other hand on their arm as well. It'll mean more to them.

Stop and visit

Ultimately, people need people, and the more intimacy we include helps out more than just the text or the email, or even when saying, "How's things going?" as you pass by them at church.

CONVICTION #15

I Believe In Using Time Well

"Therefore, my dear brothers and sisters, stand firm. Let nothing move you. Always give yourselves fully to the work of the Lord, because you know that your labor in the Lord is not in vain." I Cor. 15:58

What Have We Done With God's Gift of Life?

One of the wonderful things of being a Christian is knowing that our guilt has been done away with at Calvary's cross. The judgment for our personal sinfulness has been adjudicated in the court of God, and Christ's atoning sacrifice has washed it away…what a Savior!

However, though no longer eternally accountable for our sinful attitudes and activities, we will still stand before Christ and answer to him for what we've done for the Gospel and for him. There will be no eternal penalty for sin, but there will be an accounting of our lives, which will determine the amount of rewards we will receive. Apparently, our future place in heaven will also somehow be affected by the results of that judgment seat of Christ. Hence, the question of great importance is, "What have we done with God's gift of life?" Again, it's not about trusting or not trusting Christ as Savior. It's about how have we lived out this new life in the Spirit once we were saved. Let's look at this in four strategic categories:

- What have we done with our time?
- What have we done with our spiritual gifts?
- What have we done with our work situations?
- What have we done with our family relationships?

WHAT HAVE WE DONE WITH OUR TIME?

I used to deliver time management workshops both to area businesses as well as to high schools (The High School program was called Character Coach). Those in adult businesses had some ability to manage their time, but the teenagers had no clue in most cases. That was essentially true, because the teenagers generally used the easy way of managing their activities (called "shooting from the hip.") For them, managing time simply meant getting to one class from another on schedule, when the next test was coming, or remembering when a paper in English class was due. Pretty easy stuff. However, those seniors getting ready for college found the presentation very helpful, knowing what lay ahead for them.

I believe that time management should have a different slant and degree of importance, when looking at spiritual things. From God's point, time management is *more than* correctly handling a schedule, for we need to be seriously concerned with **what we do in our schedules** that counts with him. Listen to the Apostle Paul as he instructs the believers at Colossae:

> *"And whatever you do, whether in word or deed, do it all in the name of the Lord Jesus, giving thanks to God the Father through him."* (Colossians 3:17)

Time management for the believer, then, contains ***significant responsibility***. We are to be cognizant of what we do with the minutes, hours, days, weeks and years of our life. Paul stipulates this clearly in II Corinthians 5:10:

> *"For we must all appear before the judgment seat of Christ, so that each of us may receive what is due us for the things done while in the body, whether good or bad."*

So, as believers who love God and seriously want to please him, we must look at our schedules from this spiritual point of view and ask again, "What have we done with our time?

- Has our time been too occupied with non-essential concerns/pleasures?

- Have we carved out a necessary and revitalizing time of daily devotions for ourselves that enables us to faithfully do what God's called us to do?

- Has our time been frequently overstuffed with entertainment and relaxation activities like television, golf, shows, social events or hobbies?

- Is there a proper balance of spiritual commitment to church ministry, evangelistic endeavors, and personal witness in the workplace?

- Have we really made a significant effort in our families to encourage their spiritual growth and well-being?

- If we're young in age, do we realize the present and future rewards of putting God first in all we do? ...and the spiritual liability for *not* doing so?

- If we're older and looking back, are we happy with how we've filled our time, or are we embarrassed, perhaps even ashamed of our lack of spiritual productivity.

I'm not trying to give us a "guilt trip," which some like to do, but I do believe all of us can certainly carve out more time for God and his agenda here on earth. In this light, I'm thinking of a friend of mine at church, whose name is Al, a Thoracic surgeon working out of a local hospital. It's truly amazing to review his schedule on an average day, which begins sometime around six in the morning, the time he usually schedules his first surgery of the day. After that, he's making the rounds at the hospital to visit patients, then back at the office to do administrative things. In the afternoon, he meets with new patients, schedules new surgeries, and does additional hospital visits. At the end of the day, one finds Al at a Tuesday Elders meeting at church, attending a weekly Bible Study, or preparing a sermon for occasional pulpit supply needs in area churches. On weekends, he's usually to be found teaching a Sunday School class or attending the worship service... of course that's after his Sunday AM visiting of hospital patients. I should mention that he regularly travels as well to yearly physician conferences in order to properly keep up with new advances in technology that frequently occur, and for which his certification demands. As for me, *I'm tired just thinking about his schedule!*

The amazing thing in all this is that even beyond all the professional and ministry assignments he performs regularly, I can't think of anyone who so consistently shares his faith with others in his day-to-day work environment. Many people have come to the Lord because he took the time to share the salvation message with them at the hospital...both patients and other medical personnel. Truly, God has used well this spiritually enthusiastic and "available" man for kingdom priorities through the years. What a pleasure to know him, as he continues to be as active in Christ's work as he always has been, even at the age of *83!*

WHAT HAVE WE DONE WITH OUR SPIRITUAL GIFTS?

"...it will be like a man going on a journey, who called his servants and entrusted his wealth to them. To one he gave five bags of gold, to another two bags, and to another one bag, each according to his ability. Then he went on his journey. The man who had

received five bags of gold went at once and put his money to work and gained five bags more. So also, the one with two bags of gold gained two more. But the man who had received one bag went off, dug a hole in the ground and hid his master's money. After a long time, the master of those servants returned and settled accounts with them. The man who had received five bags of gold brought the other five. 'Master,' he said, 'you entrusted me with five bags of gold. See, I have gained five more.' "His master replied, 'Well done, good and faithful servant! You have been faithful with a few things; I will put you in charge of many things. Come and share your master's happiness!'

Then the man who had received one bag of gold came. 'Master,' he said, 'I knew that you are a hard man, harvesting where you have not sown and gathering where you have not scattered seed. So I was afraid and went out and hid your gold in the ground. See, here is what belongs to you.'

"His master replied, 'You wicked, lazy servant! So you knew that I harvest where I have not sown and gather where I have not scattered seed? Well then, you should have put my money on deposit with the bankers, so that when I returned, I would have received it back with interest. So, take the bag of gold from him and give it to the one who has ten bags. For whoever has will be given more, and they will have an abundance. Whoever does not have, even what they have will be taken from them. And throw that worthless servant outside into the darkness, where there will be weeping and gnashing of teeth.'

Christ continually referred to believers as working in his kingdom garden, performing the daily responsibilities of sowing new seeds, weeding, and cultivating the ground so that a productive spiritual crop can be harvested in due time. To do this, God has equipped each of us – that's each of us - with specific spiritual gifting to do the job well. There are teachers, encouragers, evangelists, elders, deacons, musicians, administrators, counselors, etc., each one employing God's given strengths and enablements as He has determined. Now, that's fairly simple and obvious Biblical truth. But, the personal question inherent in all this is:

"What have we done with our spiritual gifts? Have we used them wisely and faithfully in kingdom work, or have we selfishly kept them collecting dust in the spiritual closets of our lives?"

In the example at the beginning of the chapter, the one worker lost out, for he was too afraid and too lazy to be productive, while the other used his talent to bring a good return to his master. Unfortunately, in spiritual matters, many of us will find ourselves embarrassed before the Lord at judgment day, because we shirked our responsibilities to energetically employ our time (above) and our talents (spiritual gifts). All of us should be busily ministering to both the "least and the lost," as one teacher has described it, as well as to the "found but floundering!"

Yes, each of us needs also to be pruned and cultivated as well. Unfortunately, we often find ourselves too much of a struggler ourselves to be much help to someone else (which can sometimes be just an excuse, right?). I've found, however, that as we become involved in meeting the needs of others, we are also encouraged and enlarging our own spiritual garden. Remember, even broken and stressed vessels can carry some water to a thirsty soul. God doesn't need or wait for perfect water carriers, just available and focused people ready to meet the needs of a stumbling brother or sister in Christ.

A good example of this is a lady from church I knew, who was hospital bound and suffering from the later stages of Lupus. The disease gave her a lot of pain and kept her in bed, with plenty of "reason" to complain and avoid people and their problems. However, those that visited her found her kind, positive and always concerned about others. Her faith in the sovereign will of God remained strong up until the day of her death. When visiting her, folks would often leave feeling that *they* were the ones being ministered to!

Overall, God has given us the capacities to be used in kingdom work, and he expects us to faithfully and energetically use those capacities. Across the whole spectrum of ministries, it's not the abundance of spiritual gifts that often falls short, it's the presence of committed believers that's lacking.

Involvement in personal lay ministry, frankly, is so exciting, I find it difficult to imagine folks not stepping up to the plate and serving the Lord more than they do. If you don't know for sure what your spiritual gifts are, ask your pastor to help you. There's plenty of tests out there in church leadership situations that can help you assess those gifts and give you some additional confidence to get started in some area of needed ministry.

Those involved regularly in ministry know the joy of helping others and reaching out to them for Christ. Not every ministry is sharing the Gospel, nor is every service a glorious, people-moving, life changing program! But, everyone's involvement at all levels of ministry is necessary, and God will bless those faithfully committed on a regular basis. Paul reminds us of the following:

> *"Therefore, my beloved brothers, be steadfast, immovable, always abounding in the work of the Lord, knowing that in the Lord your labor is not in vain."* (I Cor. 15:58)

WHAT HAVE WE DONE WITH OUR WORK SITUATIONS?

Where do we spend most of our time? Usually, the answer to that question is at our job, if we simply look at it from a daily context. We're up no later than 7 o'clock in the morning getting ready, then travelling to arrive at work at 8 am. For the next 8 hours we're busy communicating, socializing and thinking about a bunch of people that we don't live with and probably aren't people we would call friends...though we strive to get along with them all, of course. We get back home say around 5:30 pm, say "Hi" to our spouse, and promptly settle into some more comfortable clothes to enjoy dinner. Of course, that's if there is no one to take to the football game at school, to cheer leading practice, or to some other pressing event. In addition, instead of cooking, we might need to stop off at Kentucky Fried Chicken for a fast-food dinner. Many Americans eat such quick suppers simply because parents and kids are just going in too many different directions. Of course, throw in a couple of youth programs at church, a mid-week service or a Bible Study, and you have a crazy mixture of time pressure and strained relationships. My point is that, when it's all said and done, the job is the major "normalcy" of relationships all through the week.

Okay, that being the case, we've all had enough personal experience with this type of thing to know that work easily takes our minds off our Christian focus. We're so involved that we usually don't have much of an inclination to share our faith with someone at work. Yet, as opportunity arises that's just what we *should be doing*, as long as the work environment and policy is not antagonistic to it. God has placed you and I in our work situations – like any other life situation - to be a light for the Gospel in both *character* and in *word of mouth*, as opportunity presents itself.

I'm usually on the road delivering workshops and seminars in various parts of the country to large groups of people. However, I do try and share as I have opportunity, but, as I say, those opportunities are not frequently there. I do remember an opportunity near home, where after several times of sharing my faith with a salesmen friend of mine, I asked him if he wanted to settle things with the Lord and invite Christ into his life. He was quite enthusiastic about it, so I invited him to meet me a church, where we could take the time to pray (not that we had to go there, of course). It was a quiet morning and no one was at the church other than the secretary, so we went into the auditorium and kneeled at the altar. He prayed the prayer of salvation, and in the weeks following this I was able to disciple him and answer his ongoing questions. Over the years I've lost tract of him, but my point is that in that instance I was available and looking to share my faith in the context of work. It was a great experience for me, and I thank the Lord for his kindness in using me.

That brings up an important caution, which is to avoid becoming a nuisance by badgering co-workers regarding spiritual issues. If the policy discourages such sharing on the job itself, then respect it. Disrespecting and abusing it only gives one a reputation of someone "hard-to-get-along-with," perhaps arrogant or fanatical, someone with whom one should avoid conversations. In other's minds, such a person becomes just another "religious nutcase," instead of someone to respect and admire, whose personal faith is attractive, considerate, even admirable. Certainly, there will be folks that can't stand us at all simply because of our faith, but let's not invite their distain or add to it by rude and stubborn attitudes and/or behaviors. Look for those times that are more acceptable for raising a spiritual topic to a co-worker, for work is primarily a place to...well...*to work!* Remember, when the Bible says that "they'll know us by our love," it's assuming we're modeling I Corinthians, chapter thirteen, where genuine love is described as being "patient and kind."

I knew someone at my church who got in trouble for always trying to share the Gospel at work. His co-workers tried to shun him as much as they could, and the supervisors reprimanded him several times. Finally, the time came for him to be released from his job for his actions, but his stubborn attitude remained. He was convinced that he was doing God's will by sharing the Gospel anytime he chose to do so. What a shame, actually, that the very people he could have won to the Lord were those who really didn't reject God's good news, *they rejected him!*

> *"And the Lord's servant must not be quarrelsome but kind to everyone, able to teach, patiently enduring evil, correcting his opponents with gentleness. God may perhaps grant them repentance leading to a knowledge of the truth..."*
> (II Timothy 2:24-25 ESV)

WHAT HAVE WE DONE WITH OUR FAMILY SITUATIONS?

This is a tough one to deal with, for our emotions and love for our family runs deep in all of us. But the truth is that most of us have some regrets for the way we've failed to be all we should have been in our families for Christ. Again, I'm not interested in fostering a guilt trip, but I would like to probe carefully and compassionately what we've done or failed to do with the life God has given us regarding family responsibilities.

Family life involves choices already made and new choices to continue making. So, I made a choice to marry my wife, Kathy, and what I have chosen to do in the past with that choice has had significant ramifications. Any husband or wife has made thousands of decisions regarding their spouse and children, and each has influenced family life for the good or the bad. When Christ interviews us at his judgment seat, he will probably ask a husband or wife the following type of questions.

Question: *Do you love your spouse & family as I have loved the church?*
Jesus: *"I've always exercised kindness and forgiveness in both attitude and speech, even when justice demands some sort of reckoning or discipline. I don't explode in anger, harm anyone or show uncontrolled or revengeful rage in my dealings with my precious church. Instead, I speak the truth in firm but loving correction, never trying to crush anyone or intentionally distancing anyone from my mercy and healing grace…and I expected you to do the same. Did you?"*

Question: *Do you spend significant time with your family members?*
Jesus: *"I exercise continual relationship with my spiritual family, which is my church. I help each believer to understand who I am and what is required of them in order to maintain a blessed and intimate relationship with me. I am constantly talking with them through my Scriptures, through the church body, and through my indwelling Spirit. In this way, I assure them of my deeply personal love toward them, my unswerving compassion for their lives and my sovereign presence, which is always available to assist them in their spiritual and life needs. Did you model this in your family?"*

Notice first that **both** questions demand an explanation that has ramifications in how we spent our time. The first question is a **qualitative** one, which asks for details in what we've said to our family members and the way we've communicated with them.

That's, of course, extremely important for developing harmony, meaningful, and positive relationships.

However, the second question deals more in the realm of **quantity** and is equally important. I played golf with someone the other day, who got into a discussion about fathers, and how they should discipline and handle their kids. My heart was touched when he shared that his father didn't really spend any meaningful time with him, he tended to be distant and aloof. He was a strict disciplinarian, so the five boys in the family had to get their fill of love from mom.

Well, I hope you'll use this chapter as just a starting point to begin a practical and responsible approach to exercising Christ's love toward others. Small things do matter to the Lord, and he greatly appreciates our commitment to do so.

CONVICTION #16

I Believe In God's Favor

"...I count all things to be loss in view of the surpassing value of knowing Christ Jesus my Lord, for whom I have suffered the loss of all things, and count them but rubbish so that I may gain Christ."
Phil. 3:8

At the end of the movie, "Indiana Jones and the Lost Crusade," two groups of people are gathered in an ancient cave carved out of mountainous rock, where an immortal knight of the Crusades guards the chalice Christ drank from at the Last Supper with his disciples. The "good guys," Indiana and his friends, are trying to rescue it from the Nazi powers, whose leader wanted it because of its power to give eternal life. The "bad guys," however, overpowered the knight and Indiana's followers, then tried to take it across a

203

carved seal on the floor of the cave, which was forbidden by God to cross. Suddenly, an earthquake parted the floor of the cave and the divine goblet dropped down to a ledge a few feet into the splitting ground. The Nazi commander hangs over the edge in a last-ditch effort to reach into the gaping hole and save the precious cup. Rocks are falling and the ground is moving, but as she reaches into the widening gap, she herself slips over the edge. Indiana manages to rescue her by grabbing onto her extended hand, but he himself is stretched over the cavernous split in the ground. Hanging over the dark bottomless crevice and saved only by Indiana's outstretched grasp, she continues to reach out with her other hand for the cup, now precariously caught on a small ledge nearby. He yells at her to stop reaching, and grab onto his hand with both hands, otherwise his loosening grip will send her to unavoidable death. But, her lust for the cup weakens her grip, and she slips away screaming into the darkness below. Eventually, the good guys leave the knight to his ongoing task, escape the earthquake and leave without the chalice, but save their lives for another Hollywood quest.

The movie is fantasy, of course, and not without the typical Hollywood excesses, but it does allow for a terrific point to be made. The world is often reaching out desperately for eternal life in ways that will only bring about spiritual death and loss of life itself. That's because people are reaching for something totally beyond their grasp, thus assuring themselves of an inescapable plunge into eternal darkness.

On the other hand, those that acknowledge God's existence and set their faith upon His Son, Jesus Christ, will gain eternal life. But they will also gain a more satisfying life this side of heaven, as well, and that makes the Gospel truly "*good news!*" Salvation brings us into relationship with God, but it also provides us with the *blessing* of God...his mercy, grace, love, and blessing.

Blessing means "benefit or favor." To be a believer means great benefits, even though the average non-believer thinks that a Christian gives up everything and can't really enjoy life. The truth is, of course, that he or she still experiences most of what a non-Christian might experience, but experiences it within the will of God.

God established that there are boundaries within which all of us must stay. Staying within the boundaries will bring us God's favor in what we do, while moving outside of those boundaries brings significant loss of blessing. Without the favor of God, we benefit little or nothing from what he wants for us. We are instead just stuck, trying to satisfy life's pursuits on our own and apart from the purposes and provision of Almighty God. That's like taking your vacation this year on foot, instead of by car, train or plane. As you plod along, you keep working hard to enjoy yourself, but in point of fact, you're really not going very far or enjoying what's available, for you decided instead to live life *your way* instead of *God's way!*

So, let's explore this wonderful F.A.V.O.R. of God that all believers now share. It's theirs to enjoy, even though many lose some of it unnecessarily.

Favor and Forgiveness

Believers are forgiven and, therefore, freed from the penalty of personal guilt they own because of their sinfulness. The non-believer has no such relief from his/her guilt. He or she lives in a world that is often oblivious to the fact that one day people will be accountable to God for their sinful attitudes, choices and behaviors.

Forgiveness, however, is more than that which deals with only our original guilt and separation from God. The *believer* has a precious and permanent place of forgiveness made especially for him or her in Christ. Heb. 4:16 informs us that we can *"...approach God's throne of grace with confidence, so that we may receive mercy and find grace to help us in our time of need."* Wow...how blessed we are!

This precious place is **confession**, for God never rejects those who come before him in humility and seek his forgiveness.

"My sacrifice, O God, is a broken spirit; a broken and contrite heart you, God, will not despise."
(Ps. 51:17)

Even a king like David found restoring favor from God. This was after a real bad year in which he lusted after a woman by the name of Bathsheba, had an affair with her, murdered her husband, lost the child of that affair, and had his future kingship and family suffer significantly because of his sin. Again...even he found mercy and grace. God could have killed him on the spot, taken his entire family in judgment, let Israel suffer unrepairable defeat or, well, you fill in the blanks, for it was a terrible series of sinful choices David gave in to. But he confessed his sin to the prophet Nathan and humbled himself before God.

"Have mercy on me, O God,
according to your unfailing love;
according to your great compassion
blot out my transgressions.
Wash away all my iniquity
and cleanse me from my sin."
(Ps. 51:1-2)

I've often thought that David even could have avoided some of the judgment God pronounced upon him, if only he had confessed things quicker and not waited for God to have to step in and correct him. It reminds me of the necessity and practicality of what we sometimes refer to during communion, *"Judge yourselves lest you be judged."* Nevertheless, in Christ, we have a place to find peace from the daily failures and guilt that we sometimes wallow in...to our loss. Confession restores us to a place of favor and of intimacy in our relationship with God. Truly, what a blessing it is to return as often as necessary to that place of peaceful renewal and gracious restoration.

Favor and Blessing

My wife, Kathy, and I went to the mall today with one of our grandchildren in order to find out what type of Christmas presents she might like (she's 13). We do this with all the kids, and they enjoy it immensely. However, on this day, my granddaughter came into the car with an attitude, and remained that way for most of our trip to the mall. She just mumbled answers, kept walking ahead and away from us, and didn't participate in much conversation at all. I asked Kathy why she was allowing this to go on, and she replied that she did so, because this was one of the few times she could take this particular granddaughter shopping before Christmas. Apparently, she was "pouting" because Kathy wouldn't allow her to take a friend along (she's normally a lot of fun to take out).

It was kind of funny, frankly, because along the way my granddaughter dropped a few hints about being taken out to dinner. My wife and I knew that her persistent attitude issues, if not corrected, meant losing such "Grandparent benefits" normally given to her. She lost out today, but hopefully she'll recognize the "rightness" of our decision, and we'll being eating out together some time soon.

But, here's the thing about physical and material blessings... they're often tied to works. Not always, of course, but often we are blessed because God asks us to do something, and we simply please him by doing it. Listen to James' thinking on the subject:

> *"Do not merely listen to the word, and so deceive yourselves. Do what it says. Anyone who listens to the word but does not do what it says is like someone who looks at his face in a mirror and, after looking at himself, goes away and immediately forgets what he looks like. But whoever looks intently into the perfect law that gives freedom, and continues in it—not forgetting what they have heard, but doing it—they will be blessed in what they do."* (James 1:22-25)

So, being in favor with God can be a wonderfully enjoyable thing, as he watches over our needs and provides for us economically and materialistically. It's his good desire to do that, for I don't think he finds pleasure in keeping his saints in a constant struggle for survival. Yes, there are times of difficulty and stress this side of heaven, and God uses such times well for chastisement, correction and character building. But, let's not make the absence or struggle for such things the norm, folks, for Jesus said:

> *"If you, then, though you are evil, know how to give good gifts to your children, how much more will your Father in heaven give good gifts to those who ask him"*

> *"So do not worry, saying, 'What shall we eat?' or 'What shall we drink?' or 'What shall we wear?' For the pagans run after all these things, and your heavenly Father knows that you need them. But seek first his kingdom and his righteousness, and all these things will be given to you as well." (Matt. 6:31-33; 7:11)*

Favor and Victory

There are four challenges in life that we could rightly address in the context of "spiritual warfare." I believe we are regularly waging war on the front lines in four battle zones, which are the following (I've mentioned them before):

- Dealing successfully with our own, personal responsibilities for Christ.

- Dealing successfully with our family responsibilities for Christ.

- Dealing successfully with our work responsibilities for Christ.

- Dealing successfully with our church responsibilities for Christ.

All other more specific areas can be folded into these four, things like relationships, friendships, habits, entertainments, communication, etc. So, let's briefly review how we should maneuver around in these critical areas of responsibility. God gives victory in these areas to those who seek him with consistency and faithfulness.

Personal Responsibilities

"No one can serve two masters. Either you will hate the one and love the other, or you will be devoted to the one and despise the other. You cannot serve both God and money."
(Matt. 6:25)

Jesus is saying above that each of us has the personal, moral responsibility of following God's will, or we will suffer the consequences inherent in disobedience. For believers, this doesn't mean eternal death, but it does mean a loss of God's favor to some degree.

Here's an example. Pete was a person in a men's Sunday school class I had years ago (not his real name). One day he shared how he was struggling with lust and occasional indulgence with porn. He was single, had a decent job, but was pretty much of a loner. He truly wanted to find a gal to marry, but God didn't seem to be answering his prayer. We continued to pray for him and for each other in the months ahead.

Sometime later, he came to class and confessed that he had thrown away all of his pornographic videos he had acquired through the years into a pile and lite it up with a match (it was quite a bonfire, I remember him saying). We all were exceedingly happy for him, of course, and encouraged him to stay on the straight and narrow. It wasn't too long after this event that he "coincidently" attended a singles ministry at another church, met a girl he really liked, and later on married her. Now, that's the blessing of God manifested in one who is willing to do things God's way and wait for his blessing.

Victory over sin is not an easy thing to acquire, and to some degree, all of us will struggle with it at times in certain areas of weakness. God wants us to bring all of our lives into a circle of consistent obedience. The degree to which we block the Spirit's control over our lives in any given area, means we will experience some sense of loss regarding God's blessing.

Moral responsibility is not an option for the believer for we are called to be light and salt to a lost world, and nothing short of complete surrender and obedience is acceptable. My friend above made a decision to get his life back into the blessing of God and found what he was really searching for in life, once he decided to get serious with God's will.

Though God is merciful and gracious, he wants to bless us, I believe, so much more than we even realize, if we would only get our personal walk to align with his will. God really wants to graphically bless us, according to Ephesians 3:19-20:

> *"the love of Christ that surpasses knowledge, that you may be filled with all the fullness of God... who is able to do infinitely more than all we ask or imagine, according to his power that is at work within us."*

Family Responsibilities

We touched upon this before, but it's good to revisit it again in the context of finding God's favor. I believe that family life is a testing ground for bottom line spirituality in a believer's life. It's there that a person can really be seen for who he or she is...mature, consistent and loving...or immature, inconsistent and unloving. One can fool a lot of people in life, but the family reveals in great detail the believer's true self and spirituality. God wants to bless a family with his favor, but often the participants aren't willing to comply with God's "family rules."God's rules aren't burdensome, but necessary and uncomplicated guidelines for the generally welfare of everyone concerned.

Here's a list of questions that highlight role and relational responsibilities, which in large part assure a family of God's favor,

regardless of occasional seasons of financial struggle, loss, job change, etc.
- Are both the husband and wife spiritually focused and on the same general path, when it comes to faith, obedience, and spirituality?
- Is the husband's role one of final authority...not making every decision, of course, but realizing that he is *ultimately* responsible for his family's direction?
- Is the wife supportive of his decision-making authority in the family?
- Is the husband aware that without spiritual consistency, his wife will lose respect for his family position and probably resist supporting him?
- Does the wife realize that without spiritual consistency and support for her husband, his love and attraction to her will tend to wane?
- Does the husband realize that he is the one primarily called to provide income and security for his family, not his wife?
- Does the wife realize that her main responsibility in the family, regardless of her work, is to be there as a loving nurturer to them, as well as a supportive and suitable helper to him?
- Do both the husband and the wife recognize that discipline can be exercised by either parent, regardless of the situation at hand?
- Does the husband realize that he is a primary model for his daughter in terms of identifying for her what a loving and strong father should be?
- Does the wife realize that she is a primary model for her son in identifying for him what a godly, loving and supportive wife should be?

- Does the husband realize that Scripture clearly says that treating his wife with respect and kindness greatly affects God's blessing upon him?

- Do husbands/wives realize that roles don't need to be spiritual "strait-jackets?" There is always room for flexibility in the details of things, especially when considering partner strengths and/or weaknesses.

- Do the children, if any, understand that they are to obey their parents regardless of their own feelings or wants, unless such direction would be physically harmful to them or in direct violation of God's will?

- Is the family in regular attendance at their local church for needed spiritual teaching, counsel, fellowship and support?

- For the most part, are the family relationships full of loving attitudes, including acceptance, compassion and understanding?

- Does the family enjoy doing things together and supporting one another in relational things, for instance, such as in sports, vacations, hobbies, and in other social contexts?

In summary, I'm not suggesting that every family will be perfect and without challenge in any or all of the above areas in question. However, family blessing is affected, according to God's will, by how it falls in line with the principles found in God's Word. To be consistently in the favor and blessing of God, therefore, does demand that husband, wife and children function in harmony with the will of God as outlined in the Scriptures. When one's family life exists in antithesis to the precepts and principles of God, not only isn't such a pretty picture to behold, but it doesn't engender the favor of God either.

Professional Responsibilities

Life is not about a job or a profession. Yes, there are many professions that require great commitment in terms of training and time in order to become a success. But those that put career first in their priorities and life agenda will face the fallout from such a decision. Life for the believer must be about Jesus and our faith commitment to him above all else, as we integrate everything we do into the overarching spiritual agenda of *pleasing God first*. This would include things like use of time, family involvement, church, and the things we discussed above in our Personal and Family concerns.

Secondly, and professionally speaking, we should be pursuing a career that doesn't violate spiritual integrity or principles, whether it's marketing, manufacturing, money management, sales, retail or…whatever. There are some jobs that are simply off limits for sincere believers in which to be involved. Now, it's not a matter of the Pastor telling folks which career is acceptable or not, but we are responsible to make sound judgments and avoid "worldliness" in our decisions.

Unfortunately, the world today is becoming so blended together by megalithic corporate ownerships and control that it seems everything is tainted somehow by some sort of tie-in to greed, sex, liberalism, political correctness, etc. For example, while believers want to successfully spend time in their families and establish sound relational ties, the world's idea of success is a materialistic one. In their eyes, moving up the salary ladder is the way to monetary success, enabling one to provide substantially more material goods, including home ownership, two cars in the garage, a built-in pool in the backyard, 20 pairs of shoes in the closet and a 401K that's bursting at the seams just waiting to provide seniors with lavish vacations as soon as they retire.

Now, that' all beautiful, but it may not be…yes…*it may not be God's will for you or me*. God is **not** primarily interested in providing a smooth sailing trip through life and an easy ride into retirement for all believers. Being on the poorer end of things can be a great blessing at times, for those who are willing to let God guide them through it. There are many blessings to receive and to give by those who accept whatever calling God seems to be assigning them at the time. Such godly, humble, and satisfied attitudes aren't easy to come by, for they take strong conviction and commitment to maintain in today's world. But they do bring some hefty rewards…some in the present…but perhaps most in eternity.

Not that the principles of hard work and wise career planning are wrong or without merit…please, they're not. But, learning about patience, contentment, thrift, and economic *long-term* success can be both a temporary learning experience and/or a tremendous modeling opportunity for everyone. Of course, the world mostly sees this type of thinking through socialistic colored glasses, preaching that everyone ***deserves*** to own their own home, buy those two cars, get that wonderful wardrobe, indulge those expensive vacations and enjoy that relaxing retirement…but, such is not necessarily the case with God.

> *"And whatever you do, whether in word or deed, do it all in the name of the Lord Jesus, giving thanks to God the Father through him."* (Col. 3:17)

> *"I am not saying this out of need, for I have learned to be content regardless of my circumstances. I know how to live humbly, and I know how to abound. I am accustomed to any and every situation—to being filled and being hungry, to having plenty and having need. I can do all things through Christ who gives me strength."* (Philippians 4:11-13)

But it gets worse in this enablement driven world. Many companies *require* new employees to take initial training classes in how to accept and promote diversity, homosexuality, multi-culturalism, and other morally questionable philosophies in the workplace. Such things aren't done just to help people get along, they're often there to satisfy the militant agendas all around us that want to re-shape our culture with morally relativistic values. In my opinion, it's going to become extremely difficult for believers in the future to commit themselves to such spiritual "gobbly-gook" and stay working in the corporate setting. Christians will, therefore, continue to become marginalized and ignored in the marketplace, government and educational institutions, while diversity becomes the god of culture.

So, how should we continue to act and pursue advancement in our career paths and job situations? Knowing there will be increasing struggles to mold into life the controlling agenda of leftists and liberal thinking goals, assignments, and causes, *we should stay the course and remain true to the principles and precepts of Jesus Christ*. We should avoid personal involvement or support for questionable and compromising activities, while also realizing that we can never fine a perfect or godly employment situation. It's a difficult road to follow at times, but a necessary one.

We need to work and provide for our families, so having a sense of humility in the workplace is also commendable. Grandstanding in front of everyone with the Gospel and judging every detailed sin on the part of employers and corporations, is not the answer. Such immaturity only justifiably angers them and brings unnecessary repute upon believers and the church. Non-believing society cannot be corrected by continual condemnation for that which they are not in agreement. Yes, speaking your mind in the appropriate channels and settings is necessary and right, for we are called by the Lord to be light to a fallen world. But, let's do it with a strong sense of propriety and love that finds no joy in overzealous criticisms or diatribes of destruction. Agreeing to disagree is most often the best choice.

Church Responsibilities

This is the fourth area for discussing the favor of God. Too many folks see church involvement as a time-consuming social involvement than that which is the life blood of our faith. They'd rather sit home on Sundays and flip on the television to hear a more "professional" church service by a well-known media Pastor. This isn't the will of God nor is it healthy for individual believers. We NEED the encouragement and support of our brothers and sisters in Christ, if we are to effectively and successfully manage our spiritual responsibilities and growth.

> *"And let us consider how we may spur one another on toward love and good deeds, not giving up meeting together, as some are in the habit of doing, but encouraging one another—and all the more as you see the Day approaching."*
> (Hebrews 10:24, 25)

Notice the word "spur" in the above verse, for it sums up the role of the church in its relationships and teaching. To neglect regular fellowship as some do is to make oneself liable to unnecessary struggle and failure.

The recent covid19 "pandemic" closed down many churches for months, including ours. I jumped into a Zoom platform for my Monday Men's Study Group and found it to be fantastic. Because of my creative training background, I include many fly-ins, video inserts, musical selections, and general techniques to keep people involved and interested. I also continually involve the guys by asking key questions, reading verses, and other techniques. So, it's really been great for the group of about 15 to 20 guys who attend. However, there is still no substitute for personal, eye-to-eye, in person fellowship.

So, we desperately need one another. As the Bible instructs us above,

> *"Let us not give up meeting together..."*

CONVICTION #17

I Believe Balance Is A Virtue

"Yet to all who did receive him, to those who believed in his name, he gave the right to become children of God - children born not of natural descent, nor of human decision or a husband's will, but born of God."
John 1:12

It was another Memorial Day parade in my home town of Cheshire, Connecticut. I was 16 and riding horseback in the parade with my friend, Rich, who had a couple of beautiful Palomino horses. He lived in the rural part of town, and we would often go into the surrounding hills during the summer months, enjoying the many colorful trails that wound throughout the area. This day, however, was a special day, for I had never before been in the parade on horseback, though I had marched in it with the High School band, the Cub Scouts and other kid-type organizations.

The parade went well. The streets were lined with vendors carrying balloons, colorful holiday trinkets and parents pushing strollers or holding hands with their excited children. Kids peddled their shiny decorated bikes up the blocked off streets, while bystanders waved all sizes of American flags in the breeze. People clapped after every band number, and the crowds waved enthusiastically. Everyone was truly enjoying this hot, sunny day's festivities.

On the way home after the parade, we stopped at a friend's house to show off the horses. Both horses stood resting side by side as we sat in the saddle and talked. Suddenly, my horse just dropped to the ground! All four of its legs just gave way, sending 1400 lbs. crashing down on the blacktop driveway. I went flying off to the side, while Richard's horse jumped out of the way.

"What in the world," I mumbled, as I rolled over on the grass next to the driveway. Just as quickly as it had fallen, the horse jumped back up upon its feet. It was extremely nervous and started to back away from us, but I rushed over and quickly grabbed the reins. Apparently, the horse got spooked over the slippery driveway, which had been recently resurfaced. In fear of losing its footing, it caused itself to stumble. The horse was fine, though a little uptight about driveways for a while, so we stayed on the grass by the roadside for the trek home.

Balance is important for more than just staying upright on a horse. Imagine a trapeze artist, a gymnast or a mountain climber without it. Similarly, I believe that balance is very important for believers in their Christian life, for without spiritual balance all kinds of issues and problems can occur. Let's look at a few areas.

GUILT AND GRACE

One of the hardest things to understand is how God's sense of justice interacts with his love. We fail to completely understand why some folks will be saved and others will not, why some believers experience swift and decisive judgment for sin, but others do not, etc. There are other examples to use, of course, but you get the picture, I think. Certainly, there's no definitive answer this side of heaven, but I want to share some thoughts that may help.

Let's imagine that Joe, a fairly new believer, has some personal issues to deal with in his new life in Christ. Perhaps he is dealing with anger toward others, failing to have patience with people when they do "stupid" things or do things without thinking them through first. This really bothers him, for his father always told him to "think before you act," which his father drilled into his mind at an early age by severely reprimanding his failures, even in the presence of others. Since becoming a Christian, Joe is struggling to be more patient and forgiving with others, but is having a difficult time doing so.

Let's also imagine a young woman, who we'll call Mary. She's quite the opposite of Joe, having been a believer for years, and she is quite patient with others and their sins or failures. She understands that Christ's death completely covers our sins, of which she had many as a younger person. She grew up in a dis-functional family and got into a lot of trouble as a teenager, with such things as shoplifting, sexual promiscuity and other rebellious types of issues. However, she went forward at a Billy Graham rally at college, and God just came in and transformed her thinking and lifestyle immediately. But she so embraced God's grace in her life, that she's really never had much problem being patient with others or giving them forgiveness, if they've offended her. Two different believers, with opposing feelings and interactions when dealing with issues of guilt verses grace.

My point is that all of us have a wide range of varying preferences and reactions to the way God measures out his judgment or his grace in handling our lives. Those that see the need for guilt to be recognized and emphasized, want the justice part of God to call down judgment, chastisement, and righteous retribution upon a person or people, who repeatedly disregards the moral expectations and laws of God. Others, who recognize and rejoice in the merciful and loving grace that God often provides for sinning believers or even non-believers, expect God to more readily overlook sin, and instead provide forgiveness.

First, when it comes to understanding and systematizing such Biblical truths, we must always strain to interpret the Scriptures accurately and in a balanced way. This is why Paul tells his young Pastor protégé, Timothy, to do the following:

> *"Do your best to present yourself to God as one approved, a worker who does not need to be*

ashamed and who correctly handles the word of truth." (II Timothy 2:15)

Secondly, when it comes down to justice verses grace, one must realize that God has a perfect blend of the two within his essential nature. In fact, when considering any part(s) of God's nature, always remember that he is never just one or the other in any characteristic. He is completely harmonious in all of his attributes and is *incapable* of being out of sorts, out of balance or unjustified in anything he does.

As good students of God's Word, therefore, we recognize the reality of each (guilt *and* grace), and wisely blend both when counseling someone or even discussing doctrinal truth. For instance, God is fully able to deal with guilt, asking for repentance, bringing necessary chastisement, or doing whatever else is appropriate within this aspect of his nature. But he is *also* fully able to provide needed mercy and grace to someone in need of encouragement, forgiveness and spiritual support (and, so should we). He will always act in perfect harmony and moral goodness when deciding which (or both) to bring into a person's life. Our omniscient God never forgets, overlooks, reconsiders or stumbles in any of his decisions toward us, but perfectly distributes and decrees his will. In the end, we should rest in the glorious and eternal reality of who he is, giving him unwavering trust for his sovereign will in our lives. His is always just *and* gracious in whatever life circumstances we face, and we must keep that in mind in whatever doctrinal differences we have.

Here's a helpful saying I've learned to accept and apply. When you have trouble integrating two seemingly opposed ideas about God, "Don't let what you don't know keep you from doing what you do know." God hasn't chosen to reveal every nook and cranny of his will into our finite doctrinal bag of answers. We couldn't contain it anyway, nor integrate it successfully, so the target for us here is to trust Him. Deut. 29:29 reminds us of this by saying:

"The secret things belong to the LORD our God, but the things that are revealed belong to us and

to our children forever, that we may do all the words of this law."

Also, when it comes to his providential oversight for our lives as believers, understand that God is always tirelessly and eternally at work...yes, in every situation and facet of our lives. Nothing takes him by surprise nor falls short of his moral goodness and majesty, for *"...we know that in all things God works for the good of those who love him, who have been called according to his purpose." (Romans 8:28)*

BIRTHING AND BUILDING

Churches today seem to be stuck on one side of the issue, leaning in their ministry agenda either toward evangelism or discipleship. Some churches, for instance...mostly the megachurches...seem to think that it's all about bringing new people into their buildings in order that one day those folks might receive the message about Christ and salvation. Their teaching is fairly shallow and non-doctrinal so as to not unnecessarily offend those non-believers in the congregation (which is usually a significant %). Other churches are not that interested in bringing non-believers into the building, though they are committed to evangelism through special outreaches, for instance. So, their teaching often strictly doctrinal, and their worship tends to be dry and traditional, aimed essentially for believers. *What should we believe about all this?*

Well, by way of example, I love dogs. Having lived in rural Connecticut in my early years, I had a Collie named Dutchess, which had three litters of pups over the years. One of those pups we kept, which we named Duke, but all the others we sold or gave away. In one of those litters, there was a one pup that came out last, and it was smaller and weaker than the others. As it tried to grab onto a nipple for nourishment, it just couldn't climb over the other 10 to 12 siblings well enough to nourish itself consistently. Unfortunately, it only lasted a few days, then it died.

By application, each of us needs to be spiritually born, which Nicodemus learned from Jesus. Churches that do not aggressively reach out to non-believers and bring the opportunity for spiritual birth to others assure themselves of one certain result...they won't grow very much.

    I provided a couple of months pulpit supply for a small, dwindling group of believers (30 - 40 attendees) in a church located in a significantly growing area of Western New York, where I lived. I was filling in while they were searching for a Pastor, so I asked them how I could also help them out in the area of outreach... perhaps some door-to-door visitation. Their response was telling, indicating that they just wanted to stay where they were and hold things together, so to speak. I must also add that it was a fairly "in-grown" church, where the head Elder...who taught from the pulpit...was married to the woman who played the organ and organized the weekly worship service, and who also was a primary leader in the Deaconesses. In other words, there were not many other voices involved in church goals or decision making (there were only 2 Elders anyway, as I remember it). I was just involved in preaching on Sundays, which I did for a while, hopefully providing some practical teaching. But, of course, I was limited to what I could say in order to avoid too much emphasis on "reaching out." They just didn't get it...outreach is a significant part of the great commission:

> *"Therefore, go and make disciples of all nations, baptizing them in the name of the Father and of the Son and of the Holy Spirit..."* (Matt. 28:19)

    HOWEVER, it is not the ***only part*** of the great commission. We are to do the following as well:

> *"...teaching them to obey everything I have commanded you. And surely I am with you always, to the very end of the age."* (Matt. 28:20)

    Birthing must also be equally and aggressively followed up with *building*. If not, the Gospel seed within us will not bear any evidential or significant fruit (see Matt. 13:1-23). In fact, without such nurturance, it will die. Nurturance is critical for new believers, and is the primary concern of the Holy Spirit in the life of the newly birthed believer in whom he has taken up residence. I Peter 2:2 tells us:

> *"Like newborn babies, crave pure spiritual milk,*
> *so that by it you may grow up in your salvation,*
> *now that you have tasted that the Lord is good."*

This balance is fairly obvious, until it comes to culture and methodology. Some folks in leadership think that the church is more of an evangelistic tent, while others see it more of a religious temple...both of which miss the point. The church's **mission** is to reach out to the world with the Gospel. It is not a gathering of exclusive, "don't come in here and spoil it" folk, who never want to have relationship outside of Sunday services. That type thinking makes for very small church bodies, small-mindedness and, frankly, prejudicial spirituality.

However...and here's the balance...*its regular fellowship should not be focused upon non-believers either!* It is *not* a weekly tent or evangelistic meeting. Believers *need* in-depth teaching and intimate spiritual relationship with other believers in order to maintain personal discipline, moral steadfastness, doctrinal maturity and godly character. This they cannot get in a "tent mentality fellowship," which has been watered down and softened to allow for non-believer's acceptance.

So, it is critical, spiritually heathy, and commanded that our church meetings and/or fellowship times are to be *mostly composed of and focused upon believers*. Otherwise, such get-togethers must of necessity become shallow in their teaching, soft in their call to godly living and dull in their discipleship training. Thus, our primary methodology is to have worship services, bible studies, classes and small groups that nurture and build up believers, once they are birthed. Of course, small groups can be easily created and focused for non-believers, thus forming good outreach opportunities...which is great, for instance. But, the main body of the church meets weekly for discipleship teaching, where it can edify the family of God, energizing itself for engaging mission opportunities outside of fellowship gatherings. Let's listen to the Apostle Paul's spiritual and practical agenda in all this:

> *"So Christ himself gave the apostles, the prophets, the evangelists, the pastors and teachers, to equip his people for works of service, so that the body of Christ **may be built up** until we all reach unity in the faith and in the knowledge of the Son of God and **become mature,** attaining to the whole measure of the **fullness of Christ.** Then we will **no longer be infants,** tossed back and forth by the waves, and blown here and there by every wind of teaching and by the cunning and craftiness of people in their deceitful scheming. Instead, speaking the truth in love, **we will grow** to become in every respect **the mature body** of him who is the head, that is, Christ. From him the whole body, joined and held together by every supporting ligament, **grows and builds itself up in love**, as each part does its work."*
> (Eph. 4:11-16)

Do you see the balance here? It's not a matter of choosing a church agenda, for there's only one agenda...a great commission established by Christ Jesus. That agenda involves the ongoing responsibilities of *both* birthing and building. This takes common sense and wisdom, of course, when thinking about structures, organization, meetings, etc. But it balances these two Scriptural mandates of "reaching and teaching," and never mixes them in some sort of cultural compromise. Paul makes this clear above, if we're serious students of God's Word. All churches should essentially have the same general venue and structure, with only *minor* differences due to perhaps culture settings, locations, and economic issues. Unfortunately, in today's world of technical and marketing gurus, common sense in all these issues has bowed to number getting.

Again, we never want in-grown, unattractive, self-serving, or doctrinally stale representations of the glorious Gospel of Jesus Christ to dominate the horizon either. So, let's have a practical balance in all this, resting firmly on the foundation of which Paul describes for us in the passage above. We can be creative, culturally sensitive and relentlessly seeking to birth spiritual babies, *while never doing this at the expense of building mature believers in the things of God.* Maintaining this critical balance will determine the quality of our fellowship and the success in evangelism all of us want to attain before the Lord.

PRAYING AND PRACTICING

Over the years, I've had the wonderful opportunity to lead in small group Bible studies and fellowship groups. One such men's Bible study recently has been on my mind, because it seems that the same prayer requests at the end seem to be uttered without much change or result in the ensuing weeks. I've inserted a few below, followed by a response I think that Jesus would probably like to give.

- *"Lord, help me to make the time to have more meaningful personal devotions."*

   "That's great, Tom. Now, how about self-disciplining yourself, setting your alarm clock in the morning and following through. You keep your doctor and dentist appointments, why not keep your appointments with me? And, remember, I don't charge you anything, you know. Perhaps, I should, in terms of loss of personal blessing in your life...what do think?"

- *"Lord, I pray for (name) at my work, that he'll get through the difficult time is having at home."*

   "I'm glad you're compassionate toward your friend at work, Mary. It means you're not just thinking about yourself, which is good. But, have you had any opportunities to talk with her and mention my name or share your own testimony? Have you decided to specifically share my Gospel with her, or have you just been putting it off?

- *"Lord, I pray that my family and I can get along better."*

"What a fantastic prayer, Paul! Thanks so much. Your family is an important responsibility in your life, and I very much want to help you there. But I won't do everything for you, okay. I mean, it's up to you to implement some things, too, you know, and put some wings to your prayers. Give me something to work with, Paul, okay...like spending more fun time with your kids, or taking your wife out for a surprise date night, or adjusting your nightly, 4 hour "couch potato" time at night so you can have some bed time prayers with your kids. Show me that you want me involved, Paul...I promise, I'll definitely show up!"

Well, it's easier said than done, isn't it? It's even fairly simple to write down the above, but it's more difficult to implement such things in our lives. Our prayers are generally sincere, but we're busy and things happen. Our schedule gets interrupted, someone gets sick, the water heater breaks down, or there ends up being more month at the end of our pay check. I understand all that...I face the same issues, too. But...there does come a time when excuses show themselves to be just that...wishes without fuel. My car doesn't move without gas no matter how much I pray and wish that it would, which means taking the time to visit the gas station and refilling the tank. Similarly, my spiritual life doesn't more forward...praying or not praying...without acting upon what we sense is God's will. We must do more than pray for opportunities to happen, we must look and seek those opportunities, so that God will have something to bless. Think about it, okay!

KNOWLEDGE AND WISDOM

I remember a mandatory course I took in college called, "psychological statistics." My major was Psychology, which I chose as a helpful undergraduate degree for pursuing a Masters in Christian Education later on. I enjoyed most of the other courses except that class, primarily because of two reasons. One, I wasn't mathematically focused or motivated, so working with numbers and statistics just didn't rock my boat. Second, the professor teaching the class was new and brought in from China, because of his apparent reputation in the field. This reputation would bring in a lot of dollars to the college from the projects he would work on for the local corporations. There was one major issue…from the students' point of view, however…he hardly spoke English well enough to teach *anything* in a clear and understandable fashion. And, when he did, he sort of dumped out a load of facts without much application. Now, there were a *lot* of complaints from the student body, but that didn't seem to bother the college, so he remained on staff. I'm not being too critical here…it was that bad.

I also remember that there was only one final exam, which made up 90% of our grade, but I didn't have a clue about how to pass that exam in the midst of all this poorly presented information. However, a top student in the class was a friend, so I pleaded with him, "Pete…please tell me what to do here. I know some formulas and equations, but I have no clue as to where to plug them in, let alone what they really mean."

Pete essentially identified 4 or 6 psychologically related issues and told me how to plug in the correct statistical formula for making behavioral assumptions. "Don't try to understand it, Ed," he said, "just plug it in, arrive at the statistical answer and move on." Well, it worked, for I passed…barely…and moved on to the next truly enjoyable and genuinely valuable course. I survived, but there were many who did not.

My point in this example is to show that wisdom is more important than just accumulating large amounts of knowledge. The college lacked wisdom in not providing the paying students someone who could do the job well. The Professor lacked the skill of good communication, but also the wisdom to recognize it and correct it. And, the students ended up with little "psychological wisdom" to use in life or profession. All were no doubt sincere believers and committed individuals, yet wisdom bowed to meaningless and unproductive dispersal of facts

Spiritual wisdom is key to life success for believers. Factual

"Knowledge enlarges the mind, but wisdom engages the soul."

knowledge is not sufficient with which to live the Christian life, for it must be accompanied by wise discernment in order to apply it correctly. Like a spiritual puzzle, wisdom always sees the "bigger picture," enabling a person to successfully join the tiny bits of knowledge together to form what is true, what is best, what is pure and what is God's will. Again, balance is important, for wisdom can't exist without knowledge, either. But wisdom is the most important thing to target, for knowledge doesn't necessarily change anything on its own. Sunday morning pews are filled with spiritual sponges ready to have their knowledge banks enlarged, but their lives will only be changed, if wisdom is disseminated from the pulpit as well.

> *"And so, from the day we heard, we have not ceased to pray for you, asking that you may be filled with the knowledge of his will in all spiritual wisdom and understanding..."* (Colossians 1:9)

TALKING AND WALKING

I just had lunch with a good friend, Jeff, and we enjoyed discussing Christian ideas, values and ministry opinions. One the things upon which both of us agree is the difficulty getting believers to balance their lives between what they know and what they do. Here's an illustration.

A pastor has been at a church for a couple of years, but feels the need to do something to get people more involved in personal ministry and sharing their faith. He senses overall that his church body just isn't very spiritual. Oh, they're believers no doubt, but most seem to have plateaued in their faith. He would say that his parishioners know Christ as Savior, but rarely share their faith. They probably attend on Sundays, but don't involve themselves in a small group, either. Perhaps they have never...at least for a long time...personally led someone to Christ. So, he tries to get more people involved in areas of their giftedness, but things pretty much follow the 80/20 rule, where 20% of the people are involved in some degree of ministry, yet 80% are not.

What does it take to move people beyond the essential and foundational stuff of our faith? One of the key things my friend and I discussed was the concept of rebuilding folks' sense of "conviction." When we're new to the faith, most of us were excited about growing in the Lord, sharing our faith and getting involved in fellowship and/or ministry. What happens, I believe, is that those strong convictional beliefs about God, Christ, salvation and spiritual living tend to settle in at a comfortable level, where we become more relaxed and eventually quite complacent. Our outward walk with God is sort of chugging along, but our inner relationship with Christ isn't deepening very much.

How this happens is difficult to predict or describe, but life becomes busy, kids grow up, the job gets more demanding, and our basic knowledge base or outward spirituality *seems* sufficient to support everything (which it isn't). So, unless we acquire some sort of challenge or chastisement, our "neediness" for God diminishes. Oh, we still acknowledge our need to a point, but only to where we sort of float along somewhat adrift and slowly move along down the river called contentment (perhaps compromise). I believe the average church is chuck full of this type of spirituality, and I've seen it in my own life at times.

I believe that part of the answer is to rebuild the believer's sense of conviction, beginning with faith. We discussed at the beginning of this book, and Peter addresses this in his 2nd letter, *chapter one:*

> *"For this very reason, make every effort to add to your faith goodness; and to goodness, knowledge; and to knowledge, self-control; and to self-control, perseverance; and to perseverance, godliness; and to godliness, mutual affection; and to mutual affection, love. For if you possess these qualities in increasing measure, they will keep you from being ineffective and unproductive in your knowledge of our Lord Jesus Christ. But whoever does not have them is **nearsighted and***

> *blind, forgetting that they have been cleansed from their past sins."* II Peter 1:5-9)

Peter is highlighting some key character perspectives to maintain in our spiritual walk. At the end, he suggests that anyone not consistently growing within these areas has forgotten the roots of why he's a believer in the first place (highlighted above). So, folks caught in this "malaise of complacency" really need a new dose of *salvation conviction*. They don't need to be "re-saved" or anything like that, they just need to *revisit* their salvation roots at a heart level and jumpstart their convictional engine anew.

Regarding this issue, we've almost come full circle from the beginning of this book. If you find yourself in such a situation, remember that God's Spirit never ceases to call, remind, and convict us of our desperate need for God's grace in our lives. Spiritual contentment is a killer of all that is good or productive in our daily walk with Christ. It lets us slip into casual sin, cold spirituality and unproductive lifestyle choices. Such living also keeps the blessing of God at a minimal level in each area of our walk with Christ. Like boiling the frog in science class, we can easily slip silently away into spiritual lethargy, lukewarm faith, and relational distance from Jesus Christ. That doesn't *only* affect us and our family, but enough of it can dull and diminish the spirituality of a church body as well.

How can we stir this sense of conviction and rekindle it? It will ultimately come from the God's Word, as it is disseminated in various ways...the pulpit, small groups, fellowship opportunities, Christian friendships, etc. Something will click, a testimony will hit home, a verse will challenge you, or a teacher will motivate you by what he or she says. Most importantly, however, it often comes by recommitting oneself to deeper and more disciplined times of personal devotions and Bible study.

Bottom line? If you want it bad enough, you'll seek it... and if you seek it with focused and impassioned determination, you'll find it!

Conviction...is it alive and well in your soul?

CONVICTION #18

I Believe In God's "Free" Sovereignty

"In him you also, when you heard the word of truth, the gospel of your salvation, and believed in him, were sealed with the promised Holy Spirit, who is the guarantee of our inheritance until we acquire possession of it, to the praise of his glory."
(Ephesians 1:13, 14)

It was a hot and cloudless day at Disneyworld. My wife and I were enjoying the Florida sun, while sitting on the sandy beach created by Disney, called Typhoon Lagoon. If you haven't been there, it's a water park with a huge "swimming pool" and a cannon type wave maker at the far end, surrounded by a lazy river with people carried along by a slow-moving current.

Every five minutes or so, the underwater cannon goes off, sending a five-foot-high wave catapulting toward everyone in the giant pool. In the deep end, where the wave starts, one is floating in about 10' of water waiting for this powerful wave to carry you 25 feet and then wash over you in an overwhelming surge of power…great stuff!

However, when you're out there waiting for it and keeping yourself on the surface, you can get a bit tired, even before the wave hits you. But you don't want to be tired after the wave hits you, for you've got to "right yourself" and either stay dog-paddling or swim closer to the shallow end of the pool.

On this particular day, I was probably too tired from just swimming around and shouldn't have stayed for another wave. After it hit me, I was a bit disoriented in the surge of all that water and got scared, frankly, that I might not be able to make it into the shallower waters. So, I felt exhausted and started swimming fast, deciding to make a dash to the wall on the left side, which was twelve feet high and about 30 feet away (there were places to hold onto when you got there). The life guards patrolled along the top and end of the pool, and one of them shouted down, "Are you okay?" He must have noticed my overly aggressive attempt to reach the wall. Of course, I didn't want to be hauled in by a lifeguard in front of everyone, so I shouted up to him, "No, everything's okay," and then continued to the wall where I held on until my breath and stability came back. In a minute or so, I swam slowly back to the beach area and rested a while, before going back.

FAITH IS A REQUIRED CHOICE FOR SALVATION

Two pertinent spiritual realities emerge from this misadventure. First, I was very much involved in the process of swimming to safety. No one was forcing me to stay too long in the pool or keeping me from having the common sense to rest a while. I knew it was up to me to keep swimming and stay above the water as long as I could do so. Similarly, action is required on the part of those seeking forgiveness or relationship with God, and it's called reaching out to Him ***by faith***.

The Greek word for faith means *"believing, trusting in, and relying upon."* By application, we all have been given **freedom of choice** to make decisions and to do things that acknowledge God and seek him and his will. This has been the reality of life from the beginning. Adam and Eve were free agents, who were prisoners or puppets of no one, including God. They were given certain freedoms with boundaries for their activities, and God would hold them accountable for their choices. Before the fall, those choices were not influenced by sin, so they willingly obeyed their Creator, for there was simply no desire to do anything else but that.

However, after the attack of Satan, they succumbed to the primary temptation of enticing them to be like God...and they partook of the forbidden fruit. From there on, human beings were infected with a rebellious nature that constantly dogged at their spiritual feet, making the choice to have faith and to follow God's will distasteful and hard to obey. Still, in times past, God continued to reveal himself by sending prophets and teachers in order to inspire faith, to remind them of his will, and to give them opportunity to find atonement through the sacrificial system (for Jews).

Now, to the entire human race, Jew or Gentile, Paul teaches us in Romans, that **God's essential nature was also revealed in creation**. This told people broadly that they were required to live morally sound lives of accountability to him. Of course, no one did so completely and consistently (Jew or Gentile), but chose instead to create their own religious ways to please him (if at all) on the basis of works and self-effort.

Nevertheless, along the way, God kept a door open for those willing to find relationship with him. It always involved to some degree an essential faith in his existence, a recognition of one's own sinfulness and separation from God, and need to seek forgiveness.

> *"And without faith it is impossible to please him, for whoever would draw near to God must believe that he exists and that he rewards those who seek him."* (Heb. 11:6)

However, as the human race grew, people willingly wandering away from the Truth of God revealed in Creation, in Commandment (Jews), and in Conscience (all of us). Eventually, God sent his own Son to speak to mankind, but many even rejected the CHRIST (Messiah) as well. No wonder that the Apostle Paul says the following regarding mankind's nature and situation:

> *"As it is written, "No one is righteous, no, not one;*
> *no one understands; no one seeks for God.*
> *All have turned aside;*
> *together they have become worthless;*
> *no one does good, not even one."*
> *"Their throat is an open grave;*
> *they use their tongues to deceive."*
> *"The venom of asps is under their lips."*
> *"Their mouth is full of curses and bitterness."*
> *"Their feet are swift to shed blood;*
> *in their paths are ruin and misery,*
> *and the way of peace they have not known."*
> *"There is no fear of God before their eyes."*
> (Romans 3:10-18 ESV)

Now, to those who will never have heard the Gospel, Scripture says that God will offer judgement based upon the light that each man or woman has received in their lives. Though Scripture is clear to say that no one can be saved apart from faith in Christ as the norm, some verses in Romans 1-3 seem to indicate at least the *possibility* that Christ's atonement *might be applied* to some who never heard the Gospel, **if they possess a simple, but genuinely humble belief in God's existence and who reach out repentantly to him for forgiveness.** Please know I understand that this *is not* a clearly taught doctrine in Scripture. I'm simply wondering, however, if our compassionate God would accept a simple, repentant, and genuine faith in God's existence as grounds for salvation for unusual situations, similar to that of OT folks like Abraham, for instance. His simple faith and obedience *did* find mercy and favor with God (though we assume it was also stimulated in part by

God's Spirit). In support of this, theologians also understand that infants/children who die before what we call an "age of accountability" are given special mercy and grace by God, and allowed to enter heaven (this is not a clearly taught doctrine either, but inferred...see below).

> *"And the LORD afflicted the child that Uriah's wife bore to David, and he became sick. David therefore sought God on behalf of the child. And David fasted and went in and lay all night on the ground. And the elders of his house stood beside him, to raise him from the ground, but he would not, nor did he eat food with them. On the seventh day the child died. And the servants of David were afraid to tell him that the child was dead, for they said, "Behold, while the child was yet alive, we spoke to him, and he did not listen to us. How then can we say to him the child is dead? He may do himself some harm." But when David saw that his servants were whispering together, David understood that the child was dead. And David said to his servants, "Is the child dead?" They said, "He is dead." Then David arose from the earth and washed and anointed himself and changed his clothes. And he went into the house of the LORD and worshiped. He then went to his own house. And when he asked, they set food before him, and he ate. Then his servants said to him, "What is this thing that you have done? You fasted and wept for the child while he was alive; but when the child died, you arose and ate food." He said, "While the child was still alive, I fasted and wept, for I said, 'Who knows whether the LORD will be gracious to me, that the child may live?' But now he is dead. Why should I fast? Can I bring him back again? I*

shall go to him, but he will not return to me."
(II Samuel 12:15-23)

In any case, only Christ's atoning sacrifice will bring efficacious atonement to any seeker, of course. But, perhaps in the lives of a some who have never actually heard of Messiah Jesus, there was or will be special allowance for their genuine faith in the existence of God and sincere cry for forgiveness. Perhaps, they too will apprehend God's mercy and grace, similar to children/infants who die before the age of "accountability," or Abraham, whose faith was "credited to him as righteousness." (Gen. 15:6) If this is true...and I don't know this for sure...the Spirit of God would still have to be involved in the process of saving such folks.

On the other hand, *the New Testament doesn't clearly teach* any other definitive and Scriptural option for adults or children to be saved who haven't specifically heard the Gospel. God clearly says that people who live in continual disbelief and disobedience to the will of God are standing in the cross hairs of his wrath by virtue of *their repeated refusal* to seek God and his will.

Now, Paul would also say that people *are* always free to seek him, for God doesn't turn people away nor want anyone to perish (II Peter 3). However, they are so antagonistically bound by their fallen natures and self-centered hearts, that they continue to ignore God, refuse repentance, and continue to reject Christ unless God's Spirit first draws them to salvation. So, though mankind is free to seek God, it refuses to do so, because of the inherent and utter depravity of its sinful nature.

But, again, what about the faith part of it? Would man *of his own will* be able to genuinely repent and believe, honestly receive his son, and thereafter walk in harmony with His will? For Paul, the answer is resoundingly, "No, not apart from the mercy and grace of God's Spirit!" Man's heart was eternally scared and singed by sin, such that he would never on his own inclination or intention reach out in in obedience to God...however free he was otherwise to do so. God's Spirit would of necessity be instrumental in effectually calling a person to repentant faith.

ELECTION AND REGENERATION

Regeneration is experiencing new life, being born anew (again) by the implantation of God's Holy Spirit within the heart (or soul-spirit) of a repentant sinner. However, because mankind's hearts are so **depraved** of spiritual desire and determination to believe and obey God, God has to "tap on their shoulder" in order to start the process going, which is what the Bible refers to as Election. The foreknowledge and predetermination of God enables him to know from before the world began who would be receptive to the call of Christ. His graciousness and loving kindness, therefore, sovereignly allowed (and chose) those so willing to respond to the call of faith.

> *"All of us also lived among them at one time, gratifying the cravings of our flesh and following its desires and thoughts. Like the rest, we were by nature deserving of wrath. But because of his great love for us, God, who is rich in mercy, made us alive with Christ even when we were dead in transgressions—it is by grace you have been saved. And God raised us up with Christ and seated us with him in the heavenly realms in Christ Jesus, in order that in the coming ages he might show the incomparable riches of his grace, expressed in his kindness to us in Christ Jesus. For it is **by grace** you have been saved, **through faith**—and this is not from yourselves, **it is the gift of God**—not by works, so that no one can boast. For we are God's handiwork, created in Christ Jesus to do good works, which God **prepared in advance** for us to do."* (Eph 2:3-10)

That's why John also refers to our being "drawn by the Father," for no one would do so without this spiritual "pull" in the right direction. Unfortunately, men and women just love their sin too much.

> *"No one can come to me unless the Father who sent me draws him. And I will raise him up on the last day."* John 6:44

So, the Spirit "calls" and the wayward sinner responds by faith not because of his or her innate goodness, but because of God's compassionate and merciful grace. Please remember, there is no merit on the part of anyone called to receive Christ, he or she just falls within the predetermined plan of God for the world. The Spirit calls those the Father ordains to eternal life, enabling the sinner to respond in obedient faith. The choice is a free one on the human side, though he or she may have resisted for a while or even vacillated over the Gospel truth. But ultimately, the person listens to the Spirit and chooses to obey him, receiving Christ as Savior and Lord. There is no coercion on God's part, perhaps just an enabled sensitivity to Truth, which gets things going, a spark if you will of spiritual light and sight. I'm not sure how, nor does the Bible detail it, but God's foreknowledge and fore-planning work together to purposely allow it. God wants all to be receptive, but realizes such is impossible on its own, so he preserves man's free choice, but somehow fuels faith, allowing spiritual enlightenment to enter the hearts of some.

Why all aren't enabled to have faith and repentance remains a mystery, perhaps revealed when we get to heaven. However, we must understand with certainty, that no man or women *deserves* anything but punishment, not for Adam's sin, but for their own sinful choices in life. Each will face judgment for not doing what he or she inwardly knew they should have done, which is to believe and obey God. Each will also receive an appropriate, compassionate and just punishment. Each person's accountability for his sinful choices will be measured appropriately as it measures alongside of the perfectly compassionate and just nature of God.

> *"Why should the living complain when punished for their sins?"* Jer. 3:39

SANCTIFICATION

Sanctification, however, offers something that should give all of us as believers plenty of hope and peace.

> *"And you also were included in Christ when you heard the message of truth, the gospel of your salvation. When you believed, you were marked in him with a seal, the promised Holy Spirit, who is a deposit guaranteeing our inheritance until the redemption of those who are God's possession—to the praise of his glory."* (Eph. 1:13-14)

Believers have become "set apart" to become family members with God. They possess the "family seal or crest" of God, which is in reality the indwelling Spirit of God. As an example, the seal to the right is similar to many that have emerged through history, whereby a family heritage is helped to preserve its identity in public and private affairs. Essentially, it carries the authority of a particular family or social organization, telling others that a person or document, for instance, is authentic and trustworthy. In a similar way, God's Spirit came to dwell within us in order to establish a family relationship. Along with that came a new identity for all of us...we are the people of God, which carries with it significant authority and authenticity.

First, let me assure you that only the family of believers have been given the ***right*** to be called children of God. A "right" is an authority given to someone by a higher authority. In John 1:12, 13 we read:

> *"Yet to all who did receive him, to those who believed in his name, he gave the right to become children of God - children born not of natural descent, nor of human decision or a husband's will, but born of God."*

There are many in the secular world who unknowingly say that everyone is a child of God, but such is not the case. Family members with God also have a more visible crest, if you will... the cross, a sign of faith, sacrifice, and obedience to God and his will for us in Jesus Christ. Believers are those who have been born anew (ie. spiritually, of God). Only those who have repented of sin and trusted in Christ's death for atonement and forgiveness of sin ...only those are genuine members of God's family (which the Bible refers to as fellowship).

Of course, this thinking understandably doesn't sit very well with non-believers, for mankind has always tried to save itself from God's wrath and ultimate judgment. However, in that task they will always fail, for only a perfect life can appease the perfect expectations of God's nature. This is why Christ came to save man from swimming around hopelessly in spiritual death. Christ's perfect nature and sacrifice is the *only thing* that can atone for man's spiritual guilt, though again, it requires one to believe in him and to respond to the providential call of God's Spirit.

Second, our sanctification means that we are now in ***"right standing"*** with God. By way of example, consider that you have been called to the bank for a bounced check of $400, which you wrote for a car payment. The bank teller tells you that you have been assessed a fee of $35 for this, because you used a check that was an "illegal check." You ask what he means by that, and he says that the check was not recognized in their system. "What does that mean?" you ask again. He says it was not printed by any one of the vendors with whom they normally do business. You tell him that you make up your own checks by writing in all the account information, routing numbers, name and address, etc. However, he remains firm...your intentions were good, you had plenty of money in your account, but your checks just weren't good enough. You inform him that you've written about 5 other similar checks, and he says that you will be assessed a $35 fee for each one and lose all bank benefits until this matter is adjudicated in court.

So, you ask to see a manager and complain. After an hour of negotiations, the manager lifts the penalty, telling his staff to accept your "home-made" checks from here on. He also puts $200 into your account to cover the costs involved and any associated fees. He informs you that it's the law to always let the bank know of the company who prints your checks, because they have to be registered and "okayed" by the bank first. Then, he takes your bounced check from the hands of the teller, signs his name on it, and puts it in a file so that it will secure your position with the bank going forward. The manager shakes your hand on the way out and has a sincere and apologetic smile, "Sorry about all the hassle, but from here on know that you're in *right standing* with the bank, for I've intervened on your behalf and made it so."

What happened in all this? Well, you've been forgiven, released of all penalties, reimbursed for all costs, and stand justified in your relationship with the Bank...all because of a compassionate manager who interceded on your behalf. Similarly, believers have all been put in "right standing" with God because of their faith in Christ's atoning sacrifice upon the cross. The eternal penalty for sin has been lifted, and they now have access to God's relational benefits and blessing going forward...forever.

Thirdly, however, just like the bank manager, Jesus has *signed-off* on our spiritual indebtedness, forgiving it and securing that transaction by the authority of his name. In our example, the bank teller couldn't do it, for only that compassionate bank manager carried the full authority to do so. In the same way, only Jesus could intercede for us in our spiritual indebtedness, for it was he who paid the costs for our sins by his death. You asked for the account manager in heaven to resolve your spiritual issues... Jesus...and he graciously secured your position with the Father. From here on, your relationship with God is safe, guaranteed by the blood of Christ. There is no need to fear any longer, you can now rest in the strong hands of God's Spirit, "*...who is a deposit guaranteeing our inheritance until the redemption of those who are God's possession—to the praise of his glory.*" (Eph. 1:14)

Lastly, however, the person in the example above has been freed to use his redeemed bank account, but he must **continue** to live by the bank rules. Those rules (before the incident) couldn't forgive his indebtedness, they only intensified his obligation to the bank. But now he must show "good faith" by continuing to obey all the rules as discussed and revealed to him.

Practically speaking, then, though Christ has set us free to make decisions, choices and plans...*there are boundaries. First,* Scripture informs us of those boundaries, and we are accountable and responsible to avoid having our choices "bounce back" to God in the way of sin and immaturity. *Secondly,* on God's side of the contract/covenant of faith, he can enforce boundaries of his own as well. Listen to Paul's letter to the Corinthians, chapter 11, verses 27-32:

> *"So then, whoever eats the bread or drinks the cup of the Lord in an unworthy manner will be guilty of sinning against the body and blood of the Lord. Everyone ought to examine themselves before they eat of the bread and drink from the cup. For those who eat and drink without discerning the body of Christ eat and drink judgment on themselves. That is why many among you are weak and sick, and a number of you have fallen asleep. But if we were more discerning with regard to ourselves, we would not come under such judgment. Nevertheless, when we are judged in this way by the Lord, we are being disciplined so that we will not be finally condemned with the world."*

God's boundaries can hurt, but thankfully they are provided to stop us from throwing away our spiritual mindset and our faith commitment to his will. This is the "guarantee" he promises in the Ephesian passage above as well as in many other Biblical passages. For instance, John tells us in I John 3:9:

> *"No one who is born of God will continue to sin, because God's seed remains in them; they cannot go on sinning, because they have been born of God."*

Again, this doesn't mean we are robots incapable of further acts of sin, seasons of carnality or even nagging doubts at times. It does mean, however, that our compassionate God has allowed us a degree of freedom in life, but also set some boundaries for us, beyond which, because of his love, we are not allowed to go. And, as he sees fit to do so, he can and will step into our secure relationship with him to purge it from sin at times, to correct us when wandering too far into danger, and to remind us of our responsibility to love and serve the Savior.

So...we have freedom, but within boundaries...that's the joy *and* security of our faith in Christ. Remember that it came with a significant price, and God holds us accountable for our choices and life goals. The judgment seat of Christ will reveal our faithfulness and persevering commitment to the things of God (or lack thereof). It won't be a matter of judgment for eternity, but it will affect to some degree how we spend eternity in heaven with our Lord.

CONVICTION #19

I Believe Sin Is Never Sophisticated

"I believe that today in the west, and particularly in America, the new barbarians are all around us. We have bred them in our families and trained them in our classrooms. They inhabit our legislature, our courts, our film studios, and our churches. Most of them are attractive and pleasant; their ideas are persuasive and subtle…Today's barbarians are ladies and gentlemen."
Chuck Colson, "Against the Night," from the book, "Discovering God's Will,"

Sophisticated sin! Unfortunately, too many folks have wandered into this dark forest of compromise, trying to soften what's morally wrong in order to make it acceptable, even laudable. Here's an example.

I have a friend named, Bob, a science teacher at a local high school, who attends a weekly men's Bible study at my church. The other night we were studying Ephesians chapter two and discussing how Satan influences the world's thinking today. We discussed the usual examples of how movies negatively influence society, how corrupt politics has become and how sexual boundaries have been attacked in our country. He frowned and said the following:

"You have no idea, guys. In my class alone I have 4 high school age young people who are changing their sexual identities."

"Are they going the whole way, Bob, and having surgery?" I asked.

"No, they just want to be identified by the opposite of their biological gender."

"Well, how to you treat them...you know...address them in class?"

He responded, "If a boy wants to be called a girl, that's what I've got to do. It doesn't matter what's right or wrong any longer. Sexuality is a fluid type of choice!"

We were quite shocked, frankly, and kept asking him more questions, but the answers were mostly the same. He couldn't do anything but treat them by the gender they choose (probably just for the week!). School bathrooms now have to accommodate their sexual choices by giving them transgender facilities in gym and elsewhere.

Many larger corporations have felt the social pressure to install other facilities for folks with various sexual identities. A talk show program yesterday that I was listening to said that there are over ten, differing gender descriptions one can identify with on various governmental forms. Why have they caved to such nonsense? As always, just follow the money!

For instance, when you talk with those who espouse this type of agenda, they will say that it's a new age and people won't fit into...nor should they fit into...any stereotypical guideline for sexual identification. They would say, "It's wrong to do so, for people need to "feel" accepted in the name of diversity. They may be different and need to be encouraged to be *who they perceive themselves to be*." Accepting who you are...regardless of the spiritual ramifications...is the supreme moral tenant in liberal theology and lives up to its name by blurring, erasing and/or expanding all moral boundaries beyond fact or sensibility.

Yes, our liberal culture has pursued absurdity in these matters, throwing common sense and moral absolutes out the window. To them, God is apparently dead and has been replaced by the idol of "self-esteem." This now rules alongside "political correctness" in a co-regency of moral license, guided by the following new age commandments:

- Thou shalt not hold people accountable to any standard that doesn't allow people to do what they want sexually. Standards are always fluid, regardless of biology, history, common sense, or God.

- Thou shalt not deny right of expression or identity to any person regarding their sexual orientation or gender for the day. Wait until next week, next month...whenever... they're particular inclinations will no doubt evolve.

- Thou shalt not say or do anything that hurts a person's feelings about anything, including *his* or *her* (my bad... no genders) sexual identity or moral *beliefs* (better, illicit intentions). It could cause unnecessary emotional *damage* (socially pampered feelings and unresolved guilt).

- God is love, wanting to condemn no one, but always accepting and approving of all personal choices or opinions...except His own, of course.

- The greatest commandment is this: "Do unto yourself what gives you pleasurable feelings, and let others do the same unto themselves."

We chuckle, but it's a shame what *moral pluralism* and *inclusive* thinking has done to this country in the last 50 years or so. I guess the pot smoking, LSD tripping, bead wearing, flag burning, rock blasting, veteran denigrating, sex perverting, and truth denying deviates of the 60's have finally grown up into the "politically correct," morally perverse proponents of modern-day liberalism! America is, in fact, being held hostage by these folks, who really think, talk and act like disobedient children. They satiate themselves with the moral candy they were never allowed to eat, but in which now they can fully indulge. As my friend Bob above also quipped, "Today, they even *praise* themselves for doing those things!" To these folks the Bible says the following:

> "Woe to those who call evil good and good evil, who put darkness for light and light for darkness..." (Isaiah 5:20)

So, let's define things here. **Sophisticated sin**, unfortunately, is what the world calls cool, "in," and sheik. It's thought to be glamorous and certainly considered courageous to practice, particularly in front of those who oppose it (check out the "Academy Awards" presentations each year). The proponents of sophisticated sin rejoice that they are breaking free from the strangleholds of traditionalism and the straightjackets of "puritanical" Christianity. They offer beliefs that oppose sound doctrine and solid Biblical conviction. Here's some more detail....

Compassionate Sophistication

This is new age type stuff, where people want to "feel" good about their relationship with everyone. "God is love, so we mustn't judge anyone for being different...we're better than that in the 21st century. We must think inclusively!"

Frankly, there probably won't even be a 22nd century (apart from the millennium), due to the disintegration of the world into such moral chaos and corruption. In fact, in modeling God's standards for love, I wouldn't say mankind in general has moved forward one bit (eg. a crime is committed in this country every 2.5 seconds!). His love does offer unending mercy and grace, however, to those who seek it, but it doesn't excuse or exonerate those who don't. The Bible makes it quite clear that sin is not to be tolerated.

> "The soul who sins shall die. The son shall not suffer for the iniquity of the father, nor the father suffer for the iniquity of the son. The righteousness of the righteous shall be upon

> *himself, and the wickedness of the wicked shall be upon himself."* Ez. 18:20

In Christ, of course, the repentant believer does find God's merciful love by the shed blood of Jesus upon the cross, where atonement for sin has been provided by God. But Paul reminds us that this doesn't justify being casual, tolerant or lackadaisical sinners, rather we should always be vessels of purity and holiness.

> *"So then, brothers, we are debtors, not to the flesh, to live according to the flesh. For if you live according to the flesh you will die, but if by the Spirit you put to death the deeds of the body, you will live. For all who are **led** by the Spirit of God are sons of God."* (Romans 8:12-14)

The non-believing world wants desperately to destroy the concept of sin, unless it's in the legal sense only. It overlooks many societal evils calling them "different strokes for different folks." One should not be disparaging, they say, but accepting of just about any behavior, as long as no one gets hurt. It also propagates a host of *false* ideas about God's love in order to justify such personal indulgence, denying every hint of a moral absolutism in order to support evil.

For instance, in his book, "Seeking Allah, Finding Jesus," Nabeel Qureshi describes his journey out of Islam into Christianity. He clarifies how the liberal establishment only wants to see the "loving" part of Islam, instead of the whole picture.

> *"So, if we define Islam by the beliefs of its adherents, it may or may not be a religion of peace. But if we define Islam more traditionally, as the system of beliefs and practices taught by Muhammad, then the answer is less ambiguous.*
>
> *The earliest historical records show that Muhammad launched offensive military*

> *campaigns and used violence at times to accomplish his purposes. He used the term jihad in both spiritual and physical contexts, but the physical jihad is the one Muhammad strongly emphasizes. The peaceful practice of Islam hinges on later, often Western, interpretations of Muhammad's teachings, whereas the more violent variations of Islam are deeply rooted in orthodoxy and history."* (Seeing Allah, Fining Jesus, Nabeel Qureshi, Zondervan, Grand Rapids, Michigan, 2014, p. 116)

This one "loving" response of worldly love for Islam may indeed be the final one God uses to bring about the end of the world. Now, I'm not suggesting this out of some foolish, ultra-conservative, conspiracy-grounded notion, or because I don't like Muslim folks. Rather, I'm suggesting the foolishness of naively trying to see only good in some things can come back and bite you viciously.

In WWII, Britain's Nevil Chamberlain was later seen as one who really didn't know his enemy…Hitler. However, the capacity for evil resident in that German demigod soon became evident. It would take the conviction and commitment of another man on the historical stage named, Winston Churchill, who would focus Britain and the world upon the reality of what they faced. He eventually got the world on the right road they needed to travel in order to save their very national existence. Similarly, *recognizing* inherent and intentional evil…no matter how well it is camouflaged…is the key to winning international confrontations as well as spiritual battles with the enemy of our souls…Satan. Syrupy definitions of morality and love will not do, particularly when facing Almighty God at the end of our tenure on this earth.

> *"…we must all appear before the judgment seat of Christ, that each one may receive his due for the things done in the body, whether good or bad."* (II Cor. 5;10)

By application, I am targeting the tendency all believers have to "just scoot by" and espouse attitudes such as *"loosen up a little, will ya!"* type of thinking in our personal walk in Christ. Now, I'm sure God doesn't want to "nail" us to a coffin each and every time we sin, but it is also true that *he has boundaries* for which we always will be accountable. I'm thankful for God's gracious mercy surrounding our failures to please Him, but we are not free to disregard sin's ugly nature or dismiss the possible consequences it brings into our lives.

In the context of communion, for instance, Paul says that we should carefully and regularly evaluate how we stand in our relationship with God in order to avoid His judgement. For,

> *"...if we would examine ourselves, we would not be judged by God..."* (I Cor. 11:31)

These are not words of "permissive love." They are clear warnings regarding times we "miss the target" of God's expectations and indulge in unwise and/or sinful behaviors. We should appreciate God's compassionate nature, but *not at the expense of understanding his powerful dislike for sin. Compassion is never sophisticated* when it comes to sin, for love is not an excuse to indulge the flesh at the expense of godliness.

MORAL SOPHISTICATION

It's considered praiseworthy in today's politically inclusive thinking to believe that morals have no absolutes, a philosophy called "moral relativism." It believes the following: *"Morals are simply socially-grown concepts that do not find any transcultural or eternal values in them. One culture believes one thing, and another believes the opposite, so we must all become tolerant."* There are people in high places that not only believe this dribble, but actually maintain strong convictions about it, willing to do whatever it takes to shape our society after it.

Philosophically speaking, however, if there were no absolute truths in life, then all thinking would be pointless, nothing more than foundationless assertions and assumptions...just unsubstantiated chatter in a meaningless moral vacuum. Yet, everything in life, including science and creation, functions on assertions about what is true or false. We call some of this natural law, which operate in trustworthy and repeatable ways, such that it forms the basis for mathematics, history, science, ecology, geology, and philosophy, though we will always approach and understand it as finite beings. Somethings in life are undeniably just that way... knowable, practical, repeatable, and reliable.

In the spiritual world, where God dwells and oversees his creation, truth is just as real as in any other field of study or belief. Absolute truth exists there *because He exists* and has authored reliable, functioning and knowable ***moral realities*** as well. We approach these spiritual truths by reason and by faith, just as the scientist does through testing, evaluating and making assumptions. It is evidential, yes, but it nevertheless exists as the world in which we move and have our being, both for the believer and the scientist, at every level.

In addition, truth is always by definition singular, trustworthy, reliable, repeatable and unchanging...that which is and always will be true. One can't have two truths or multiple moral values that contradict each other. So, one who thinks that cultural morality is true and that any society's beliefs are valid and true, is logically on the level of a first grader (there can be only one *author* of such Truth as well...God). So, logically speaking, listening and accepting moral relativism is listening to the winds of moral imagination. Such thinking may sound sophisticated, but it's really nonsensical and illogical moral escapism and has now allowed over 50 years of cultural confusion, political tension, societal breakdown, and moral mayhem.

So, where is absolute truth to be found? Well, as Christians, we believe that it is found in the living Word of God, Jesus, and in the written Word of God, the Scriptures, both of which have been given to us by God in order to understand the truth of life and salvation.

> *"In the past God spoke to our forefathers through the prophets at many times and in various ways,*

> *but in these last days he has spoken to us by his Son...The Son is the radiance of God's glory and the exact representation of his being, sustaining all things by his powerful word..."* (Heb. 1:1-3)

Now, sophisticated thinkers, whether they be scientists, philosophers, historians, politicians, or presidents, can get things wrong at times (so can we), but especially when it comes to moral truth. That's because *man's thinking* is always ethnocentric, tending to trust in itself in these matters. However, as believers in Jesus Christ, we trust the Bible, *for it clearly claims to be the Word of God and that it's principles and precepts come from revelation*, not reason. Of course, one can disregard its claim, if he or she would like to do so, to their own loss.

Biblical Truth rests upon prophesized events shown to be historically accurate and trustworthy, including Jesus' miracles, his resurrection, his sensible explanation of God's existence, his teaching about sin and evil, the reality of future judgment, and God's pathway to eternal life in Christ. Here's how I would arrange in sequence what we believe about our "non-sophisticated," but nevertheless trustworthy belief system.

- Life apart from our Creator God is evolutionary lunacy, because of the obvious interconnected, intelligent design embedded into our world and universe around us. Intricate natural laws hold everything together, giving evidence of the Master Designer who created and maintains it.

- Man is more than "an accident suspended between accidents" (Briscoe), because he is uniquely created above all animals with a sense of logic, self-identity, purpose and behavioral accountability.

- Spiritual and moral realities are just that...real...and they cannot be ignored. We are moral creatures to the core, which clearly reveals the existence of both good and evil, as well as the God who created moral standards to begin with. Absolute principles of moral truth exist, but if one differs from another(s), only one has standing with God.

- Prophetic utterances permeate the Old Testament and have either already been fulfilled or are soon to be fulfilled as we approach the 2nd coming of Christ. Christ's birth, Israel's past experiences, the global landscape of warring nations at the end of the age, Israel's coming into its own land in 1948, the accurate predictions of physical catastrophes in the end times…all these and more form the basis for a reasonable and reliable trust in Biblical Truth.

- Sin is real, whether one calls it evil behavior, wrong decisions, or psychological maladjustment. It has corrupted mankind, destroyed families, destroyed nations and wrecked-havoc in lives and cultures upon the earth for millennia. Thus, judgment for sin is both necessary on earth and affects man's relationship to a holy and righteous God. Good works can't erase accountability and guilt, only the blood of God's perfect and sinless Son could atone for these at the cross. By accepting this gracious act as true and trusting in its efficacy before our merciful Lord, we can find forgiveness and reconciliation with our Creator. Then, one day, we will enter into life eternal, prepared for us before the foundation of the earth.

In summary, one shouldn't give way to those wanting to make moral truth into something personal, social, "evolutionary," or political. It can't be the result of blending everything together in some sort of compromising spiritual stew. Truth doesn't exist that way. Such rabid and relativistic blending we see today as taught in liberal universities, for instance, is really nothing more than unaccountable defiance and profound deviation from the moral will of our Creator God.

CULTURAL SOPHISTICATION

American culture has undergone a colossal transformation since the fifties. The days of family roles and relationships portrayed by 50's television shows such as "Ozzie & Harriet," "Donna Reed," "Leave It To Beaver," and "Father Knows Best," are long gone. The conservative values of many of the old Walt Disney shows such as "The Hardy Boys," "Spin and Marty," "The Adventures of Davy Crockett," and "The Parent Trap," became smothered in the murky, anti-Christian agendas of liberal producers such as Normal Lear. *"Soap was truly ahead of its time, driving head-long into taboo subjects like murder, prostitution, and homosexuality."* (https://www.ign.com/lists/op-100-tv-shows/100) He led the way in the nineties with "Archie Bunker," then spun off many similar programs featuring buffoon type fathers, broken family situations, teenage sexuality, homosexual characters and lousy language to say the least. Soon, entertainment degenerated into risqué night-time comedies like "Golden Girls," "Will and Grace," and "Soap." Listen to Hollywood's sophisticated praise of itself regarding the comedy "Soap."

Of course, the topics, programming, and entertainment today (2021) has surpassed anything in the 90's as far as influencing culture with cable vulgarity, rampant sexuality, extreme violence, and social corruption (HBO, Cinemax, and other adult focused venues are popular avenues for this stuff). It's only a matter of time before the window of complete carnal indulgence will be opened without *any* controls or standards of decency. Welcome to the 21st century!

> *"Soap was truly ahead of its time, driving head-long into taboo subjects like murder, prostitution, and homosexuality."*
>
> (https://www.ign.com/lists/op-100-tv-shows/100)

Christians live in a world culture that does not set boundaries for personal moral behaviors. As a kid, I used to play a board game called, "Careers." The way to win was to accumulate fame and fortune by setting a goal for yourself at the beginning of the game, and then entering various fields or careers to get there. Even in the game, one could go far and accumulate much by entering politics, education, media, etc., for these were quickest ways to acquire power, financial success and life position.

In today's real world, however, media, entertainment, education and politics have been hijacked by "flesh driven" thinking and philosophy, stimulated by Satan, and exert controlling influence in our present-day culture. Go along with these people in power, and the road to success becomes smooth; oppose them, and the that same road becomes strewn with pot holes and ruts. Conservative values are not acceptable, if you're seeking a media position or a political position, for powerful, liberal-driven groups will oppose you. Even non-influential types of jobs demand that new trainees go through rigorous training modules on relational and moral acceptance, restricting one's Christian based views from being shared or discussed in the workplace. If one doesn't get on board and embrace such thinking, he or she will have only limited promotion, if any, and probably the possibility of eventual separation.

Believers have always had struggles in human culture, but in America it's never been as oppressively immoral and oppositional as it is today, essentially because we've left our Christian roots behind. That which is still good is quickly deteriorating, and culture is no longer "Christian" to the same degree as it once was. Biblical evil is no longer seen as sin, but as sophisticated pleasures and/or pursuits to be enjoyed without guilt (because God is no longer honored nor are moral absolutes recognized).

So, in the midst of this, where will *your* convictions lead you? Will you cower and compromise? Or, will you be willing to lose things of temporal value in this life to gain what is eternal in the next? I believe that it's time for all of us as believers to accept that fame, fortune and success may no longer be attainable for genuinely committed believers. Jesus warned us about this, saying:

> *"No one can serve two masters, for either he will hate the one and love the other, or he will be devoted to the one and despise the other..."*
> (Matthew 6:24 ESV)

So, again, the question persists: *Will believers follow their Christian **convictions** about moral choices and behaviors, or will they follow the well-trodden path of temptation and compromise. In other words, will they bow to Christ or acquiesce to culture?*

CONVICTION #20

I Believe Loss Can Be A Friend

―◆―

"Faithful are the wounds of a friend"

I was watching a well-known Pastor on the television last night, who delivered a fantastic talk on the role of loss in our lives. I sat glued to the set as he passionately shared how the difficulties, pains, and struggles believers experience at times doesn't mean that they've slipped from God's loving care or that he's abandoned them. So, let me pick up on his thoughts, add a few stories of my own and see if together we can gain some helpful insights for our walk with the Lord. Let's use the story of Jonah to form a foundation for our focus.

A Runaway Prophet

"So, bub, you can't stand those folks, huh?" remarked a man wearing a heavily tattered blue shirt. His rough, weather worn face looked up to the heavens for a sign of good weather that didn't seem to be as evident as he wanted. The winds were kicking up and clouds were moving in rather quickly, which made him scowl.

"I didn't say that, sir. I just don't think they deserve anything good from God, that's all," returned the young man named Jonah.

He was hunched over the side of wooden ship sailing west toward a darkening sky and looking intensely at the endless waters that surrounded him. Tarshish was a Mediterranean port on the southern coast of what today is Spain, 2500 miles away. Jonah seemed lost in thought, contemplating something deep within, seemingly as deep as the ocean itself. The incessant tossing of the waves and the constant movement of the small ship, though, was also making him a bit seasick.

"*Well, sonny, you'll not find it out there with them sharks,*" the older man replied, while securing a loosened rope to a rail.

"*Take it from this o'l barnacle bruised bum of a sea shark, life's as mysterious as a wave that hits the side of this he're boat...you just can't fig're it out. No, sir, you just can't do it!*" The sailor's name was Thomas, who had struck up a conversation with Jonah, a young lad he felt was just out of place on this Mediterranean voyage. He seemed like a nice young man to Thomas, but in need of some encouragement, so he continued.

"*Look, I've been to Ninevah, son. Yeah...it's a scourge, 'tis true. But, if ya ask me, God's not gonna be in'tressed in them no matter what's go'in on anyway. They're just rich folks hav'in their kicks, not car'in about us poor, strug'lin bums. Pitiful bunch of fat, lusty o'l freeks...just pitiful. Why should God even give a care!*" Thomas reached down to a bucket of tar and began patching a small crack in a floor, while Jonah quietly scanned the horizon in profound silence.

Suddenly, Thomas looked up in excitement. "*Hey, bud, I know what God's up to. He's gonna fix those folks up, patch 'em up with tar...and he wants you to do it!*" Thomas laughed heartily, not knowing that this was exactly what Jonah was called to do for that immoral and wayward crew of Ninevites...minus the tar, of course. They were sailing the seas of life toward their own spiritual destruction, but Jonah wanted no part of correcting their spiritual compass.

Startled, Jonah jerked his head around and looked a Thomas, who was laughing away. Jonah, frowning obviously, was taken back by the old man's insight, though he knew he was just joking.

Still, it bothered him, so he grumbled to himself and started to walk away.

"*Hey...I was just kidding,*" Thomas said, not wanting to hurt Jonah's feelings.

"*You're right, friend...that's exactly what God wants me to do!*" Thomas stopped laughing. He wasn't a religious guy, though the rest of the crew all had their own gods and idols. But a chill came over him that had nothing to do with weather. Would this young man really be running from God? That meant potential danger to the voyage, and he would later share that with the crew. Jonah, however, walked away and returned to his berth in a lower deck of the ship.

Let's pause in the story for a moment and make some applications. All of us are experts at running from God, even though most of us know how to cover it up well. No, not everyone is running because of some terrible sin, though often it's the case. Mostly, however, it's just not wanting to do what God want us to do, or believe, or think. We just get stubborn and resist his Spirit, whether subtly or with obvious intention. Spiritual maturity is not an easy thing to accomplish, and we "chomp on the bit," rebelling from the will of God. That brings trouble from both resulting difficulties we could have avoided and/or from the purposeful chastisement that God brings into our lives to straighten us out.

Things Get Worse

"*Throw him overboard! Do it now!*" The degrading weather situation had brought on a sudden and terrible storm, which was now unleashing its full flurry of pounding rain, powerful winds and raging seas. The small ship was only meant to handle a few passengers and crew, but it was now being thrown from one 20' wave to another, fighting for its very existence. Jonah's escape plan wasn't working too well at the moment, either, for the whole crew had heard about his situation and were worried that their own gods couldn't calm this storm and save them.

> "*Appease his God and throw him in the water...then we'll be safe. Let his God's anger kill **him**, not us!*" cried one sailor to the others, who were trying to tack the sails and keep the ship from being crushed in the tumultuous, wind-swept waves.

Poor Jonah, he's about to be caught up in a series of events beyond his control, where God will be teaching him important spiritual principles in the context of difficult circumstances. Ever been there yourself? It's not fun, but God certainly can "turn up the volume" on his communications with us at times, can't he!

So, here's Jonah, simply trying to get away from a prophet's responsibility. But, it's more than that, for he's in direct, conscious and deliberate rebellion against the clear command of Yahweh (not a good thing, right?). We all make poor choices at times and disobey God, but there are choices...*and then there are choices... big ones*! So, this was no little act of disobedience and, frankly, he knew it. He was harboring a real hatred toward others and trying to withhold God's mercy from them. As a prophet, he was seriously devoid of love, and the Lord was now going to forcefully and expediently remind him of it. However, from Jonah's point of view, I think he would argue his case against Nineveh in the following way.

> "*Those Ninevites are deeply corrupt, and they spurn everything your law says for us to follow. Such immorality and idolatry I've been taught to hate since I was just a child. How can I just forget all that and give them opportunity to be forgiven? That's not what I think should happen, anyway. They deserve to be judged!*"

Now, that was his intellectual argument. But, again, the real issue was his cold heart. Like an arrow shot into his chest, his prejudice and hatred burrowed into his spirit, causing him to fight God's will.

Finally, the sailors threw him off the boat into the sea, hoping that the wrath of whatever gods they served would be appeased. Though they were a group of idolatrous wayfarers themselves, they still recognized that man is accountable to God, so they dumped Jonah into the sea.

Please notice that Jonah admitted his guilt in part and tried to save the men. The Bible says:

> *"Pick me up and throw me into the sea," he replied and it will become calm. I know that it is my fault that this great storm has come upon you."* (1:12)

I wonder...do you and I quickly recognize our guilt after doing something outside of the Father's will? Or, do we harbor it for a while, refusing to listen-up and bring needed repentance of heart and behavioral change? Jonah had some pockets of self-will that remained, but at least he was beginning to recognize his own rebelliousness.

Secondly, the men realized in a moment of faith that Jonah's God was real and that they needed his help to get to safety in the midst of the overwhelming storm. They cried out to Him, and God in his merciful grace calmed the storm and saved their lives. Isn't it interesting that God even used this miserable and rebellious prophet to accomplish something good in someone else's life.

> *"At this the men greatly feared the Lord and they offered a sacrifice to the lord and made vows to him. But the Lord provided a great fish to swallow and Jonah was inside the fish three days and three nights."* (1:16, 17)

When Consequences Catch Up

But the story goes on for Jonah, for his heart wasn't so easily broken and made pliable to the plans of God for his life. More pressure was needed upon this piece of coal to turn it into diamond.

"What? I can't believe it. I'm...I'm alive," cried Jonah as he gulped some rancid stomach contents from inside the huge fish that had swallowed him whole.

"Yuk! And, this goo floating around me and...hey...what this? My gosh, it the guts and bones from this creature's last meal. God... help me!"

But no divine voice parted the silent darkness.

Jonah calmed down over the next few hours as he tried to float around in all that gunk, finally resting himself upon a half-digested shark carcass. The stench was unbearable and the stomach acids were already causing his skin to burn.

"Lord God...you're bigger than all this. Okay...okay...I may have been a bit rash about those Ninevites, but surely you wouldn't let a good Jew...you know, one of your own...just die in this stink'in mess, would you?!"

But the Lord remained silent.

Jonah started to doze off for a second, when something bit him on the foot. *"Ouch!"* he shouted out. He yanked his foot out of the watery goo and slid back into it again. All around him something was nipping and biting, causing tiny bloody cuts on both legs. The pain was excruciating, wracking his mind with the dread of what might be happening to him...being eaten alive by something he couldn't even see. He hit the watery goo wildly to scare away whatever was there, but it took the better part of an hour before it seemed to leave him completely alone.

"God...I'm a prophet, not a plate full of flesh for some detestable snake from the deep. Don't let me die this way...please! Get me out of here!"

But the Lord remained silent.

Why is it that when difficulties come, we want easy answers and quick fixes, not fully accepting that such hard times may be the very result our own immaturities and sins? Jonah was in the depths of despair and simply wanted out. But, that's a place of great potential, because it makes the heart susceptible to the Spirit.

However, at this point, he wasn't out of deep trouble yet, but his pain and despair were wearing on him greatly. Jonah needed to be *broken* so he could compassionately understand that those Ninevites were in dire need, too, and that he was the one chosen to offer them forgiveness.

Pain changes one's perspective, especially when it's from God...and when one **listens** to it! It focuses the mind upon what's truly important and also what consequences may be in the making for the one who doesn't want to listen to it.

Here's another point worth remembering. We need to realize that God wasn't punishing Jonah as much as he was lovingly chastising him to become a better person and a more useable prophet. I remember a time of my life when I wasn't listening to God, but continued down a disobedient path of my own self-will. God created a season of physical pain for me, something the doctors or I couldn't heal. Nevertheless, I also found God blessing me with a degree of compassionate help and comfort in the midst of it all that got me through it. I found that God's merciful grace can accompany his stern discipline, blending the two in a providential poultice of spiritual comfort and healing. God is so loving and good.

But at this point, Jonah was still hanging on to his stubborn and prejudicial mindset, and he clearly wasn't ready to accept the truth about himself, God, or the Ninevites. Nevertheless, after three days in the pit of despair, he did finally open up his heart in genuine repentance. Listen deeply to his words:

> *"In my distress I called to the Lord, and he answered me. From the depths of the grave I called for help and you listened to my cry. You hurled me into the deep, into the very heart of the seas, and the currents swirled about me; all your waves and breakers swept over me. I said, 'I have been banished from your sight; yet I will look again toward your holy temple. The engulfing waters threatened me. The deep surrounded me; seaweed was wrapped around my head. To the roots of the mountains I sank down; the earth*

beneath barred me in forever. But you brought my life up from the pit, O Lord my God. When my life was ebbing away, I remembered you, Lord, and my prayer rose to you to your holy temple. **Those who cling to worthless idols forfeit the grace that could be theirs.** *Bit I with a song of thanksgiving, will sacrifice to you. What I have vowed I will make good. Salvation comes from the Lord."* (Jonah 2:1-9)

Yes, Jonah was listening with his heart instead of his ears, and God freed him from his life class on "Seaweeds and Spirituality." However, the pain and distress he went through must have impressed upon him three, key truths:

1. He, Jonah, was deserving of death for his *own* sins. In his heart and in his dealings with pagan people, he was no model of perfection, rather just as selfish, carnal, closed-minded, stubborn, prejudicial, lustful and pride-filled person as any Ninevite that ever walked on the planet.

2. God's mercy has no boundaries to those who genuinely reach out to receive it. There is no sinner so wicked or sin so despised that God cannot forgive and find God's merciful grace.

3. If one wants to live securely, it's time to confess one's sins to God, get on the right side of things, and then get plugged back into God's perfect will for his or her life.

I can remember another time in my life where I refused to deal with some significant life issues that I needed to correct. I could even sense my lukewarm heart as I read God's Word, though from an outward point of view I was doing well before all who knew me. But I was flying under the radar, serious in my desire to serve the Lord, but never really

"To return to what you've found, requires realizing what you've lost."

putting an end to some of my spiritual immaturities. I was just as stubborn as Jonah.

The key to Jonah's (and our) turnaround was realizing that life within the will of God needed to be more important than life outside of it. *All of us will continue to cling to our sins until we realize what we're losing, when we're outside the will of God (2:8).* The loss of ministry, the loss of intimacy, the loss of purpose, the loss of blessing, the loss of peace and provision from God... all these and more are the result of not accepting and following God's Will. Rebelling only makes it worse, of course, and God may also have a *choice* place for us to visit in order to restore our perspective to what it should be. Losing God's daily, sustaining grace is a costly mistake.

Wait...You Mean There's More?

Great ending, but...opps...it's not over, yet!

"Okay, Lord, I've preached to these spiritual scoundrels and... alright...some will rightly be saved from your coming destruction. That's good. But, I'm still angry over those who still haven't repented, so I'm just gonna sit over here on that hill and watch the fireworks!"

"Ah, Jonah, there's not going to be any fireworks, Jonah," replied the Lord.

"Wait, what? There has to be. You promised."

"Jonah, there's enough repentance and genuine confession going on over there such that the "fireworks," to which you so callously referred, will not be necessary."

"Awe...that's just not right, Lord. I mean, they're still getting away with stuff, just like I said before leaving on this journey. I'm so angry, Lord, I could just die!"

"Jonah, I could make that happen, if you'd like?"

"No...it certainly wouldn't be on the top of my list," returned Jonah nervously.

"Well, then, you best reconsider your right to remain angry, okay? Something good is happening over there, and I think they

need my merciful grace just as much as you do. Would that be a fair statement, my opinionated young prophet?"

A little while later, Jonah was resting on that hill and watching to see if God would change his mind. A huge vine grew up over him to cool him from the sun, and he was quite happy. But God sent a worm to eat it up overnight and then sent a scorching east wind to vex him under the day's blistering sun. He was miserable.

"So, Jonah, can we talk? You were distraught about that vine dying and making your life uncomfortable, but you could care less about saving those lost folks who were without hope in Nineveh, along with all their animals. So...why is that again?"

Some things cling to us like glue, and as the writer to Hebrew says, *"...let us throw off everything that hinders and the sin that so easily entangles, and let us run with perseverance the race marked out for us."* (Heb. 12:1)

The question remains, "Did Jonah finally learn his lessons?" I'm sure he learned a lot and that there was some degree of genuine "conviction" going on in his heart. How much? Well, we'll have to ask him in heaven someday.

But the better question is, "Have you and I 'fessed up' lately to *our own issues?"* Perhaps you're stuck in some tenacious and odiferous seaweed of your own, and God is trying to get your attention in order to turn you back to him. Like Jonah, could

"Surrendering To God Brings Power

Waiting For God Brings Hope

Listening To God Brings Direction

Trusting In God Brings Peace

you still be clinging to a "worthless idol," in persistent opposition to the will of God? If so, Jonah's experience can be very helpful to you.

You see, I believe that Jonah was eventually so impacted by God's grace in the Nineveh revival that he was freed from his stubborn prejudices. The key to whatever repentance Jonah had in the end, would have been a result of the pain he went through in the belly of the great fish that swallowed him. It caused him to evaluate judgement and chastisement in light of his own personal experience with God's grace and mercy. That's what broke him and allowed God to have the fish vomit him out of its stomach.

Eventually, I imagine he genuinely considered the sad spiritual condition of these folks and their unavoidable eternal destiny. I think he realized how seriously they were lost in their own sin and separation from the love of God. And, in the process, surely he thought about what **he had lost in his own rebellion**...the closeness he knew with God, the love relationship he had previously enjoyed with Him, and the challenges of ministering in previous situations. Perhaps it was time to finally repent and turn from his hatred. Perhaps it was time to joyfully and fully embrace God's will. Perhaps it was time to rejoice and find healing from God.

So, if you find yourself entangled in the seaweed of some sinful attitude or behavior, think about what you have in Jesus and what you've lost since cohabitating with sin, rebelling from your Lord, or just living a compromising spiritual existence. You'll find the following statement to be a road which can bring you back to God's mercy and blessing:

"When you think about your sin and how much you've lost;
You'll once again recognize what you found at the cross"

CONVICTION #21

I Believe God's Will Outshines Everything!

"Set your minds on things above, not on earthly things." Col. 3:2

"**B**oy, is that a beautiful thing or what!" I remarked, after polishing up my 1960 Chevrolet Impala with its sport rims, bright red interior and white exterior paint. It was my first car and cost me (that is, my dad) just $450. I needed a car with which to go to college in the fall, and my dad had just purchased it for me through a newspaper ad. Yes, it was an old car, but it was still in good condition.

"You couldn't make it shine more than it is," returned my dad as he entered the house for some lunch. He had been watching me for a while as I cleaned and waxed it, though it was in such good shape that it really didn't need it. That was my first car, and it lasted me through my college years into my marriage.

Then, a couple of years after I got married, I spotted a shiny, deep blue Volvo in a commercial on television that really got my eye. So, my wife and I checked the finances and decided that we could afford it, and we made the plunge into our first new car. That 4-door sedan really was a quality car, and I held on to it for about 3 years, until it seemed a good time to trade it in for something a bit bigger, because of family needs. Rather than list all my cars since then, I'm sure you get the idea that a shiny new car every few years is nice to have. Though it isn't always necessary, we all have a tendency to "move up," particularly if we listen to the stuff advertising executives dish out on television and in other outlets.

To begin, the shiny sensualities of the flesh aren't necessarily evil, just over stimulating at times. Media advertising and entertainment venues bombard us all the time with such things for the explicit purpose of increasing their profit margins. They want to draw our attention to what we want and need, whether or not such things are materialistic, sexual, financial, or otherwise.

In and of themselves, our basic wants or needs may not be intentionally wrong, unless of course the content is obviously inappropriate in attitude or behavior. But, the sheer *overload* of such influences all around us will nevertheless over-stimulate any healthy or spiritually sound desire, if self-control and wisdom are not present to draw a line in the sand.

> *CAUTION...Too many believers are seeking the flashiest church building, the sharpest pastoral communicator and the best worship-band led church. Think of the pressure that's put on smaller churches to keep up with the quality of music, preaching, and programming available to those attending megachurches that also have larger budgets with which to work. Please understand that it would be great to have a Chuck Swindoll, a John McArthur, or a Charles Stanley in the pulpit every week, but that's just not going to happen for most of us.*

Secondly, however, let me ask this of you: "What makes us so susceptible to evil? Why is it that we can either fall into casual sin so easily, or, perhaps fall headlong into destructive and addictive habits…even as believers? Where do we get the inner conviction so critical for *warding off* these evil influences?

EVIL AND SOURCES OF TEMPTATION

Actually, there are probably only three sources of evil…the **first** being temptation that comes from the *outside*. Outward issues are often a tricky blend of several things working together, often unintentionally so, to cause such intimidation that we fall on our spiritual faces. For instance, something as common as losing one's job can set us off in doubt or anger. *"Why would God let us go through such loss, if he truly loves us and our family?"* we ask. We might even start blaming the boss, the company, or the world's economic instability instead of just accepting God's unseen purpose. Didn't God tell us that *"In the world you will have troubles?"* (John 16:33)Of course, whether we have a specific answer or not doesn't really matter in the end, for the ultimate attitude to adopt is trust, knowing he *"is working in all things for good."* (Romans 8:28).

Or, perhaps, we start being attracted to a person at work, looking to talk with him or her through the day, though in the beginning, it just seemed a friendly thing to do. But as time progresses so does our level of pleasure, and soon we're wanting to make those casual contacts more often. Before long we're starting to talk about things far too intimate than is necessary and the closeness that comes from that provides opportunities to increase our fantasies and possible intentions to do things that are sinful. Yet, most of us know that the Scriptures tell us, *"…among you there must not be even a hint of sexual immorality…"*

Or, how about that young, Christian couple, who buys a house too soon, getting "things" instead of security and spiritual maturity first. Yes, I know about the need for more room for the kids, for entertaining others from church, for investing in a non-depreciable item for your future, etc. These ideas can be good, of course, when seen from a healthy and discerning point of view. But sometimes they can also be not much more than simple excuses to indulge our immature desires to acquire pleasurable possessions...understandable at the time, but perhaps inappropriate looking back. There are many other situations where we step into things we shouldn't, and then get stuck in the mud of either subtle or significant sin. But the point is, however, *how can we avoid them, right?*

Secondly, *evil also comes from within*...what and who we are inside of ourselves, with all of our inclinations, impulses, and intensions. Two strong influences make up who we are on the inside...our DNA and our experience (nature vs. nurture, if you like). Our nature is unique, for it's a blend of mom and dad and who they were (I'm sure one day some foolish geneticist is going to mix the traits of more than one person...I have no idea how... and come up with some super person, or perhaps a freakish, dangerous and demonic aberration). Nevertheless, the DNA part of us, however tweaked, is what each of us will have to deal with, and it holds great influence over our lives.

We also understand that on the inside of us dwells a sense of moral conscience, and wants us to be "moral and ethical" to some degree. It pushes us to think with a degree of compassion along with an overriding sense of right or wrong, when making decisions regarding people or events around us.

Another inner influence upon our lives is called *experience*. Here, we acquire knowledge and store it within, which we use to make to make future assumptions and decisions about life. When our experiences are good and/or healthy, experience leans us in the direction of good and God. When they bring evil, pain, abuse, and harm into our lives, such things can easily push us away from doing good or seeking God.

The interaction of both nature and nurture makes up who we are in the long run, building or attacking godly character and commitment. From a Christian point of view, of course, we understand the Scriptures to say that, *"All have sinned and have fallen short of the grace of God."* In fact, just before Noah floated his boat to the top of the world, God told him the why of it all:

> *"The Lord saw how great man's wickedness on the earth had become and that every inclination*

of the thoughts of his heart was only evil all the time. The Lord was grieved that he had made man on the earth..."
(Gen. 6:5, 6)

Thirdly, there is the influence of Satan, which frequently intimidates us into making immature decisions in favor of evil. Satan and his demonic servants, all of whom are devoid of goodness at any level, have the singular purpose of attacking God, harming his creation and undermining his rule over us. This spiritual influence toward evil operates both on the outside of us as well as on the inside of us, for Satan can be the cause of both disease and demonic oppression. For instance, he can *stimulate* our inner person toward lust, fear, pride, jealousy, hate or other inner propensities. Now, he can be resisted and rejected, but we need the power of God's indwelling Spirit to make that happen with any level of consistency.

So, losing a job, having a questionable friendship with someone of the opposite sex, or wanting a new home are not necessarily irresistible encroachments of Satan into our personal lives. However, they can be opportunities for him to intimidate and tempt us to be attracted to the "shiny things" all around us. Anything that appeals to us can also be something Satan uses to allure us, anger us, or antagonize us to reject God's will. Scripture warns to be wise, not simple, in these matters, saying, *"...in order that Satan should not outwit us. For we are not unaware of his schemes."* (II Cor. 2:11). Remember:

> *"...our struggle is not against flesh and blood, but against the rulers, against the authorities, against the powers of this dark world and against the spiritual forces of evil in the heavenly realms."* (Eph. 6:12)

Convictional Review: Overcoming Evil

In all the convictions we've been discussing so far in this book, there needs to be a foundation upon which everything rests. Remember in chapter one how we identified that conviction is a combination of Perspective, Passion and Purpose? Okay, be aware that *what we believe and understand to be true **forms*** that foundation (based upon the Word of God, of course). W*ithout spiritual perspective (deep seated belief in God's Truth)*, our passions, purposes and practices will be sporadic and inconsistent. It's like lighting a candle and watching its flame diminish quickly as you gradually lower a glass over it. When you deprive it of oxygen, it simply loses its flame.

So, perspective is ground zero and the spark of every convictional flame. It's what ignites your passions, drives your purposes, and determines your practices in serving the Lord Jesus. Such *godly thinking is always* at the heart of every spiritual conviction, beginning with faith. But, if it is to root itself within us and become the inner pinions of spiritual character, it must be driven deep into one's heart through Scriptural study, devotional prayer, fellowship, pastoral teaching, worship, etc. Understanding God's Word is the seed of life-changing attitudes and behaviors. Mark 4:20 reminds us of this:

> *"Others, like seed sown on good soil, hear the world, accept it, and produce a crop...thirty, sixty or even a hundred times what was sown."*

However, perspective understanding *by itself*, can't overpower evil, for it's essentially just intellectual and logical thought. It must *inspire* something within us, which *motivates and moves us* somehow...if it is to be a life changing force God's Truth is meant to be. Otherwise, perspective is just impersonal facts and detached wisdom, etc. To initiate personal changes in attitude and behavior, one needs *some degree of inclinational passion* (desire or emotion). This only happens when the truth of God's Word impassions us deeply enough that we *finally and purposely* put our perspectives into action! Remember Paul's prayer?

> *"I pray that out of his glorious riches he may strengthen you with power through his Spirit in your inner being, so that Christ may dwell in your **hearts** through faith...that you, being rooted and established **in love** may have power together with all the saints to grasp how wide and long and high and deep I the love of Christ, and to know this love that **surpasses knowledge** that you may be filled to the measure of all the fullness of God."* (Eph. 3:16-19)

Paul is saying here that the Holy Spirit is the one who is actively strengthening (empowering) our inner person at the heart level by faith. But that comes by way of rooting ourselves in a "love" relationship with Christ (impassioned and personal), which is itself is *more than* just perspective, for it "surpasses" knowledge." So, godly perspectives *must breed passion,* if intentional behavior are ever to "kick in" later on.

Consider Tom, for instance, who's having a problem with lust. Every time a beautiful woman walks by, he has an overwhelming urge to fantasize about her. Yes, he tries to think of verses that deal with purity, and that helps him to control his mind to a degree, which is good. And he renews his faith commitment to Christ in the midst of such temptations, as well, trying to renew his determination to obey the Lord, instead of his feeding his lewd mindset... another good strategy. But he's only about 50% successful in all that, because over a week or so all that self-discipline and determination evaporates, and he indulges himself again in either an impure entertainment choice or unguarded fantasy. He's just a mixture of sincere commitments and sorrowful confessions, a cycle with which he's regrettably and remorsefully too familiar. And the same overall cycle would be the same with whatever appetite seems to masters us from time to time, be it uncontrolled hunger, anger, jealousy, pride, etc. *But why does Tom fail so often?*

I believe there's a misfire or disconnect between what he understands about God (perspective) and what he wants to do for God (*passion*). His perspective of purity and immature spiritual desire has not yet become a ***driving force*** of his heart. He's been *influenced* by God's Word in those areas, yes, but he hasn't yet been fully *impacted* by it…to the point where it brings ***significant*** spiritual desire, enough so to change his lifestyle. Unless that misfiring connection is restored and strengthened, Tom's cycle of success/failure will repeat itself continually.

Similarly, as immature and carnal believers, we do at times continue to return to a sin or temptation, just like Tom. Again, why is that? Because it *feels good*, right, in one way or another! Yes, of course. But strategically speaking…it's because we don't ***profoundly*** believe what God is saying in his Word, and that weakens the convictional passion (later purpose) so necessary to overcome sinful desires with consistency. Our spiritual understanding is too shallow and weak, unable to move us deeply enough to want and choose God's will over our own!

Satan's part in all this, of course, is to ***dull*** our spiritual discernment (perspective), inviting temporal pleasures *in place of passion* for God and his will, thus dissipating any significant, intentional drive to stay holy and pure. Never the less, the Spirit's job is to continually ignite and re-ignite one's passion for God. *It's the fuel in our tanks, the fire in our spiritual bellies and the motivational force of godly conviction.* Perspective must acquire such transforming passion in our spiritual walk, or we will either just get by or begin to dangerously compromise our standards and become a replica of King Saul. Let's become a King David, instead, and let our beliefs go deep enough that they become impassioned for God and make us vessels of true, lasting honor in his hands for his purposes.

On top of this, if Satan can get us into habitual sin of some sort, then our spiritual reserves really fill up with improper attitudes, which only erode our thinking. Did you ever seriously think you and I could indulge our evil desires and not have residual effects upon our memory, our thinking, our emotions, even our physical body and health? Such repetitive sins break into our personal walk, our marriages, our families and our careers, bringing a whole lot of unplanned and debilitating debris. It also incapacitates our willingness to obey and serve God.

However, when spiritually impassioned thinking *is* developed instead, (if grounded in God's Word), it brings *persevering determination* to obey the Lord in our daily challenges and choices. Yes, full and lasting conviction happens when we raise our impassioned perspectives to the level of *full surrender and yieldedness to the will of God's indwelling Spirit*. It's believing in God and his will, wanting God and his will, and submitting to God and his will in spiritual **submission**...*regardless of anything to the contrary*. Now, that's what can change a weak, vacillating believer into a powerful servant for the Lord. Yes, I know that no one will be perfectly grounded in godly conviction such that he or she is untouched by sin or above temptation. But this is still the underlying process...a spiritual roadmap...for successfully traveling forward in Christian living.

To summarize, then, **perspective** *thinking is foundational* for implementing spiritual growth or change...mental focus, yes, but mostly one's mindset and belief system (Romans 12:2). Secondly, it follows that we believers still cannot be the men and women God wants us to be until *we also want to be* what God wants us to be...that's the **passion** part of conviction. Thirdly, men and women cannot consistently obey God's will until they become *surrendered* to it...*that's the* **purposeful** *part of conviction*. Again, the inner *perspective* to obey God will never be effective enough on its own to consistently resist sin or habit until it *moves our* inclinations and ultimately *empowers* our intentions. All three functionalities are necessary to maintain convictional strength, ongoing purity and lasting spiritual growth.

Please keep in mind, too, that *weak or compromising perspective thinking* facilitates *dissipating desire* and *determination* to obey God. Saul was a great example of this, for he continually strayed from the prophet Samuel's words to his own demise. He never learned to "think right" and have the deep-seated belief in Jehovah that would have overcome his own propensities toward fear and depression, occultic involvement, demonic oppression and habitual disobedience. Only when God's Truth resides deep within us (at the heart level) will spiritual conviction bloom. Again, here's how to diagram it:

Perspective +> Passion +> Purpose => Practice

Deep discernment of God's Truth develops the spiritually impassioned perspective necessary to intentionally and consistently overcome evil

So, build your own personal library of *spiritually impassioned* and *empowered perspectives*. This process is the key for developing spiritual stamina and success over sensuality and Satan. This in turn produces men and women of conviction that God can use mightily.

At this point, I must point out a *critical* factor in our discussion...our foundational conviction is always faith. *Paul tells us to, "take up the shield of faith, with which you can extinguish all the flaming arrows of the evil one." (Eph. 6:16)* There are many convictions to be acquired in our spiritual walk with God in Christ, but faith is the one from which we primarily fight our enemies... Satan, the world and fleshly desires. Inside of our hearts God planted a small seed of belief, trust and reliance upon Christ as our Savior and Lord. *That essential faith seed is a small,* Spirit-planted powerhouse of godly desire and determination to love and serve our heavenly Father. Yes, there are many convictions we must come to adopt, if we are to live with spiritual purity and consistency, but without faith undergirding it all, everything can easily topple to the ground.

So, whatever you believe and acquire for your convictional library, don't forget the source of it all...your *faith* conviction. As you face the challenges of life, always believe in Christ deeply, desire his blessing passionately and commit yourself fully to the Lord. Without this primary spiritual love for God constantly being resourced, any of us can fail to be what we should be in our Christian walk.

Building Your Convictional Library

How do we build and maintain our convictions? Perspective, Passion and Purpose come from the Spirit and his Word. As we meditate and study Biblical Truth and its spiritual precepts and principles, we will gradually develop a mental library of impassioned and empowered spiritual convictions. This is more than acquiring just head knowledge, though, it's adopting significant *heart* knowledge and wisdom. Peter reminds us of this critical difference in II Peter 3:18:

> *"But grow in the grace and knowledge of our Lord and Savior Jesus Christ."*

The word for knowledge in this passage means "experiential knowledge," not factual knowledge (https:/biblehub.com/greek/1108.htm). It comes out of our <u>relationship</u> with Christ on a daily basis. Do you want greater discernment, deeper desire and unwavering determination in your conviction(s) for God? Then, get deeply and prayerfully involved with the Word of God, for it's the primary resource for renewing your heart passion and faith/commitment Jesus Christ. John tells us:

> *"The Spirit gives life, the flesh counts for nothing. The words I have spoken to you are spirit and they are life."* (John 6:63)

God's Spirit within us responds to Jesus' words, and then moves us within toward righteousness by Truth. That's why the Spirit encourages us to trust in the Scriptural truth and feed upon it, for it alone can stir and empower us to overcome our carnal, compromising and wayward impulses. We must *"fix our eyes on Jesus, the author and perfecter of our faith,"* which implies that we must focus upon God's Word with consistency. By doing so, we will, *"approach the throne of grace with confidence, so that we may receive mercy and find grace to help in our time of need"* (Heb. 4:16). Ultimately, this practical, yet personal, relationship with the Scriptures will purge us from evil influences. Jesus said, *"Sanctify them by the truth; your world is truth."* (John 17:17)

Let's highlight 5 practical avenues for strengthening our spiritual convictions

1. KEEP RECONSECRATING YOURSELF TO GOD. As I said, consecration is the presenting all of yourself in obedient faith to Christ. Most people, when they think of this, remember a time when they went forward at a youth rally or at an altar call in a church service. They think that it might be something to do maybe once or twice in your whole life. On the contrary, though it's true that these may be special times of recommitment to the Lord, I'm suggesting that it's something you and I need to do daily. Presenting our minds and hearts in faith obedience to the Lord is a critical part of spiritual growth, for it seals and reseals our covenant with Christ on a regular basis. It may be accompanied by Scriptural study or devotions, confession of known sin, personal worship and a humble surrender to the lordship of Jesus Christ over our lives. But it doesn't necessarily have to be a dramatic or lengthy point-in-time thing either. For instance, just by sitting on the edge of the bed at the start of the day, you can bow before God and present yourself to Christ in faith and obedience for everything that's ahead of you. No other posturing is necessary, just a humble prayer of love for God is all that's necessary:

> *"Yes, Jesus, I believe in you and seek to do your will today. I want to put you first in everything today and to love you with all my mind and heart. Keep me from sin, Lord. I trust you to direct my life and I will rejoice in your timing and providential leading. Make me a fruitful Christian, and bless me according to your will in all that I do."*

Throughout your day feel free to repeat that prayer...freely and in similar words...and so align yourself with God and restore your spiritual and relational intimacy. Remember,

Satan and fleshly desires cannot over power a believer whose heart is full of faith and love for God:

> *"Create in me a pure heart, O God, and renew a steadfast spirit within me. Do not cast me from your presence or take your Holy Spirit from me. Restore to me the joy of your salvation and grant me a willing spirit, to sustain me...The sacrifices of God are a broken spirit, a broken and contrite heart, O God, you will not despise."* (Ps. 51:10-12, 17)

2. DISCIPLINE YOUR MIND. Make the time to delve into the Bible *every day* and prayerfully digest its teaching. This allows the Spirit of God to *renew, rebuild and re-motivate* your convictions with his impassioned truth. I'm not talking here about a 5 minute Our Daily Bread read through, even though that's a helpful thing, of course. I'm talking about a "biblical relationship" with God, where we take sufficient time to seek God in his Word. We desperately need to understand, review and focus upon its principles and precepts under the oversight of God's Spirit. In this way, the Spirit of God will plant new thoughts and convictions within your inner person: "Sanctify them by your Truth; your Word is Truth." (Jn 17:17). We might call this, *"Mental Meditation."*

But another key to maturity is to practice *"Mental Management."* By this I mean simple mind control, where you protect your heart from listening to and lingering thoughtfully near things that stir up unhealthy or evil desires and intentions. All of us have roving fears, anxieties, lusts, hate, pride and many other thoughts that "drop into" our consciousness from time to time...even random uncategorized thoughts. If we give questionable, unwise, sinful or just bothersome thoughts time to germinate, they will, and cause havoc! However, if you're into the Word, prayer, fellowship, etc., then the Spirit will help you to manage your thought life in such moments, enabling you to resist potential and/or obvious sinful thought patterns.

We're in a spiritual war, folks, far beyond anything flesh and blood can win. As Ephesians 6 reminds us, victory over such enemies comes not by fleshy tools or human efforts alone, but by putting on the full armor of God...and by offensively wielding *"the sword of the Spirit, which is the Word of God."* (Ephesians 6:17) So, fill up your heart and mind with the Word of God cognitively and consciously. Carry some verse cards with you to work or have a Scriptural phone app ready to fire up at first notice of temptation. Remember, the outer person will only do what the inner person has considered and allowed, so think right and you'll begin to live right.

3. MAINTAIN REGULAR FELLOWSHIP opportunities and close Christian friendships every week, which greatly enables us to build up our impassioned reserves for God. Examples are regular church services, of course, but also home study or small groups, lunches/breakfasts with Christian friends. Please remember that this is also not just an idea, it's a command:

> *"...let us not give up meeting together as some are in the habit of doing, but let us encourage on another, and all the more as you see the Day approaching." (Hebrews 19:24)*

Remember, if your spiritual tributaries are pouring good things into your life...such as fellowship, service for the Lord, love from other believers, solid teaching, etc., you'll find that those things will **replace over time** the unwanted flow of sin and temptation into your spiritual reservoir. We can't eliminate temptation from time to time, but we can diminish its overall impact by managing our spiritual infrastructure with discipline and wisdom.

4. PRACTICE REGULAR CONFESSION. When genuinely and contritely done with consistency, confession restores spiritual balance in our walk with Christ. Just like those valves on the back of a dam let out small amounts of water from

time to time to manage the water level and relieve mounting pressure, confession releases the hidden or tolerated sins that have seeped into our minds, hearts and lives. Re-consecrating ourselves then reaffirms our spiritual convictions and restores our spiritual dam's integrity.

5. DEVELOP A WORSHIPFUL RELATIONSHIP WITH CHRIST. Your personal Bible Study and devotions aren't meant to be stagnant or emotionally dry. Allow time to lift up your heart in praise to God for his goodness and grace in your life. Eagerly engage in personal worship and prayer, while expressing your thankfulness to the Lord, who saves and sustains you each and every hour. Sing a song by yourself, listen to your favorite worship leader's podcast or CD...in other words, enjoy the Lord and praise him for who he is and for what he's doing in your life!

In a world where sinful attitudes and activities shine so ostentatiously, we've got to focus upon God and his Will for us as revealed in the Scriptures. That's how we stimulate our spiritual convictions and make everything around us seem like temporary sparks of a camp fire, which quickly die out in the dark. We want our lives instead to be a penetrating flame of light reaching into the sky, providing spiritual warmth for ourselves to enjoy and that by which others can be enlightened. Then we all can say, "Nothing shines more brightly or is more valuable to me than the Lord Jesus Christ!" Amen and amen!

CONVICTION #22

I Believe In An "Unbelievable" Future!

"Then I saw "a new heaven and a new earth," for the first heaven and the first earth had passed away, and there was no longer any sea. I saw the Holy City, the new Jerusalem, coming down out of heaven from God, prepared as a bride beautifully dressed for her husband. And I heard a loud voice from the throne saying, "Look! God's dwelling place is now among the people, and he will dwell with them. They will be his people, and God himself will be with them and be their God. 'He will wipe every tear from their eyes. There will be no more death' or mourning or crying or pain, for the old order of things has passed away." Revelation 21:1-3

Ed, what in the world are you saying? Believable, unbelievable...make up your mind, will you? No, the truth is, our future in Christ is both believable and "unbelievable." It's coming and it's real, but at the same time it's so exciting and indescribable, it's beyond our mind's understanding of how wonderful it will be:

> *"No eye has seen, no ear has heard, no heart has imagined, what God has prepared for those who love him."* (I Cor. 2:9)

This is the context that I use the word, "unbelievable," for we just can't *fully* understand what life will be like beyond the grave. Truly, our future with God is going to be an eye-opening, ear-pounding, heart enlarging and out-of-body experience! (a *new* body experience, let's say). So, let's take a limited look at what lies ahead for you and me in Christ Jesus.

First, the clock is ticking!

The Bible says that no person knows the day or hour when Jesus will be coming back to this earth, but we can know when it's close. Jesus clearly gives a description of the times and life just before he comes.

> *"Now learn this lesson from the fig tree: As soon as its twigs get tender and its leaves come out, you know that summer is near. Even so, when you see these things happening,* **you know that it is near, right at the door.** *Truly I tell you,* ***this generation*** *will certainly not pass away until all these things have happened. Heaven and earth will pass away, but my words will never pass away."* (Mark 13:28-31)

Okay, but what generation? Well, the generation "of the fig tree." The fig tree is often used to describe Israel in the New Testament. So, Jesus is saying that when you see that Israel is back as a nation, growing and producing fruit, then THAT generation won't all die off before He comes back the 2nd time.

Okay, Israel became a nation in 1948, after almost 2000 years of disruption and international fighting. Since a generation in Scripture may be interpreted to be somewhere between 70 and 100 years, we're already into that range of time by 72 years (2021... the time of this writing). So, without putting too fine a point to it,

I suggest that Christ will come back sometime within the next 28 years! Thus, we may not know the day or the hour, but we are told to *watch* for his coming...when we see this particular sign, as well as other accompanying signs beginning to be fulfilled.

Second, the signs are clearly happening.

A couple of years ago, I gave a presentation at our yearly men's winter retreat about all the signs of Christ's second coming that seem to be happening. So, let's review that list now, after first reading through Christ's words directly.

> "Do you see all these things?" he asked. "I tell you the truth, not one stone here will be left on another; everyone will be thrown down." As Jesus was sitting on the Mount of Olives, the disciples came to him privately. "Tell us," they said, "when will this happen (temple destruction...70 AD), and what will be the sign of your coming) and of the end of the age?" Jesus answered: "Watch out that no one deceives you. For many will come in my name, claiming, 'I am the Christ,' and will deceive many. You will hear of wars and rumors of wars, but see to it that you are not alarmed. Such things must happen, but the end is still to come. Nation will rise against nation, and kingdom against kingdom. There will be famines and earthquakes in various places. All these are the beginning of birth pains. Then you will be handed over to be persecuted and put to death, and you will be hated by all nations because of me. At that time many will turn away from the faith and will betray and hate each other, and many false prophets will appear and deceive many people. Because of the increase of wickedness, the love of most will grow cold, but he who stands firm to the end will be saved. And this gospel of the kingdom will be preached

in the whole world as a testimony to all nations, and then the end will come. So when you see standing in the holy place 'the abomination that causes desolation,' spoken of through the prophet Daniel—let the reader understand— then let those who are in Judea flee to the mountains. Let no one on the roof of his house go down to take anything out of the house. Let no one in the field go back to get his cloak. How dreadful it will be in those days for pregnant women and nursing mothers! Pray that your flight will not take place in winter or on the Sabbath. For then there will be great distress, unequaled from the beginning of the world until now—and never to be equaled again. If those days had not been cut short, no one would survive, but for the sake of the elect those days will be shortened. At that time if anyone says to you, 'Look, here is the Christ!' or, 'There he is!' do not believe it. For false Christs and false prophets will appear and perform great signs and miracles to deceive even the elect—if that were possible. See, I have told you ahead of time. So if anyone tells you, 'There he is, out in the desert,' do not go out; or, 'Here he is, in the inner rooms,' do not believe it. For as lightning that comes from the east is visible even in the west, so will be the coming of the Son of Man. Wherever there is a carcass, there the vultures will gather. Immediately after the distress of those days the sun will be darkened, and the moon will not give its light; the stars will fall from the sky, and the heavenly bodies will be shaken. "At that time the sign of the Son of Man will appear in the sky, and all the nations of the earth will mourn. They will see the Son of Man coming on the clouds of the sky, with power and great glory. And he will send his angels with a loud trumpet call, and they will gather his elect from the four winds, from one end of the heavens to the other." (Matt 24:2-34)

Generally speaking, there will be an increase in worldly difficulties, dangers and distresses. Jesus tells us that the following signs will occur, some with increasing frequency as we approach the final days (and Christ's 2nd coming).

1. Destruction of the Jewish Temple

This was fulfilled in the year 70 AD, when the Romans destroyed it.

2. Appearance of many false messiahs toward the last days.

To the right are most of the foolish "prophets" in history that tried to convince the world that they were the Son of God revisiting the earth. Unfortunately for them, they all died and met the real Savior and Lord. One of the most well-known is Sun Moon, shown to the left, a self-acclaimed Christ of the Unification Church. His true humanity revealed itself, when he died In 2012 from pneumonia, yet failed to be resurrected from the grave. Genuine Christians follow a living Savior, whose power over death is a historically proven reality. From Sun Myung Moon - Wikipedia

HISTORICAL FALSE MESSIAHS
Dositheos the Samaritan (1st C)
Ann Lee (1736–1784)
John Nichols Thom (1799–1838)
Abd-ru-shin (1875 –1941)
Lou de Palingboer (1898-1968)
André Matsoua (1899–1942)
Samael Aun Weor (1917–1977)
Ahn Sahng-hong (1918–1985)
Sun Myung Moon (1920–2012)
Yahweh ben Yahweh (1935–2007)
Wayne Bent (born 1941)
Iesu Matayoshi (1944-2018)
Jung Myung Seok (born 1945)
Claude Vorilhon (born 1946)
José Luis de Jesús (1946–2013)
Inri Cristo (born 1948)
Brian David Mitchell (born 1953)
David Koresh (1959–1993)
Maria Devi Christos (born 1960)
List of messiah claimants - Wikipedia

I also had the "pleasure" of being introduced to another false Christ, when I was a teenager growing up in Connecticut. Though not on the list, he called himself "Brother Julius," and his wife was known as the incarnate Holy Spirit. He eventually was said to be involved with a real estate scheme and died sometime in the 90's.

In the days just before the climactic return of our true Savior and Lord, Jesus Christ, the Bible says will be marked by a resurgence of false messiahs. They will no doubt use technology and miraculous appearing tricks to draw many to their own spiritual demise. Nevertheless, their lifestyle will reveal their trickery, for such men have always been steeped in adulterous living, doctrinal fantasies, and financial schemes. They often prey upon those whose backgrounds are scared by broken families, social rejection, and dissatisfaction with the organized church in some way.

3. **International tensions and struggles** The world is hemorrhaging with political tension. Political factions that have been somewhat scattered throughout the world are beginning to coalesce into three key philosophical areas... communism, socialism and capitalism. Europe has greatly moved toward socialism, China remains communist, and Russia is a hybrid capitalism with remaining roots of autocratic controls still strongly entrenched. Both Africa and South America have both Marxist and socialist surges vying for dominance. America remains a republic led by the people with free enterprise thinking, but it has been corrupted beyond repair by the enrooted thinking of liberalism as its moral base. Thus, it has become clearly divided into two opposing views... free enterprise and socialism...but socialism has mostly won the day, particularly in the recent election of Joe Biden. It's only a matter of time before the greatest nation ever formed upon Christian beliefs collapses under the weight of its own diseased political structure and social immorality.

> *The purveyors and perpetrators of godless socialism seek to corrupt the American ideals of individualism, free enterprise, religious freedom, limited government and personal economic success through responsible self-effort. They have confiscated media outlets, invaded culture*

with entertainment immorality, and usurped key positions in local, state and federal government in order to espouse their bankrupt political agenda. The Christian ideals of earning what you have and being content therein before God and man has been corrupted with materialistic jealousy, that which steals from those who have in order to feed those who simply want.

Why Do Liberals Hate Christianity?

- Christians believe in absolute truth.
- Christians are intellectually inferior.
- Christians are hate-mongers.
- Christians impose their religion.
- Christians are hypocrites.

Yes, the world is struggling to survive, but the pot is boiling over in its quest to find a secure answer for economic and political peace. We know the answer is found in a return to the principles God has laid out for us in the Bible. But Satan has always been the ruler of this fallen world, and he continues to infect people, governments and nations with his insidious disease of self-satisfying and godless self-reliance.

> *"But the natural man receives not the things of the Spirit of God for they are foolishness unto him: ...they are spiritually discerned."* 1 Corinthians 2:14

4. **Wars and rumors of wars.** The 20th century was the bloodiest ever, which is a sure sign of the coming end of times. But, along with Communism, Socialism, Liberalism, and Nazism, a huge threat to world order has been the Muslim faith, which by its own mission as stated in the Koran is to conquer the infidel world. Many believe that the final battle against Israel,

led by anti-Christ and his 10-nation confederacy, will be led by surrounding Muslim nations. Christ will come, of course, and bring defeat. But the inherent jealousy of the Arab-Muslim world over Israel's land has fueled itself for 4000 years, ever since Isaac was born as the promised son of God's covenant with Abraham. Ishmael, his son by Sarah's handmaiden, Hagar, was ultimately rejected from that promise and its fulfillment in the land Israel now occupies. Ishmael settled in Arabia, which ultimately gave birth to Mohamed and Islam in the 7th C.

20th Century Death-In-War Statistics:	Question:
20 to 50 M...Stalin's purge of Russian	What is the "greatest war machine in history?"
30 M...Chinese cultural revolution	
15 M...killed by Hitler in WWII	Answer:
2.5 M...killed in Cambodia 1975-1979	Mohammed & Islam: 200+M people killed in 1400 Years*
1.35 M...killed in the Vietnam War	
120+ M...worldwide in 20th Century	*various internet resources

5. Worldwide famines and earthquakes

It's obvious the EARTHQUAKES have significantly increased in recent years (see chart). In addition, famines have increased as well, though some of this has resulted from the after effects of ongoing wars. Over population also leads to economic struggles, hunger, disease, and crime: *Over 800 million people worldwide are in starvation mode each day.*

Mag. 6.99+ Earthquakes
- 1863 to 1900   12
- 1901 to 1938   53
- 1939 to 1976   71
- 1977 to 2014   164

Report has been based on data available from USGS

Famine Statistics

There have been **6M** deaths by famine from **33 A.D. - 1699 A.D.**
(and 50 recorded famines)
But there have been **500M** deaths by famine **- 1700 A.D.**
- 2012 A.D.
(and 97 recorded famines)

6. Hatred and persecution of believers

In times past, the political world in America achieved a positive landscape of many thoughts coming together through compromise and common sense. This seems no longer to be the case, for there are now two fairly well-defined and differing perspectives regarding society and government, namely conservatism or liberalism. These two world views have become clearly observable in all areas of life. Essentially, conservatism believes in these:

- Market driven economics & free enterprise…work that achieves.
- Limited government and control over people and their pursuits.
- Welfare is a helpful, *temporary* solution…a safety net for the needy.
- Moral absolutes and clearly defined "rights & wrongs."
- Societal standards of morality based upon Christian principles.
- Cross-cultural moral standards, which guide social behaviors.
- Racial integration through opportunity enhancement.
- Family defined as husband (male), wife (female), and children.
- Emphasizing people's responsibilities, without idolizing their rights.

- Sexual common sense and purity in entertainment and lifestyle.

The other side of the coin, liberalism, looks at life quite differently. It sees the following as its societal and governmental objectives to espouse.

- The rich should support the needy and underprivileged.
- Government enforces socialism through high taxation and controls.
- Government mandates that all *equally share* in the economic pie.
- Morals are not absolute; rights & wrongs change as society does.
- Christian thinking must go, for they are unapologetically exclusive.
- Multi-culturalism is the new normal; people can live as they choose.
- "Social justice" must be achieved through Marxist rebellion & havoc.
- Family is a "village," gender is flexible, trans-folks are accepted.
- People's rights are far more important than responsible living.
- Sexual freedom is the hallmark of liberalism; God is multi-cultural.

There's an old Disney movie – "20000 Leagues Under The Sea" – which describes the passion that captain Nemo possesses, due to being imprisoned in a war camp and later having his family killed by those same people. He escapes, but is driven thereafter to seek revenge upon all war ships, sinking them mercilessly with his submarine boat. At one point after destroying one of those ships, he tries to justify his unloving, killing spree to someone. He first asks, "Do you know what love is?" The hearer responds affirmatively. Then Nemo says confidently, "What you fail to understand is the power of hate."

I think that perfectly describes how moral leftists look at Christians...they simply hate them. Why? Because our holy God has set boundaries for behaviors and holds men accountable for their willful choices to sin against those boundaries. They don't want to be bound by anyone, including God, for they are driven by a lust for self-pleasure and self-fulfillment. In addition, they also think that there is more than just one way to please God and gain his heaven (though the inherent contradiction in that statement is unmistakable!). Yes, in the end of days, persecution of believers will increase exponentially, particularly, I believe, in America.

7. Many will turn away from the faith

In the past, more Americans used to be people of moral conviction than today. Years of television sit-coms, dirty-mouthed comedians, erotic plays, graphic videos, and "R" rated movies have undermined our national moral conscience. We are a formerly Christian nation that has long left its belief in absolute right and wrong, except perhaps, when talking about racism.

> Every day, 8 Christians worldwide are killed because of their faith....Every week, 182 churches or Christian buildings are attacked....Every month, 309 Christians are imprisoned unjustly.

Because of all this, the church itself has been infected with satanic and flesh-driven influences. Believers are struggling with addictions and temptations in growing numbers, and those with shallow faith/commitment roots are defecting. As the end of the age approaches and Christ's 2nd coming nears, many will either ignore and/or renounce the Gospel of Jesus Christ.

However, it is also true that the "Gospel will be preached to all nations," and then the end will come. This is certainly a general sign as well, but it's hard to "insert" it into a time sequence, depending upon one's view of the rapture and the tribulation period. Let me suggest that there are very few nations remaining today that haven't heard about Jesus Christ. If the term "nations" can be interpreted as every individual ethnic tribe or culture, then there remains a bit of work to do, considering indigenous cultures in the bush of Africa, the mountains of Tibet, or the valleys of China.

In my view, however, that is pressing the point a bit too much. The main issue here is that every continent and large cultural grouping will need to have had the Gospel preached to them before the second coming of Christ occurs. Again, I believe this mark has essentially been achieved already, particularly with a world in which internet, television, radio and satellite technology is available and abounds for people to hear the Gospel even in remote places.

> "Follow the pattern of the sound words that you have heard from me, in the faith and love that are in Christ Jesus. By the Holy Spirit who dwells within us, guard the good deposit entrusted to you" (1:13–14).

8. Many false prophets will appear

Recently, I recognized a once prominent televangelist in the news, who is now stating that homosexuality can be a viable lifestyle for believers, as well as accepting that there are, at times, other ways to find God's salvation than through the Gospel. I said to myself, "Am I hearing this right?" Yes, I was, unfortunately. On another broadcast, I heard that the son of a very prominent Pastor was teaching extremely liberal things in opposition to sound and traditional conservative doctrine. Finally, I listened to an interview with one of the most well-known televangelists in the nation discussing very questionable theology regarding salvation, judgment and hell. So, it would seem that this particular sign of the last days is growing in theological prominence.

There is a word of caution in this, however. Jesus was essentially talking about those godless, wicked prophets, those who *clearly* opposed sound doctrine. There are differences that exist from one pastor to another, that do not deserve the name, "false prophet." Careful thought should be given before we start calling people names in overly critical accusations and without any sense of humility. This is not to excuse the shallow examination of Scriptural truth on the part of some, but to emphasize the opposite. There is always the necessity of sound thinking, personal study, accountability, humility and prayer, before we accept someone's teaching about the Word of God.

It's also critical that one looks behind the teaching and examines the person and/or organization involved. In Peter's second letter to the church, he discusses the indicators and motivations of false teachers, including avarice, greed, popularity, self-promotion, rebellion, satanism, etc. Such things are signs that the teaching could easily be *intentionally* erroneous and should be avoided or condemned. There may be many ways to go from Los Angeles to Chicago, but there's only one map for obeying God ... Scriptural Truth. Let's study it well and avoid shallow, over-simplified, or unsound extrapolations from it that frustrate the Spirit's sensible counsel. As believers, we don't stone false prophets to death any more, as they did in the Old Testament times. However, perhaps that might shrink the ranks of this misguided crowd today, if we reinstated it. What do you think?

9. Increase of wickedness and spiritual coldness

In talking about the world and its spiritual condition, here Jesus is saying that the last days are going to be a hay-day for hedonism, harlotry and hellish behaviors. Cold spirituality breeds sin and wickedness, and God is not going to be much of a concern for these end-times folks. There will be a "form of godliness," of course, but the work of those false prophets and the sharp increases in sinful indulgences will easily diminish spiritual sensitivity.

> **Where Is America Today?** *(2015)*
> If you fell asleep 40 years ago and awoke today, imagine how shocked you would be at what happened to "Christian" America.
> Divorce: Increased from 4% to 51% in one generation.
> Abortion: 57 million unborn babies aborted; part of socialized medicine.
> Marijuana: State legalization is the new normal for handling this issue.
> Alcoholism: 20% increase; 28.6% 12th Gr./40.1 % college binge drinking
> Cohabitation: 65% (lifestyle fornication); 1 of every 8 births today.
> Pornography: Rampant, graphic, just a "click away" on hand-held devices.
> Movies and music: Graphic nudity, gratuitous violence, prolific profanity.
> Spending insanity: A $18 T national debt and $15 K personal credit card debt.
> Out-of-wedlock births: 50% children born out of wedlock (1st time in U.S history).
> Sexually transmitted diseases: Over 110M Americans (1 in 3 infected); $16 B cost.
> Homosexual, transgender lifestyles: Promoted, legalized, honored in marriage.

Actually, we see this now in part. Politicians and political parties lie and commit fraud, even to the point of stealing votes and elections. The disingenuous calls for peace by groups like Black Lives Matter are drowned out by *their own* antics of rioting, rebellion and burning. Entertainment is inundated with sexual perversion and promiscuity, hatred, killing, fantasy, carnality, and false narratives about God and life. Luke Skywalker is better known in the teenage crowd than the name of Jesus! Big-Teck companies and media giants are merging in a powerful quest to control the freedoms we've had since the founding fathers signed the constitution...but few seem to listen or even care. Social platforms as Twitter, Facebook and Google are now "cancelling" certain Presidents, politicians, societal leaders...even everyday folks...who simply have viewpoints that offend them. They posture themselves as able to best determine what is to be heard, which is Un-American, un-scriptural and, well, just wrong!

> **Personal Corruption:** "It is ordained in the eternal constitution of things, that men of intemperate minds cannot be free. Their passions forge their fetters." Edmund Burke

I believe that biblically based teaching, preaching, writing, music, entertainment...will be held in such disrepute in the near future that they will also be "cancelled" due to "offensive" political viewpoints. Quiet dissenters will no doubt be tolerated, but aggressive protestors will be squelched in the name of either racism or religious bias. George Washington, Thomas Jefferson, and Ben Franklin will probably be "turning over in their graves," as the saying goes!

But, again, all of this falls within the permissive will of God, because his time table for judgment is on track. The glory of our true Savior and Lord will eventually be broadcast around the world as Jesus comes shining through the clouds at his second coming!

10. Abomination that causes desolation

There is a tribulation time coming, bringing to the world great distress and destruction. The Bible calls this the Great Tribulation, and it will exist for a period of 7 years. The first half (3.5 years) will be difficult enough, but the second half will be marked by global destruction and terrible loss of life. World-wide plagues (eg. Covid19), natural disasters, wars and famines will increase even within this period of time. *But where will the church be?*

Well, it appears first that there will be a western world ruler – called Anti-Christ in the Bible – that will make covenants and control nations. He is unrecognized as such by people for the first half of the Tribulation, but then is significantly revealed for who he is mid-way through it. He does this by breaking an important covenant with restored Israel and then sets himself up as a god in the rebuilt Jewish temple, where sacrifices had been resumed after two thousand years. He seizes power over a recently formed western confederacy of nations and also assumes "religious" authority over it. This act in the Bible is referred to as a "abomination of desolation."

In II Thessalonians 2:1-9, we are told how all this unfolds. The key to this is that the second coming of Jesus Christ cannot come ***until this "abomination" above takes place*** (He comes with his saints and meeting those believers still alive on the earth).

> *"Don't let anyone deceive you in any way, for that day will not come until the rebellion occurs and the man of lawlessness is revealed...He will oppose and will exalt himself over everything that is called God or is worshiped, so that he sets himself up in God's temple, proclaiming himself to be God."* (v. 3-4)

It is after this event that the door is open for Christ to come back, redeem his church, set up the *Judgment Seat of Christ* for believers, and usher in the 1000 year reign of Christ (at the end of which will be the *Great White Throne Judgment* for unbelievers of all the ages).

I might add that in this same passage, there must also be a removal of a "restrainer," before Anti-Christ is revealed and desecrates the temple. There are several interpretations of who or what this is, and it helps to know a little Greek when looking at it. But my interpretation is that the "restrainer" is the Holy Spirit (and his influence). He has always frustrated and restrained evil according to God's purposes even into the last days, where he finally removes his restraining influence, and the world is left to its own unbridled propensities for evil.. The temple desecration will then occur, and the 2nd half of the Tribulation period will commence, which will bring untold evil, physical destruction, terror, famine and war.

At the end of it all, a trumpet will sound and Jesus will THEN come with his saints in heaven, rapture those believers alive on earth, and come to face the world rulers in the battle of Armageddon. The judgement seat of Christ will occur after Christ defeats this rebellious hoard, and Satan is thrown into a holding pit for 1000 years. The New Jerusalem will then descend to mid-air, from which all believers will live and rule with Christ, enjoying peace and righteousness in that Millennium period of time.

Apparently, those non-believers remaining through the Tribulation will still be living on the earth, separate from the New Jerusalem and to some degree existing in "normal" life responsibilities. At the end of the 1000 years, however, God allows Satan's release for a brief, last ditch effort to disrupt things, but the Lord Jesus quickly squelches it, throwing him and his demons into eternal Hell. This is followed by a final judgment, called The White Throne Judgment, which is where all *non-believers,* who refused to seek and obey God and/or receive his Word, will be judged and sent to their eternal abode in Hell.

My understanding of that Hell is not a place of excruciating torture and endless pain, but of suffering, separation and loss based upon how they had lived (in whatever historical period may have been the situation). Believers, however, will continue to live and enjoy the wonderful blessings of a *renovated and restored earth and heaven*, where peace, prosperity, and productivity in Christ will continue for all eternity!

Again, if my assessment above is correct, many of us will experience the second coming of Christ within our lifetime. However, our beliefs about the details should not outweigh the conviction of it all, that it's "unbelievably believable" and coming soon! I hope the awe of it all will work to keep us in obedient faith each and every day, while we patiently await our Lord's return!

CONVICTION #23

I Believe Culture Can Be Deadly

"We demolish arguments and every pretension that sets itself up against the knowledge of God, and we take captive every thought to make it obedient to Christ."
II Cor. 10:5

For the most part, I really want this book to be a *positive* learning experience, not overly critical one. Unfortunately, however, so many times in Christian circles people seem to get high on describing and debasing evil behaviors which, frankly, is easy to do. After all, as believers we can be rightly shocked by the depths of sin some folks can get into or even by just describing the moral, political or cultural opinions they hold. I'm sure you've heard some pastors give "fired-up sermons" on the evils of our society, which, though justified, seems somewhat unnecessary to blast them upon their flocks as often as they do. Jesus did, of course, call firm attention to the hypocrisy around him at strategic times, especially on the part of the Jewish leadership. But that was seldom and only when such a tone was necessary and productive. Christians should realize that the non-believing world is doing what they do best...they sin, they enjoy doing it, and they'll try to justify it in any situation. Ranting over it isn't very productive, at least very often.

Nevertheless, for you and I today, I think it remains important to *strongly review* our American society and highlight the grievous turnaround that's been happening over the past few years (now 2021). It seems quite sudden, frankly. But the reason I believe it is necessary to do this is that there seems to be a graphic and brutal distinction between *what we were* as a nation and *what we've suddenly become*. Moral dissipation, gender revision, political corruption, and much more is everywhere, and without any platform to refute it or restore common sense and biblical values.

Now, we've never been a perfectly moral or godly nation, but at least there has been a core of Christian values upon which this country was founded and carries on some legal precedent. But, no more, for "liberalism" is the new religion and moral foundation. It's no longer just a philosophy, for it's become a belief system being taught in our schools, practiced in corporate culture, and forced down the throats of our citizenry. Yes, it's sad but true, Christian beliefs, moral absolutes, constitutional law, a strong work ethic, immigration sensibility, debt control, freedom of speech, gender distinctives and much more are no longer the acceptable norm for up-and-coming leaders on the national scene. One top democrat recently is trying to have "mom" and "dad" replaced with "parent" in all legal and social contexts. This, of course, calms the fears of homosexual agitators, and helps to avoid gender stigmas in their relentless quest for societal normalcy. So, let's look at some of the cultural convictions that are driving our nation at the present time.

Evil Conviction #1: Pluralism...Truth Without Substance

"A political philosophy that embraces social and political inclusiveness; where men and women of different religions, ethnicities, races, and political parties share power; members of these competing groups are treated as equal before the law; they live together in harmony and pursue truth together."

www.bing.com/videos/search?q=pluralism&qpvt=pluralism&FORM=VDRE

I think we should pause for a moment and sing a chorus of "Cum-Bye-Yah!" Not to be overly sarcastic, but this should be under the category of dreams, even nightmares! Yet, sadly, this is where our country is going. Now, it's a nice thought...everybody getting along and all, but in the governance of a nation, it simply can't be done. It's been tried to some extent, but it's never worked, because opposite declarations of truth cannot coexist in harmony. Truth simply cannot be divided, or it ceases to be truth. For example, if peaceful, freedom seeking Americans invite Jihadist Muslims into the Senate, who forcibly seek to establish a world-wide Islamic government under the rule of the Koran, the only thing that coexists will be the mingling of blood on the floor of the capital building and beyond. Why is that? Because the two views are diametrically opposed to each other. If each one believes it is the only truth, then compromise will never do for either entity. The fundamental, Islamic dogma dramatically declares that all infidels either submit or be killed...there is no other choice. So, Christians should never compromise and let into U.S. politics anyone declaring himself or herself to be a fundamentalist Muslim adherent. It's simply foolishness to do so, for they will either loudly or silently work toward the ultimate goal of Islamic government control.

I've put together below a list of other Christian values that simply cannot be compromised, if believers are to be seeking God's Truth and following it wisely:

...Christians cannot compromise and allow abortion upon demand.

...Christians cannot compromise and allow or approve of homosexual marriages.

...Christians cannot compromise and allow porn to be acceptable entertainment.

...Christians cannot compromise and allow child-adult sexual relations.

...Christians cannot compromise and allow the welfare state to honor sloth.

- ...Christians cannot compromise and allow suicide as an acceptable practice.
- ...Christians cannot compromise and allow a "village" concept to parent our kids.
- ...Christians cannot compromise and allow state education to teach immorality.
- ...Christians cannot compromise and allow recreational marijuana or drug usage.
- ...Christians cannot compromise and allow political rioting, destruction and chaos.
- ...Christians cannot compromise and allow Marxist leaders into political roles.
- ...Christians cannot compromise and dis-allow the free exercise of religion.
- ...Christians cannot compromise and dis-allow free speech on digital platforms.
- ...Christians cannot compromise and dis-allow traditional family roles to flourish.
- ...Christians cannot compromise and dis-allow folks to responsibly share Christ.
- ...Christians cannot compromise and dis-allow the teaching of moral absolutes.
- ...Christians cannot compromise and dis-allow schools to teach about creation.
- ...Christians cannot compromise and dis-allow the teaching about God & faith.
- ...Christians cannot compromise and dis-allow sensibility by using a disease with a death rate of well under 1% to redefine America, close down society, cripple economic stability, jeopardize national security, and control reasonable congregating all because power seeking, Marxist-leaning politicians continue to use *unreasonable fear* to reconstruct Americanism into a socialistic nightmare! (2020 to 2021)

Here's my point, however. Moral and even governmental pluralism is nonsense, even though in America we encourage the exchange of ideas and values. I understand that not everyone will agree with one another, but the old phrase calls out to all free-wheeling moralists or politicians, *"Don't throw out the baby with the bath water...please!"* There are, after all, substantial life truths, which common sense shouts out to us, "Don't mess around with these, dimwit!" Of course, those that believe in pluralism do not recognize moral or life absolutes in the first place, so their ideas are unstable and untenable from the get-go...rationally, philosophically and spiritually.

Listen, no one knows anything in the same way as God knows... with absolute certainty, that is. Omniscience is not a human trait. But the faith by which we approach and define our principles and precepts of life best be in line with moral sensibility and sound discernment, or we're only going to repeat the evils of previous hair-brained and/or demon-inspired leaders. Following biblical principles and precepts is the way to allow God's Truth to keep society...any society...safe from moral evil and satanic influence.

In the days ahead, I'm fearful of tremendous push back from this newly embraced political/religion of liberalism, because it will try to blend truth with tyranny, righteousness with irresponsibility, and moral compromise with compassion. In Isaiah 5:20, God clearly warns any people or nation if they do:

> *"Woe unto them that call evil good, and good evil; that put darkness for light, and light for darkness; that put bitter for sweet, and sweet for bitter!"*

So, one word of wisdom, when listening to compromised media types and marauding "social justice" groups burning down businesses and ripping apart our social structures: Raucous-raising rebels don't make reputable character references or even righteous leaders in free societies. They're self-appointed demagogues of destruction regarding everything this country stands for...and you can take that to the bank. If you hear politicians or media folks waffling on the convictional truths I've highlighted above, know they are sadly compromised and part of the problem itself (intentionally or not). We're not called to hate, riot or foolishly rebel against governmental over-reaches, but in this country, we can still lawfully remove them...if we have the discernment and determination to do so.

Evil Conviction #2: Pleasure...Satisfaction Without Boundaries

As I said before, human beings have been given a wonderful gift by our Creator God...the ability to enjoy things that feel good to us. The 5 senses that we possess enable us to find relaxation, release and recreation in the midst of a life that sometimes can be very difficult. But these gifts are not without boundaries.

With the implementation of various types of "manufactured" pleasure tools, mankind has opened up the door to sinful participation like never before. It used to be throughout history that there were certain places where people could go for sexual pleasure, for instance. There were brothels, temple prostitutes, street walking call girls, etc., but a wayward soul had to find those places and go there in order to satisfy his or her lust. In today's world, one can enjoy the sinful pleasures of sexual promiscuity in one's own home by turning on the television, the I-phone, or going on line. Sexual pleasure can be displayed or downloaded in an instant. Our society is reeling from the effects of such stuff in our marriages, our ministries, in our social relationships, in our entertainment, and even in our work environments. One cannot sinfully indulge all this, thereby exceeding God's boundaries for it, without harming oneself, one's family and those around him.

But, it's not just sexual pleasure that resides at the touch of a finger, for the pleasure of the eyes is magnified as well for those who are entangled with another flashy culprit...materialism.

> *"Do not love this world nor the things it offers you, for when you love the world, you do not have the love of the Father in you. For the world offers only a craving for physical pleasure, a*

craving for everything we see, and pride in our achievements and possessions. These are not from the Father, but are from this world. And this world is fading away, along with everything that people crave. But anyone who does what pleases God will live forever." (I John 2:15-17)

Advertising is a powerful platform for drawing folks into a web of improper and illegitimate life objectives apart from the will of God. "Things" do not bring satisfaction alone, and "more things" do not in any significant way supply anyone with "happiness." Acquisition of material things... houses, cars, jewelry, clothing, vacations, or money, for instance...is enjoyable, yes, but such pleasures are always limited and short-lived. Unfortunately, people (believers, too) often don't wake up to that reality until it's too late. They bury themselves in "things," hoping to find lasting satisfaction, but instead are bound to buy "more things" to keep themselves materialistically enthralled...which is impossible, of course. The need for another "materialistic high" consumes them, yet eventually evaporates into boredom and depression, when they lay their head down on their pillow at night. Suicide is often the only relief for such a cycle of revolving emptiness. Christians who subtly play this game can also end up subtly replacing Christ's joy with worldly substitutes, and experiencing the same type of personal loss and emptiness. Paul was not kidding us when he said following:

> "We need a discerning mind, which cultivates within us a deeply impassioned love for God (pre-eminent desire). Only then can defeat Satan's exaggerated lust within us for fleshly satisfaction."

"And now there remains: faith [abiding trust in God and His promises], hope [confident

expectation of eternal salvation], love [unselfish love for others growing out of God's love for me], these three [the choicest graces]; but the greatest of these is love." (I Cor. 13:13 Amp)

But pleasure is not just found in "things," either. It is available in large quantities and easily found in the drug market. The most common are over the counter remedies for headaches, body aches, fevers, colds, flu, and sleeplessness and other mild discomforts that all of us have from time to time. When used with control and responsibility, these are helpful and temporary aids to get us through a physical sickness or something similar. And, they are also necessary for treating accompanying symptoms associated with significant illnesses, as well.

But here again, the desire for wayward pleasure causes some folks to over indulge themselves in pain relievers and seek a "high" that is so subtle, it creeps in like a pleasant breeze. Then, the craving for peace and rest from normal difficulties becomes overwhelming, causing folks to abuse such drugs and crave more powerful ones.

The entertainment industry is overrun with such cases, Elvis Presley being one of the sad and more well-known cases. In a court of law investigating Elvis' death, the following evidence came to the front: *"Elvis' doctor overprescribed addictive drugs to Presley, singer Jerry Lee Lewis, himself and eight others. He prescribed over 19,000 uppers, downers, and painkillers for Presley over the 30-month period."* (Elvis and drugs – Bing)

But, drugs of a more serious nature are corrupting the moral fiber and character of adults and youth across our country. I don't need to get into all the details of all this, for most of us know the damaging result found therein. However, now we have state governors, like New York's Mario Cuomo, actually trying to legalize marijuana. The lack of moral and societal sensibility is simply astounding. The point remains, however, that convictions as to right and wrong, when motivated by pleasure or by the need to fill state coffers, can drive people to great depths of evil.

Evil can be very persuasive, and Christians in the years ahead need to hold tightly to Biblical boundaries, when considering indulging their desires for what "feels good." A believer's life is not about what *feels good,* it's about what *is good.* And, what is good, finds its source in Biblical Truth, in which believers need to be immovably entrenched in spiritual conviction.

Please remember that pleasure demands boundaries in all areas. Exceeding such boundaries brings personal loss and painful disruption into one's spiritual life with God. Such many not happen immediately, but it will come without fail.

Evil Conviction #3: Power...Pursuit Without Authority

From the time we were in elementary school, each of us learned how to control our environment and future. I remember the holiday movie, "A Christmas Story" (1981), where the main character, a young boy, gets picked on by older boys. He has to learn really quickly how to survive in the big and bad world around him, so he won't get "beat up" from some bullies. It's fun to watch, but it's also very true. Overcoming powerful obstacles in life is something in which all of us are engaged from our earliest years. When we learn and apply God's Truth correctly, we will be able to maneuver through it all with safety and success.

However, when people grow more sophisticated and self-reliant apart from God, they often travel down self-directed roads that can offend Him. They create images and beliefs about life that simply aren't true, particularly in the area of social roles and cultural beliefs. For instance, I'm thinking about how Hollywood has reinvented femininity to produce aggressive, dominating, gun-wielding, cartoonish characters such as Wonder Woman, Super Girl, Red Sonya, and Bat Woman. Real life movies such as Lt. Ripley (Alien), Selene (Underworld), and Storm (Avengers), have catapulted such imaginary superhero women into mega box office successes. The point is that TV and movie moguls have transformed women, their capabilities, their biological and emotional distinctiveness, and their God given roles into something that they were never intended to become...sword waving, muscular, masculine, aggressive, power-wielding icons of heroic achievement.

It's not exactly what the Apostle Peter had in mind when communicating God's will for the feminine role.

> *"Rather, it should be that of your inner self, the unfading beauty of a gentle and quiet spirit, which is of great worth in God's sight. For this is the way the holy women of the past who put their hope in God used to adorn themselves.* (I Peter 3:4-5)

I want you to think of the disastrous effect this has upon the young girls and boys in our society. Kids adopt as personal identity and moral values what they see in their young years. When accompanied in the context of parental fighting, divorce, and role confusion in the home, it's no wonder there has been such a significant rise in lesbianism, male homosexuality and anti-social behaviors across our land.

But the powerful have gone way beyond just sexual role identification. They've flooded our societal conscience with beliefs that foster socialism, health care entitlements, globalism, religious intolerance, welfare enhancement, broken national borders, health care for illegal aliens, parental subjugation (village concept), transsexualism (choose your sexual identity), anti-Israelism, white supremacy (anti-white), racism, religious intolerance (toward Christians), and the list goes on. These are *not* noble or moral people, but a massive movement of spiritually corrupted and self-driven power seekers.

Unfortunately, the powerful and politically strong have confiscated Truth at the expense of what is godly and right. Driven often by financial profitability, personal conviction or political advantage, they forge their godless beliefs into *powerful cultural values*. Such power, when aimed at corporate, entertainment or governmental levels, parades such exaggerated and/or false doctrines as acceptable, thereby authenticating such behaviors upon the young, the naive, the uneducated, and the spiritually ignorant. Over time, the moral frog has been slowly and methodically well-boiled into complete insensitivity to ***God's*** sense of purity and wholesome values for family and society.

But, seeking power has possibly even crippled our political system. The powerful elites of our society have finally undermined the pinions of political authority resident within our constitutional republic. They have apparently conspired to destroy the accomplishments of a conservative, populist President, who has done more good for this country than any other in recent history. It also appears that possible election rigging has taken place. By reprogramming voting machines, fraudulent and back-door voting counts, and seizure of positions of authority, that they may have highjacked the people's right to choose. And, in a stroke of media manipulated skullduggery, they made the former President accountable for a mob scene at the capital (driven in reality by a skilled group of Marxist agitators), then called it insurrection (which it wasn't), and now are using it to transform the country into socialistic reform to suit their own bias! Wow!

Free speech has also been seriously wounded by high-tech platforms, and at the time of this writing, there is serious consideration that fundamentalist Christians, and all those who oppose liberalism, should be "reprogrammed" (who knows how) into good liberal followers (or Marxist sympathizers, if you prefer). Folks, this is not fiction, but the fervent conviction of anarchists, social architects and media moguls to profit from a complete dismantling of Christian principles and precepts that have founded our nation. This is a new world order espoused by extreme leftists and radical liberals, who are now fighting to control our once godly and conservative governed nation, which was formed under biblical principles and precepts. This is ***not*** a conspiracy theory or a fantasy, folks, it's in the news, it's real, it's here, and it's being installed onto the hard drive of our social and economic system by radical extremists…frankly…just as Paul warned us 2000 years ago:

> *"But mark this: There will be terrible times in the last days. People will be lovers of themselves, lovers of money, boastful, proud, abusive, disobedient to their parents, ungrateful, unholy,*

> *without love, unforgiving, slanderous, without self-control, brutal, not lovers of the good, treacherous, rash, conceited, lovers of pleasure rather than lovers of God - having a form of godliness but denying its power. Have nothing to do with such people..Just as Jannes and Jambres opposed Moses, so also these teachers oppose the truth. They are men of depraved minds, who, as far as the faith is concerned, are rejected..." II Tim. 3:1-9*

Here's one more thing that's on the table for this misguided mob of political misfits...total blending of sexual identities into a universal, inclusive, and generic being. In other words, in our newly created social future, rarely will anyone refer to a "women" or "man" in any distinctive sense. Boys and girls will shower together, play on sports teams together, use the same bathrooms, and be able to choose their sexual "identity" on a daily basis...as they feel is appropriate. Physical changes of a more permanent basis can be had through elective surgery where men can carry babies and women can have implanted within them the ability to impregnate. Of course, sex with animals will be okay, as well as any other deviant form of pleasure, and marriage will succumb to simple relational unions. Kids will be raised by whatever union that wants them...two women, three men, etc. (sorry, I should have said two or three inclusive, sexually blended, gender free, transgendered or surgically transformed beings deciding to live together!).

Jesus said that those that have eyes to see, should see (recognize, understand), and that is particularly true about our nation at the present time. Power is up for grabs, and it won't be God's hand that brings it into leadership, but the power of demonic influence substituting what is evil for what is good.

One asks, "How can this happen so quickly?" Well, an illegitimate administration is in a power grab (owning three places of authority...the House, the Senate, and the Presidency) to quickly and forcibly (through Executive Orders) install by "edict" its ill-founded agenda. It uses the Covid19 pandemic as an excuse to do this (EO's can b *temporarily* authorized in a national emergency situation). And, if you oppose some of this stuff in the future, you may even be labeled a racist or an anarchist yourself and sent to "retraining school," possibly fined by opposing it all, or even imprisoned. Again, this is not my imagination, just start listening to media mob, disinformation specialists and "social justice" advocates.

By the way, just one of its absurd actions is to offer people the right to take unemployment compensation, *if they fear* they might contract Covid19 at work. Imagine the mob scene when/if that EO takes place. The lazy, the entitled, and all those that "feel" like it, can simply jump onto the government's pay boat. Wow, our Founding Fathers must be turning over in their graves!

Even organized socialism wouldn't go that far, for there has to be enough folks working to pay for those who aren't working. No, this is Marxism at the core, which gives you some idea of the agenda of the *far* left. Constructive "left" and "right" dialoguing, along with non-partisanship compromising on the part of people of good character, has historically brought America to its greatest heights. But it will soon be crushed to its knees by the far-reaching, freedom-squelching hands of Karl Marx, Lenin, Stalin, and other obvious culprits of godless thinking. Paul, in writing to the Thessalonians in 3:9-10, made God's opposition to socialism clear:

> *"For even when we were with you, we would give you this command: If anyone is not willing to work, **let him not eat**. For we hear that some among you walk in idleness, not busy at work, but busybodies. Now such persons we command and encourage in the Lord Jesus Christ to do their work quietly and to earn their own living."*

I could go on, but I think the words and thoughts thus far in this chapter is sufficient to express *my* convictions. Once again, I do believe that the signs of the times show that we are probably in the "last days" to which Jesus referred. The unfolding of our nation's political bottom feeding and moral corruption is no doubt one of the vehicles God is allowing to usher in those days. *So, let's keep our convictions* strong and our lives pure from the social disruption happening all around us. The Lord is always with us, whether in good times or during times of evil encroachment upon the world. Pray, stay close to one another, and stand strong in the principles and precepts of Almighty God and his Son, Christ Jesus!

Maranatha, Lord Jesus, we await your coming, when the power and authority of Almighty God will rule this world instead of the evil intentions of often demon driven folk who either deny you or ignore you. Keep us strong and pure in the time of world tribulation, maintaining a faith that perseveres and proves itself genuine.

CONVICTION #24

I Believe Convictions Build Consecration

"Therefore, I urge you, brothers and sisters, in view of God's mercy, to offer your bodies as a living sacrifice, holy and pleasing to God—this is your true and proper worship. Do not conform to the pattern of this world, but be transformed by the renewing of your mind. Then you will be able to test and approve what God's will is— his good, pleasing and perfect will." Romans 12:1, 2

People who are *consistently led* by their spiritual convictions as shared throughout this book, are by definition a *consecrated* people, those choosing to think and live according to God's Will. It's what a priest did in bringing a sacrifice to the altar in the Old Testament…he *offered* it to God as a perfect and chosen lamb fit for the sacrifice. In the same way, we as believers are to *present* ourselves as "fitting" offerings, "living" sacrifices, and a people of "obedient faith," ready and willing to do God's Will. This is the essence of *consecration*.

However, this life of spiritual consecration is not always modeled well within the church at large, though it's our mission (or should be) for all of us. Again, the overall meaning of consecration is the "setting oneself apart" to Christ in every way, assuming one has the initial faith and desire to do so (commitment without impassioned belief is just conversation!). But consecration can be viewed from differing perspectives, so let's discuss each one in this final chapter.

[*The Greek word for "offer" above also means to present. Consecration, from a different Hebrew word, means to "separate or set apart." So, believers offer and separate themselves to God's will*]

First, Consecration is POSITION.

"So, Ed, are you a consecrated believer?" asks Mike of me.
"Well, yes and no," I respond.
"Ah...excuse me, Ed, but that's a bit vague, friend."
"Yes, but let me ask you this, "Is your Pastor a consecrated believer?"
"You bet he is, Ed, and a great model of spiritual growth."
"So, has he stopped growing in Christ, then, would you say?" I returned.
"Of course not, he's not perfect, nor are we." responds Mike.
"Well, okay, then who's really a fully consecrated believer?

This imaginary conversation might be as confusing to you, as it was to Mike. But I want to assure you that I do not in any sense suggest that anyone lives a spiritually perfect and holy life. None of us do, this side of heaven. However, the Bible does say that by faith in Christ we *stand in perfect relationship with God,* sinless, and fully *consecrated* or "set apart" to him. This "positional" sense, is what *salvation* brings to us sinners as a gift, and that's what I was sharing with Mike.

> *"And you also were included in Christ when you heard the message of truth, the gospel of your salvation. When you believed, you were marked*

> *in him with a seal, the promised Holy Spirit, who is a deposit guaranteeing our inheritance until the redemption of those who are God's possession— to the praise of his glory.* (Ephesians 1:13, 14)

Salvation doesn't rest upon works in any sense, for our spiritual position regarding right standing with God was settled, when we believed in Christ and committed our lives to him as personal Savior and Lord. At that moment, we passed from guilt-ridden, spiritually deformed, rebellious, and broken creatures bound for eternal separation from God into eternally forgiven and spiritually restored family members *with* him. Now, that's a gift, and it's not dependent in any way upon anything else. We simply *receive it* with an honest and good heart...as Mark tells us in chapter four of his Gospel. Once we receive it by faith, the gift is *credited* to the new believer, and he or she is saved (forgiven) from sin's penalty and punishment. This position in the family of God remains until we die and go to meet Jesus in heaven.

I know, we've not always lived up to it perfectly, but that's the glory of it. Whatever level of spiritual growth we've achieved will not in any way add to the *efficacy* of our salvation or our right to receive forgiveness and eternal life. If our faith is genuine and our life evidences that it is, Jesus will welcome us into glory. It's every believer's *position* in Christ this side of heaven.

Secondly, Consecration is PROCESS

So, consecration can also be seen as an overall ***process*** on this side of heaven. There's much involved in God's part to mold us and change us into obedient vessels, who faithfully seek and model God's will. When we're consecrated to God on the inside, however, he can do great things through us outwardly. But, when we're vacillating on the inside, we're prone to wander outwardly and become dull tools for God to use.

By way of example, I have to tell you that I *don't* like woodworking! By that I mean the process involved in making a piece of furniture, redoing old cabinets, or even putting up new moldings around a window. It's never a simple "1-2-3" type of thing, for there's usually significant time involved between each action step.

For instance, the other day I had to re-finish the moldings around my kitchen counter tops. My good friend Mike re-did my kitchen a few years ago, installing new cabinets, counter tops, windows, etc. The countertops were Formica, but he put an attractive wood molding around the edges, which needed attention every few years. So, I first had to apply varnish remover to those moldings, which took several hours for to do its thing. Next came wiping it all down, removing the old varnish away, followed by applying some preparation substance to it, which helped bring out the grain...and then let it dry. Next day, I had to sandpaper the whole length of countertop molding, until it was again smooth enough to apply the varnish again. Do you think that finished the job? No...once that dried overnight, then I needed to sandpaper that revarnished surface once more, in order to fine tune the surface for the last coat of varnish. All of those steps involved application, drying time, repeated sanding of the wood, and a lot of waiting in between each step in the process. Ugh...such a bore! Having said that, I know that there are people who really enjoy that step by step process. Each step is something to complete and in which they seriously find great satisfaction.

Imagine Noah making that ark out of gopher wood. Month after month he cut, shaved, bent, sanded, pitched, molded, grooved, interlaced, and somehow painted that ship until it was ready for the high seas. Scholars believe that time period was between 100 and 120 years. *Talk about patience!*

Noah the boat-builder, or anyone else that builds anything, knows that such work can quickly become slowed down or halted, if one's tools are left unsharpened. When Noah had to cut through a foot-wide beam for his boat or a carpenter wants to saw a 2"x12" plank in half, both need to be sure that the saw is cutting sharply and deeply into the wood. Similarly, consecration can be seen as an ongoing process, where we *gradually allow* the Spirit of God and his Word to cut sharply and deeply into our hearts, slicing through those hard-to-reach parts of our inclinations and intentions with God's Truth. It's inviting God's Spirit to continually realign us at the core of who we are.

God was not in any hurry for Noah to finish, and the truth of it is that he's really not in any great hurry to finish working on us this side of heaven, either. Still, for both newer or older believers, time is particularly important, though sometimes it's an annoying factor, in our spiritual development. Old ways and habits seem too deeply rooted to give way and yield to the Master Carpenter's skilled hands, though they eventually will. But the Spirit is relentless and follows a uniquely designed blueprint for each believer, sometimes working more quickly than at other times, but always on schedule with the Father's will.

I know that it's difficult to endure the Master's process at times, but know that the love of God doesn't waver while the process is being worked out for our spiritual growth. From our point of view, a life of *practical consecration* can be frustrating and time consuming, as we work through the ongoing *process* of walking, falling, confessing, re-motivating, and rebuilding ourselves in the mercy and grace of Jesus Christ. However, from ***his*** point of view, his covenantal love never changes:

> *"Because of the loving devotion of the LORD we are not consumed, for His mercies never fail. They are new every morning; great is your faithfulness!"* (Lamentations 3:22, 23)

Like it or not, and just like woodworking, the spiritual *grain* of who we are in Christ must be relentlessly drawn out through difficulty, if it is to be proven attractive and genuine. The Spirit abrasively scrapes us, cuts us, and sands down the edges of our character according to his will...refining what he wants us to be. It's not an endless process, for heaven will bring forth the final product of everything we are ultimately intended to become.

Until then, our task is profoundly clear...*yield to the process and keep going* (See Eccl. 8:6). But, remember that there is effort and responsibility involved in all this, as we move forward by faith to ***continually reconsecrate*** ourselves to God's will. Let's look at this next.

Thirdly, Consecration is PRESENTATION.

> *"Therefore, I urge you, brothers and sisters, in view of God's mercy, to offer your bodies as a living sacrifice, holy and pleasing to God—this is your true and proper worship."* (Rom. 12:1)

The most common idea associated with consecration is the specific ongoing act(s) of "offering" ourselves as ***living sacrifices*** to God. Again, offering here means ***presenting yourself*** to God in an act of *obedient faith*. It's point-in-time yet ongoing acts of *giving over* (or recommitting) ourselves to God and his will by faith, and it must be done as often as necessary. Again, this presenting ourselves to God itself doesn't guarantee spiritual maturity, but it is a *necessary part* of the ongoing process. It's our core ***faith in action!***

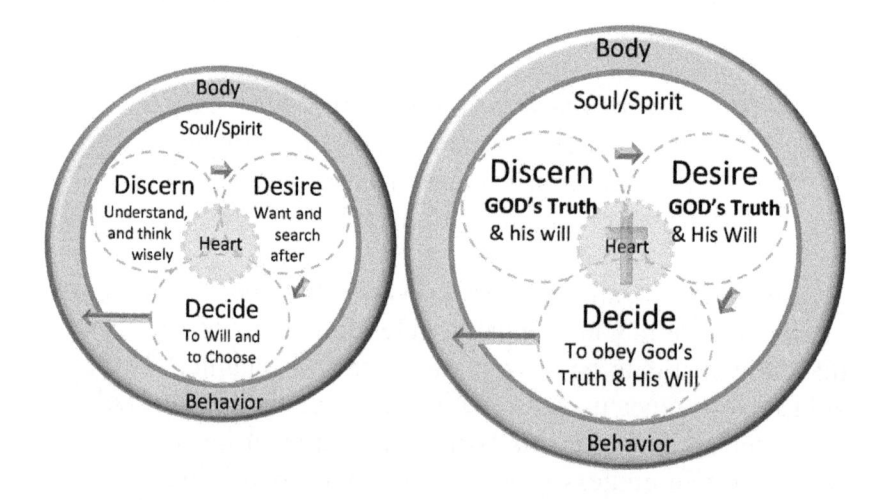

The diagram above (left side) shows how *general* convictional behavior works (believer or non-believer); it's how we're wired to live. We sense, understand and form beliefs about the world around us, which in turn motivates us to some degree. If necessary or appropriate, that will move the will toward commitment to act upon one or more of those cognitive thoughts. For example, I see an ice cream stand and suddenly feel hungry (desire). Then I decide (willful choice) if I am hungry enough to go and buy a cone for a snack. I may have other thoughts and desires as well for different types of food at that moment, too. I may also have a desire to be more physically fit, and want to resist the ice cream (avoidance desire). Any motivation(s) is possible when it comes to the fleshly part of us.

Now, **Biblical** Consecration (right side), more specifically, begins when we *discern* something that God says we should believe and act upon. Again, that will create some level of *desire* to adopt and/or obey God's Truth. Finally, we have the specific *choice to act* upon that Truth (anything God may be telling us to think or do). We may say, "Yes!" to God and lovingly yield ourselves to him then to do his will (consecration). Or, we might willfully choose to disregard God's Word and his wisdom, and suffer the consequences.

Consecration is a decisive choice and surrender to the will of God. For instance, one may be in the midst of temptation, but willfully decides to turn from sinful thinking and embrace God's will. To do so, he or she consecrates (presents) himself or herself to the Lord in obedient faith. Or, perhaps a person just discerns how blessed he is and desires to present himself to Christ out of love and adoration. Whatever the reason, consecration is the willful choice to let God realign us and reign within us at the core of who we are. It takes place because of what we think and want (impassioned perspective), but in the final sense, consecration is the choice to yield to God's will.

What brings about these willing acts of consecration? Well, we will always choose what we think is most desirable to us at the time…without fail. You see, from childhood on we acquire many perspectives about what is true, moral, best, etc. Not all perspectives have desire or emotion linked to them, but many do. Those are the ones that motivate us (2+2=4 is factual thinking, but it has little passion attached to it). Our minds store these "impassioned perspectives" and they vie for power and control over our attitudes and behaviors, particularly those dealing with sensual issues.

However, God says that we are to "present ourselves" as obedient people to his will, not giving ourselves over to every impassioned perspective crossing our minds. That's what animals do, not intelligent and cognizant human beings. We are to listen to God's Truth and let it motivate us toward godly decisions and determinations.

No one chooses to do God's will, without wanting it; and no one wants to do God's will, without understanding and believing it first. So, the secret of godly behavior is influencing and changing our thinking (understanding, beliefs) so that godly desires, decisions, and disciplined living occurs. **Right thinking brings about righteous living**. God's Word spoken to us by the Spirit in our hearts is that which gives us the *wisdom*, the *want*, the *will*, and finally the *walk (if we listen to it, for it all begins in our thinking)*. It is the inner, spiritual fuel for consecration.

> *"For the word of God is alive and active.* **Sharper** *than any double-edged sword, it penetrates even to dividing soul and spirit, joints and marrow; it judges the thoughts and attitudes of the heart. Nothing in all creation is hidden from God's sight. Everything is uncovered and laid bare before the eyes of him to whom we must give account."* (Heb. 4:12, 13)

The apostle Paul lays out a highway for spiritual success here:

> *"Finally, brothers and sisters, whatever is true, whatever is noble, whatever is right, whatever is pure, whatever is lovely, whatever is admirable—if anything is excellent or praiseworthy—***think**

***about such things.** Whatever you have learned or received or heard from me, or seen in me—put it into practice. And the God of peace will be with you."* Phil 4:8, 9

Now, I wish that "presenting" ourselves to God was a *one-time* thing, sort of a 2nd work of grace (there are some who believe this). But I don't think Scripture suggests this at all. What it says is that there are *ongoing* times where believers must carefully *re-align* themselves with who they are in Christ. No single experience will suffice, for one writer put it this way*: "Yesterday's successes do not guarantee today's victories."* That's because we're falling down spiritually and getting-up again all the time, and our hearts continually need "updating." Acts of consecration enables "heart work" to take place. Otherwise, spiritually speaking, we're just too "slippery!" As another person has rightly said, *"The problem with living sacrifices is that they can too easily crawl off the altar!"*

As an example, the back room in my house I like to call my "man cave." Kathy, my wife, doesn't go there too often, for she prefers her upstairs bedroom, where she props herself up on a pillow and enjoys watching her favorite TV programs or communicates to our grand kids on her I-Pad. But, in my "man cave" there's a couple of couches to just sit back and relax with a good book, listen to my stereo system, or enjoy some re-runs of "Gunsmoke," "Star Trek," or "NCIS" on TV.

However, there's a growing problem with that extended 12' X 12' room back there…it's *sinking* (and it's got nothing to do with me getting heavier!). Because it was built off the back of the house, it's not resting on a solid, deeply dug foundation…just cement blocks. Whereas the house rests on cement walls going down 7 or 8 feet deep, the back room only goes down a few feet, so it's begun to sink on one side. Now, it's only about an inch or so, but it's obvious, and one day I'm going to have to fix it before serious cracks and leaks start showing up.

In the same way, we need a solid and reliable *spiritual foundation* for living with God, one that is strong enough to resist the continuous movements around us that bring temptation and sin.

Reaffirming our faith and desire to obey God (consecration) *is that foundation*. Actually, this is what communion does for the believer, as well. Overall, consecration asks and answers these key questions about our relationship with God.

- First, do I really believe in Christ and want to obey him?

- Is it deeper faith and trust that God wants of me? Is there a doctrinal truth that I have been refusing to accept, and God wants me embrace it?

- Perhaps, I'm shallow on my view of some sin in my life, and God wants me to "get serious" about it...and it's now time to yield to the Spirit's urgings and consecrate myself to purity and holiness?

- Have I been jealous of someone, overly angry at someone, lustful toward someone, or revengeful toward someone and need to confess it to God?

In any of these situations above, I am seriously considering (discerning) my inclinations and intentions. If I understand that I am "waffling, wavering or wandering," then it's time to **rethink** things to the point of wanting God and his will and then ***reconsecrating*** myself to Him and his will (deciding, surrendering, submitting, yielding). The will to do so is there, if the heart motivation is there! In addition, the heart motivation is there, if our perspectives about God are aligned correctly. Overall, consecration asks this question when facing temptation:

"Do I really understand and believe with heart-felt desire that Jesus Christ is and will be my Savior, God, and Lord of my life regardless of anything to the contrary?"

Anything less than, "Yes!" is shallow faith, and consecration needs strong affirmation to overcome sin. When we sincerely consecrate ourselves to Christ, we enroot the Gospel seed and secure it more deeply into our hearts with an ever-increasing *love* for God and *compliance* to his will (see Col. 2:6,7). It releases our intellect, inclinations, and intentions to do whatever God wants of us. It softens our heart, making it receptive to the Lordship of Christ deep within our soul. Such foundational and worshipful *realignments* keep us from falling into spiritual dissipation, if genuine and frequently done. By the way, this is what true praise, worship, and good musical offerings do (or should do) for the church body.

I understand that each act of consecration can't of itself solve every problem, overcome every sin, or usher in immediate spiritual maturity, for there are many important convictions, attitudes, and strategic responsibilities God wants us to learn, sometimes the hard way, right. But presenting and re-presenting ourselves to God establishes a ***platform*** for confessing sinful thoughts and habits, embraces new and godly convictions, and yields ourselves to God's Will. Along the way, it will also bring significant change to our ***practical responsibilities as well*** (such as prayer, fellowship, Scriptural study, etc.), for these *must also be integrated* wisely into our lives.

Fourthly, Consecration is PURSUIT

When one builds an Ark, a house, or anything else, process needs time to finish its task. Houses, for instance, do not go up in a day, it takes a couple of months. But...bottom line...it also implies **doing things correctly along the way,** or the process can't be completed successfully either. The foundation must first be completed, *then* the framework is built, the plumbing installed, the insulation put in, the roof shingles nailed down, and all the inner walls painted and/or wall-papered. Similarly, we add things to our Christian walk as well, step by step, but always in line with our spiritual blueprint, God's Word.

> *"For this very reason, <u>make every effort to add to your faith</u> goodness; and to goodness, knowledge; and to knowledge, self-control; and to self-control, perseverance; and to perseverance, godliness; and to godliness, mutual affection; and to mutual affection, love. For if you possess these qualities in increasing measure, they will*

> *keep you from being ineffective and unproductive in your knowledge of our Lord Jesus Christ. But whoever does not have them is nearsighted and blind, forgetting that they have been cleansed from their past sins."* Therefore, my brothers and sisters, make every effort to confirm your calling and election. For if you do these things, you will never stumble, and you will receive a rich welcome into the eternal kingdom of our Lord and Savior Jesus Christ." (II Peter 1:9-11)

One of my favorite rides at Disney World is also one my wife enjoys, too, and it's called "Buzz Light Year." This Magic Kingdom ride is really more of a contest than anything else, for you enter a small, cup-like vehicle in a continuously moving line with many others in front and in back of you, each about 4' apart from each other. In front of you on the "dash board" is an attached laser gun, which you use to shoot at hundreds of moving, pop-up targets along the way (for about 2 minutes). You can turn your moving vehicle around and reposition your laser gun as you wish, but it's quite difficult to score a lot of hits because everything is constantly moving around (my wife achieved a higher score than I did last time!)

Pursuing God is similar to that ride in the sense that there's always a new target popping up or an old one that needs refurbishing. Though salvation begins with our faith conviction at its core (which, remember, is also a growing thing), the Spirit drives us toward a **whole-hearted** and **broader** relationship with God *overall*. This means discovering new insights, acquiring new convictions, and increasing our desire and determination to do God's will.

I can remember one stage of growth, where I wanted so much to rid myself of certain clinging immaturities. I got into the habit of reconsecrating myself by saying, *"In spite of all, no matter what, I will believe and obey."* Now, that was a good thing to do, for it helped me to spiritually forge ahead, even though I couldn't understand some issues I was dealing with. But its strength was limited, for I'd still find myself struggling with compromised thinking not too long afterwards. Why? Because my perspective beliefs (faith and/or other convictions) were off, shaky, waffling. So, until I got my thinking straight in a couple of areas, my desire and determination to obey God was correspondingly weak.

But times of struggle and failure are not worthless to sincere believers. God's Spirit is particularly busy in those times...as he was in my life then...teaching, correcting, enabling, and restoring us in ways that a life apart from such difficulties and challenges is simply unable to do.

In my case, God was gradually showing me (among *other* things, too) that in order to challenge carnal desires one must have an equal or greater ***spiritual desire*** within (motivation, passion, need) for Christ. So, by focusing more deeply upon <u>why</u> I was a Christian and <u>why</u> I wanted Christ (discernment and perspective). I was then able to build up stronger resistance to temptation. My overall consecration to Him grew stronger, too, as I **understood** more of what God wanted from me. It became easier to yield myself to Christ and love him from the heart!

Remember that Jesus said one will find his or her heart where their treasure resides (what he or she *values* the most). By application, when we wisely understand what's best and most spiritually valuable for us, a thirst for God grows and gets the attention of our will. Then, we are more likely to ***choose*** and ***pursue*** God's will with greater consistently.

Overall, a key to spiritual growth and re-commitment, then, is realizing that just *one* presentation of ourselves to the Savior *is insufficient*. There is much more to learn and much to discern from God's Word. Many growth spurts are needed to smooth out a "consecrated" flow of character down the bumpy road of sanctification.

Are we really pursuing and listening intensely to what the Spirit is trying to teach us from God's Word? Our ability to consecrate and present ourselves to God will be greatly hampered until we are so inclined!

Please remember as well that our essential faith conviction only forms the *foundational platform for growth*. We must continue to present **all** of our thinking (beliefs, understanding, attitudes), **all** of our desires (wants, needs, feelings), and **all** of our intentions (plans, purposes, goals) before God in obedience to him as the unqualified, unquestionable, and unchallenged Lord of our lives. And that, my friend, will take time and many spiritual realignments along the way. However, that's what practical consecration is all about. (See Mt. 10:37, 38; Ps 86:11)

> *"Love the Lord your God with all your heart and with all your soul and with all your mind and with all your strength."* (Mark 12:30)

> *"And we all, who with unveiled faces contemplate the Lord's glory, are being transformed into his image with ever-increasing glory, which comes from the Lord, who is the Spirit."* II Cor. 3:18

It's obvious, isn't it, that pursuing God is not just a relaxing pastime, but an *ongoing personal discipline*. As we pursue the Lord and increase in knowledge and wisdom, we became more consecrated, obedient, and useable servants for his glory. Without such genuine pursuit, however, the process becomes lackadaisical and encumbered. That's why Paul tells us to avoid "grieving the Spirit," thereby frustrating God's will. Instead, *present* yourself daily (II Chron 15:2), walk "circumspectly," (Eph 5:15, KJV) and pursue God to the fullest!

Fifthly, Consecration is PERSPECTIVE

Okay, Ed, but how do we add to our faith all these other important qualities and convictions you suggest? Paul encourages us to have a ***regenerating mindset***.

> *"Be transformed by the renewing of your minds."* (Romans 12:2)

His wording comes from one who is weeding his or her garden and then adding new seedlings. Similarly, we are to remove the detrimental thoughts/beliefs of the flesh and, instead, work into our mental soil some spiritually healthy thinking from God's Spirit. Such healthy convictions come from listening to a good sermon, talking with other believers, reading a good Christian book, or renewing our minds in personal devotions and the study of God's Word. As we cultivate these godly truths into our minds and hearts, a spiritual ***cutting edge*** is maintained. Our lifestyle will more consistently conform to God's will.

I should say that we don't need to understand *everything* about what we believe, or have *unending* wisdom, or be a "perfect" believer (if we were, you wouldn't need to do it!). We also don't have to fast for a month, spend 2 hours per/day reading Scripture, chant a "recommitment song," or join a monastery somewhere! It doesn't mean that we've arrived at sainthood, nor entered a second stage of grace, either. It doesn't mean we understand everything biblical, and, for sure, it doesn't make us immune to Satan's temptations along the way.

> *"And this is my prayer: that your love may abound more and more in knowledge and depth of insight, so that you may be able to **discern** what is best and may be pure and blameless for the day of Christ, filled with the fruit of righteousness that comes through Jesus Christ— to the glory and praise of God."* Phil 1:9-11

Again, did you notice the word discern in that passage? Life is all about discovering truth, particularly for believers...God's Truth. The Desire and Determination parts of any conviction rest greatly on the initial strength of what we discern to be true. More significant truths and beliefs will generate greater desire and determination to obey the Lord.

As Paul prays, he wanted the Philippians' love for God to abound (their primary faith conviction), and that it would continue to grow deeper in knowledge and insight such that serious discernment would transform them, spiritually speaking. The end result would be a life full of purity, blamelessness, and godly living. The key to the whole passage is DISCERNMENT. Please recall that it was discernment which gave us opportunity for reach out to God in faith, which as believers we seized that opportunity and were saved. But spiritual <u>maturity</u> demands that we continue beyond just faith. We must listen to the Spirit intensely, passionately fill our minds and hearts with the Word of God, and then conform our lives accordingly. (Matt 6:21)

Sixthly, Consecration is PERSEVERANCE

In the building process...for houses or believers...there is a key part of it that stands out and which drives the process to a satisfactory conclusion, and that's pursuing God with *perseverance.* When one is building anything of value, frankly, it will take *perseverance* to do the job well and bring it to completion. Perseverance can be defined as ***endless pursuit!*** (regardless of the difficulties)

In line with this, have you every just asked yourself *what keeps you going in consecration to Christ? What slows you down?* There have been times in my life, like yours, for instance, when I was just kind of bored, *spiritually* speaking. I didn't seem to be doing anything "great" for the Lord, and my spiritual life seemed fairly routine. God almost seemed uninterested in me and what I was to accomplish in my spiritual walk. My faith was dry. Ever felt that way? Here's a possible reason.

> *"Remember that God may pull himself away at times until we do something we've been putting off for too long. Such periods of dull and dry experience of desert spirituality can become instructive for us, if we let them. In such times, our spiritual life becomes boring, our expectations squelched and our personal ministry hampered. We've hung on to the physical at the expense of the spiritual, embracing the baubles of sin instead of the jewels of righteousness. It's not that we have walked in total spiritual rebellion, perhaps, but that we've wandered in the fields of compromise and inconsistency. Instead of enjoying the*

> *bountiful blessings of God, we've too often dined at the table of fruitlessness and poor harvests. Sin may have failed to totally corrupt us, but we've allowed it to numb us and incapacitate us from becoming the sharp, effective and fully functional sword in the hand Christ. God's door to blessing certainly remains open, of course, awaiting our decision to change our priorities instead of just rearranging our regularities."*

Let me return to King Asa once again. The prophet Azariah went out to warn King Asa of some of the things that bothered the Lord about his lackluster kingship and the Israel's lackluster spirituality at the time…around 900 BC.

> *"Listen to me, Asa and all Judah and Benjamin. The Lord is with you when you are with him. If you seek him, he will be found by you, but if you forsake him. He will forsake you. For a long time, Israel was without the true God, without a priest to teach and without the law. But in their distress, they turned to the Lord, the God of Israel, and **sought him** and he was found by them…."* (II Chron 15:1-7)

Immediately after receiving this warning, Asa "took it to heart" and went through out the land, eliminating idols and teaching the people to follow the Lord. What happened? Great revival came, because the people began **seeking the Lord wholeheartedly**.

Spiritual perseverance demands, to begin with, that we **refresh, enlarge, and stimulate our faith.** This is often the problem for us, isn't it, because all of us tend to slow down and lose steam. We too easily can put our lives on cruise control, coast along, and slipping into a lackluster faith walk with Christ. Oh, we may pray, but it's mostly perfunctory. We're willing to share Christ with someone, but we don't often reach out for opportunities to do so. We may go to church, but mostly it's just to enjoy friendships, keep up with what's going on, and because of the routine of it all. We sing the songs in the worship service, but our minds are not really focusing upon the words or meaning of them. We say a prayer or two in the morning about the day ahead of us, but mostly our day is focused just upon our work. There's really no particular goal where we ask God to use us in some way while there. When we're home, we plan our vacations to Disney, talk about the new furniture that's being delivered next week, and think about how we're going to fix up the house and make it bigger and better. We love to talk about politics, of course, and the crazed liberal agenda that is so antagonistic to freedom and to our Christian heritage. Yet, deep conversations about our relationship with Christ are noticeably infrequent, perhaps because we don't have much of one to begin with.

A *consecrated* Christian, however, is the opposite. He or she is first and foremost a **faith-driven** person, pursuing God out of intense belief, which moves him or her toward whole-hearted *desire*, and which overflows into an ever-deepening **determination to obey** (marks of genuine conviction). Like the Energizer battery, *they keep going!*

> "...grow in the **grace** and **knowledge** of our LORD and Savior Jesus Christ..." (II Peter 3:18)

By the way, it's not that the daily concerns and routines of life aren't necessary or enjoyable for us to pursue as well. It's just that such things can, if not guarded carefully, dominate or detour us from our *primary* mission in life, which is pursuing Christ with *relentless faith*. That's the quality that consistently rejects compromise and *perseveres* in consecration to God. It's fueled by an intense desire and determination to do so, rooted in initial belief, but *motivated* and *surrendered* to the living God in whole-hearted consecration!

Again, if you want to persevere and grow in Christ, be sure to cultivate your ***primary*** faith conviction first, for it's the power source for everything we do. ***Then, "add to your faith,"*** as Peter reminds us, the other necessary principles and precepts that God wants us to passionately understand and willfully obey.

Here's our goal: *Seek* God's presence, his power, his provision, and his purposes in everything you do...without perfunctory obligation, but with enthusiastic pursuit of his person throughout your day. Again, it's not that we're praying every minute or reading the Scriptures at work instead of focusing upon the job. No, but it is a **relational thing,** thinking about the Lord Jesus often as we go about our daily tasks, responsibilities, plans, and relationships. Faith always seeks out relationship with Christ, and that drives us forward in relentless devotion to him, *in spite of all and no matter* what (yes, I still like that phrase, but now I use it more discerningly!). Do you recall what the prophet told Asa?

> *"The Lord is with you when you are with him. If you seek him, he will be found by you, but if you forsake him. He will forsake you."*

So, here's a challenging question: *"Is your consecration growing beyond just simple faith and toward a mature mindset of wholehearted trust, passion, love, and God-fearing surrender* **in all you think and do?"**

Lastly, Consecration is a PLACE

Consecration is sometimes used in describing our *spiritual condition*, that is, a spiritual state or, perhaps, a level of spirituality. I call it a place in our spiritual walk with God that is both pleasing to God and satisfying to us. Now, we do have to be very careful with this perspective, because as I've said before, no one this side of heaven ever "arrives" at a place of perfection in daily lifestyle. Contrary to some erroneous thinking, sainthood is never a bestowment of stature based on accomplishment, either. Rather, it's just a word that says we're a saved believer moving faithfully forward in the process of sanctification.

However, for practical purposes, I like to think that there still is a "place" in our walk with Christ that is obtainable now, where we are *mostly* "walking the talk," "living the life," "modeling the message," and consistently living in a praiseworthy relationship with God. It is consecration in full bloom, if you will, glowing bright with the spiritual colors of faith and godly living. Though we still are not perfect in our walk with the Lord, for the most part we've left behind the obstinate habits and obvious compromises that easily trip us up (see Heb 12:1,2). Instead, with the Spirit's empowerment, we've *settled into* a maturity that both pleases our Savior and satisfies us.

> "The passing pleasures of sin cannot compare with the lasting rewards of righteousness!"

> *"Man cannot please God without bringing to himself a great amount of happiness; for if any man pleases God, it is because God accepts him as his son, gives him the blessings of adoption, pours upon him the bounties of his grace, makes him a blessed man in this life, and insures him a crown of everlasting life..."* (Spurgeon, "Chequebook of the Bank of Faith")

I'll close with Paul's statements regarding his own spiritual consecration to God. Notice his overall impassioned faith commitment to Jesus, his Savior and Lord.

> *"I have been crucified with Christ. It is no longer I who live, but Christ who lives in me. And the life I now live in the flesh I live by faith in the Son of God, who loved me and gave himself for me."* Gal. 2:20

> *"Indeed, I count everything as loss because of the surpassing worth of knowing Christ Jesus my Lord. For his sake I have suffered the loss of all things and count them as rubbish, in order that I may gain Christ...that I may know him and the power of his resurrection, and may share his sufferings, becoming like him in his death, that by any means possible I may attain the resurrection*

from the dead. Not that I have already obtained this or am already perfect, but I press on to make it my own, because Christ Jesus has made me his own. Brothers, I do not consider that I have made it my own. But one thing I do: forgetting what lies behind and straining forward to what lies ahead, I press on toward the goal for the prize of the upward call of God in Christ Jesus."
Phil. 3:6-11

I hope you've enjoyed our trip together down the highway of spiritual conviction. In summary, please remember that spiritual maturity doesn't come by miraculous intervention or a singular bestowal of grace in answer to prayer. Rather, it is the result of a responsible faith maintaining a healthy diet of spiritual vitamins, a self-disciplined and often painful regiment of exercise, and a constant renewal of one's mind caught up in impassioned insight from listening to God's indwelling Spirit!

Finally, I offer you this refrain from an older hymn with a message for all times, "Living For Jesus." It captures the heart of what I've said along our journey.

*"O Jesus, Lord and Savior,
I give myself to Thee,
For Thou, in Thy atonement,
didst give Thyself for me;
I own no other Master,
my heart shall be Thy throne;
My life I give, henceforth to live,
O Christ, for Thee alone.**

*Words by Thomas O. Chisholm, music by Carl H. Lowden

CPSIA information can be obtained
at www.ICGtesting.com
Printed in the USA
LVHW051140120122
708210LV00013B/424